T0171211

NOTE *to* SELF

NOTE *to* SELF

30 WOMEN ON HARDSHIP,

HUMILIATION, HEARTBREAK

AND OVERCOMING IT ALL

Edited and with an Introduction by

Andrea Buchanan

SIMON SPOTLIGHT ENTERTAINMENT
New York   London   Toronto   Sydney

Simon Spotlight Entertainment
A Division of Simon & Schuster, Inc.
1230 Avenue of the Americas
New York, NY 10020

First Simon Spotlight Entertainment
hardcover edition January 2009

SIMON SPOTLIGHT ENTERTAINMENT and colophon
are trademarks of Simon & Schuster, Inc.

For information about special discounts for bulk purchases,
please contact Simon & Schuster Special Sales at 1-800-456-6798
or business@simonandschuster.com.

Designed by Maura Rosenthal

Manufactured in the United States of America

1   3   5   7   9   10   8   6   4   2

Library of Congress Cataloging-in-Publication Data is available.

ISBN-13: 978-1-4391-9114-9
ISBN-10:   1-4391-9114-X

For Jason

my heart, my husband, my hero.

CONTENTS

LIFE'S CONSTANT COMPLEXITIES

INTRODUCTION

s far back as I can remember, my father wrote little notes to himself about everything. They were reminders, really, little scraps of paper with nuggets of wisdom. This way, he could recall a thought or follow up on a half-baked idea or new creation. For a time he was an inventor, so ideas were his life, and he would not let one of them pass him by. Even his wardrobe functioned as a facilitator to his ideas. He would not wear shirts unless they had two pockets: one for his pens, the other for his scraps of paper. "Function over fashion" was his motto.

After the invention of sticky notes (someone else's brilliant idea), they became a staple in our home, perhaps more important than sugar or coffee or rice. They were everywhere, but most of them could be found on the kitchen table in a neatly organized row alongside the orange place mats and plastic fruit centerpiece. The notes were supposed to be relegated to his area of the table, but if they went unchecked they would creep toward my mother's, my three older sisters', or my place settings. A day didn't go by in which my mother wouldn't rightly complain about "those damn notes." While she rejected this practice of his, I embraced it. As the youngest of four girls, it was a bond that my daddy and I shared. But I took it to another level: my notes were en vogue, beautifully penned on parchment paper (I think I even went so far as to laminate a few). Canvas inside a shadow box was probably my note de force. I gifted my husband one saying, "My love guaranteed."

Let me be clear: I don't write lists. I hate them. Somewhere along the way a list came to represent structure, rigidity, and that perfect girl in class who had the color-coded markers for every day of the week. I write things down on scraps of paper, on Post-it notes, on beautiful stationery, and on my hand. I would have them everywhere—just like my dad—but my husband hates clutter even more than my mother does. So he makes piles of all the scraps and puts them by the phone, on my desk, near my computer.

I curate famous quotes, paraphrases of famous quotes, raw emotion, friends' quotes, snippets of phone conversations, ideas. To me they are like oxygen. I need them to breathe. A recent inventory yielded these gems:

"You get what you want."
"Receiving is Giving."
"Have more faith than fear."
"Breathe and breathe again."
"Listen to your instinct. It just might save you from yourself."
"Service is the rent we pay for living on the planet."

"Don't forget to exercise and drink water."
"Dream Big. You will have it all. You already do."
"She has a free pass to get the fuck out of my life." (I threw that one away.)

I have collected countless scraps of wisdom, inspiration, insight, and empathy over the years. One day it occurred to me that a book of such reflections—and the stories that surrounded them—might bring others the joy and comfort and occasional laugh that they bring me. I started to seek out stories that wouldn't fit on a Post-it but had final messages that could. Notes to self.

All of the stories were primarily about moments of redemption following what I call life's "Big Three": Humiliation, Heartbreak, and Hardship. However, as in real life, sometimes tough moments cannot be so easily compartmentalized, so I put some stories into a category I like to call "Life's Constant Complexities," which can mean anything from coming to terms with a professional setback to accepting the width of one's thighs.

We all have a "story" that helps define us, a piece of ourselves that reflects who we are today yet is somehow rooted in our past, perhaps holding us back. More often than not, we need to shed that outdated outer shell—that "story"—so that we may finally and fully move into the next phase of life with a lesson of wisdom firmly intact (and if you are like me, taped to a wall). So I asked my fellow contributors not only to share their stories but also to sum them up in a final note to self, something that a reader could scrawl on a Post-it and keep somewhere she could access for a quick dose of wisdom. What they came up with will inspire you.

Each woman in this book has a defining story from which she has moved to a new pinnacle of life, renewed and redeemed by the lessons she learned and will share with you. Punctuated by tears and laughter, these stories are full of incredible strength, invaluable knowledge, insurmountable odds, helpful survival instincts, amazing willpower, humiliation on a national level, and a hefty dose of humor. Through them, I have come to realize that no matter what life presents—however unfair, ugly, or murky it may seem—if you are willing, you can actually learn from the biggest of life's challenges and find the light in the darkest of tunnels. And once you go through it, the lesson, the takeaway, *your note to self,* can act as a reminder, a place holder, a bookmark just in case you forget, for one moment, how amazing you are and how awesome the journey has been, even with its difficulties.

It seems only fair that I now join this community of women in this book and kick it off by telling my stories of the "Big Three" that have defined me, emboldened me, and taught me lessons worthy of places front and center on my wall.

My story of humiliation came early. I should state that we all have moments when we are humiliated, but I am talking about the one humiliation I could never forget, the Super Bowl champion of embarrassing moments (think Janet Jackson).

I grew up in Lewisville, Texas, a middle-class suburb of Dallas. While some kids spent their summer vacation at camps, on lakes, or, at the very least, at the community pool, I spent mine poring over Christie Brinkley's operating manual, "How to Look Like a Model." I studied its glossy pages like a student preparing for my dissertation. I wanted to be a model, and not just for myself. There were many who deemed me beautiful, and I felt I owed it to them, too. At fourteen, I was five foot ten, 120 pounds, and wore a 34C bra. I had been voted both Sophomore and Junior Duchess. I knew my place amongst the jocks, nerds, and burnouts, and I enjoyed the view from up on high as I looked down on my adoring subjects. Senior year was primed to be a royal cakewalk to the ultimate crown, homecoming queen. At the time, this was serious business; signing each other's yearbooks as we said our good-byes for summer vacation after junior year, we all knew the crown would be mine when we returned in the fall. My acceptance speech was all but written, and my glorious future was laid out before me like my homecoming cape: my star linebacker-boyfriend and I would get married after graduation and our first child was going to be named Rush, after the band. This was the road map of my life. And it was happening just as planned.

That summer, however, my body went rogue. I mysteriously packed on thirty pounds, developed a goiter in my neck, and almost overnight suffered from a serious case of bug eyes. My mother had her theories about what was causing the sudden change. For a while she determined that I had a bacterial infection that I'd caught tubing down the Rio Grande. Not long after that, she knew in her heart of hearts that the chemicals used to perm my hair were ruining my looks. My favorite theory, however, and one that stuck the longest, was simply my cat.

My mother moved beyond these strange explanations for this sudden illness and was determined to find a diagnosis. As helpful as her determination was her sharp sense of humor, which helped us keep a bit of levity in the house during this stressful time.

My parents took me to a specialist in Dallas. As I sat in his cold office barely covered by a paper gown, he examined my body—feeling the goiter in my throat, checking under my arms for swollen lymph nodes and around my breasts for possible cancerous lumps. While he was conducting his exam, he whispered to me, "I can see why your mother is so upset. I can tell you used to be so beautiful." Though I didn't give him the satisfaction of seeing it, at that moment I broke into pieces. Life was never going to be the same for me, and I knew it.

I was diagnosed with a severe case of Graves' disease (a thyroid disorder), and the doctors ultimately had me drink radioactive iodine, which tasted awful, to kill my thyroid, which had decidedly gone berserk. This was followed by all sorts of medication to replace what they'd destroyed with poison so that what was left of my abnormal gland could function. It was a scary time as we attempted to regulate my metabolism with chemicals, and I absolutely didn't feel or look like myself.

Meanwhile, I prayed for a miracle to keep me out of school, but God wasn't listening. As I drove to class on the first day of my senior year, it dawned on me that I was an anonymous participant in what used to be my life. I was terrified to face my peers. The responsibility I had felt to my fellow students to be

beautiful and to be their homecoming queen was now replaced
with utter fear and self-loathing. I felt ugly and disgusting.

Walking through the hallways that early September morning
was the first time in my life I wished no one would notice me.
Some of my classmates stared too long, while others averted
their eyes. I could hear the whispers of concern coming from
every direction, and my head was spinning. They say kids can
be cruel, really cruel. Well, due to my previously held titles junior and sophomore years, my peers were either kind or felt
pity: they nominated me for homecoming queen. I was completely stunned.

But this was Texas, and let's get real: I knew in my heart I was
not going to be crowned queen. I went to the homecoming game
anyway, decked out in one of Lewisville's finest dresses and
wearing two gargantuan corsages made of mums pinned to my
chest, complete with streamers that hung down to the ground.
The queen was to be crowned at halftime.

When the time came, I made my way down the bleachers to
take my place with the other nominees. As I descended, I
stepped on one of the streamers, ripped a corsage out of my
dress, and tumbled down the steps. I knew that I could either
fake a serious injury or get up off the ground, brush myself off,
and make my way onto the field. I mustered every shred of dignity I had and got up. Limping, I made my way to the fifty-yard
line, escorted by my father, only to witness the crown placed on
my friend's head. She was the perfect homecoming queen:
beautiful, nice, and gracious. It was the most humiliating moment of my life. All that practice to walk like Christie came
crashing down. The one thing I depended on, my looks, had

turned on me and sent me plummeting down the stadium steps in front of the entire town. And at a young, impressionable age, it seemed like the world was coming to an end.

Seventeen years later, I was living in Los Angeles. My body had gone through changes due to my Graves' disease, but I'd regained a sense of self. Granted, I was no runway model, nor did I want to be, but I was healthy, active, and very much in charge of my life. I had traveled the world as a documentary filmmaker covering grizzly bears in the Canadian Rockies, active volcanoes in British West Indies, rock stars in Europe, and the March for Women's Lives in Washington, D.C. Lewisville felt far away and abstract, as if my darker high-school days there had been a dream from which I had awoken. I was a new brand of queen: a goddess with lip gloss, a woman grounded through meditation, a filmmaker who wanted to make an impact on the world. One night I went out to dinner with a friend, who brought along a woman and her husband, whom I had never met. The moment I saw this woman, Ayrin, I knew she was from my past. I asked her where she was from, and she said sheepishly, "I like to think of myself as being from the East Coast, but for a while I lived in a small town outside of Dallas called Lewisville."

I choked on my Chardonnay and practically yelled across the table, "Oh, my God! I grew up in Lewisville!" Ayrin asked me to repeat my name again, and it was as if she had seen a ghost.

"Oh, my God," she said. "You're Andrea Buchanan. I can't believe it!" My face flushed. I wasn't exactly sure how to handle her shock at discovering my identity.

Ayrin blushed, too. "You used to be so beautiful," she said

softly, and I felt as if I'd been punched in the gut. "Not that you're not beautiful now," she stammered, "but you were the girl we all wanted to be. You were so perfect."

She went on to tell us that she had been a misfit. Bone thin and six feet tall, with pale skin and black hair, she'd found herself in a sea of blondes when her parents had moved to our town. She used to hang out in the "freaks" courtyard and smoke cigarettes, counting the days until she could leave Texas.

Ayrin claimed to have had two friends in school. I had two hundred. She was shy. I was outgoing. She dated the mascot. I dated the star linebacker. She wanted to be me, but I wanted to be Christie Brinkley. We both wanted an identity beyond ourselves, a sense of belonging.

Ayrin cut to the chase. "And when you got sick, I was so upset. It just seemed like you were in so much pain. My friends and I tried to figure out what happened to you, because back then, you had set the bar for what was possible in life: being popular and being super-nice. If you weren't happy and perfect, then what were my chances?" Ayrin, choking back tears, went on, "One day, in homeroom, you looked at me. It felt like you were really seeing me, and that you somehow understood me. You seemed to understand what it was like to be an outcast, and that gave me a big dose of courage, strength, and confidence. I have never forgotten that."

And then she explained the perfect irony: when she left Lewisville, Ayrin moved to Manhattan and became a Calvin Klein model.

That night, Ayrin helped me realize that I needed to heal the shame I felt for what had happened to me and learn to laugh about the humiliation I'd experienced on the field that night. Through the embarrassment, I had transformed the path of my life. I now went beyond the surface in almost everything I did in my work, my relationships, and how I viewed the world. Through the pain I had learned compassion for anybody suffering something out of their control. Disease in any form is scary stuff, and it can show up when things are humming along and knock you down, however beautiful you may look. And the night I met Ayrin, I truly learned that reaching within yourself to find solace, peace, and love heals you from humiliation. When we are knocked down, we sometimes see things more clearly, below the haze of lost perspective.

Note to self: Losing your crown can be the luckiest moment in your life.

Two years later, my life was running on all eight cylinders. I loved what I was doing in my work life, and I also had an incredibly full social life. There were dinner parties, trips to New York, and—my favorite of all—spending time with my four closest girlfriends: my circle. We vacationed together, were in each other's weddings, threw each other elaborate parties, shared our most intimate moments, and held each other's deepest secrets. We even went so far as to swear our undying love to one another and made vows and promises I couldn't imagine breaking. My girlfriends and I were like the dude's version of a weekly poker group, but instead of playing cards, smoking cigars, and drinking beer, our nights were more about sharing, processing our innermost feelings, and sleepovers.

My husband, family, and other friends outside this circle often played second fiddle to the girls. Belonging to this group of women meant the world to me. My identity and my ego depended on it. At the time, I was too caught up in the intoxicating effects this group's popularity had on me. I changed so that I would fit in and then I suffered from a false sense of safety, seemingly less vulnerable to the perceptions of others. Perhaps this was my coping mechanism, developed as a result of the earlier days when I'd tried to shoulder the responsibility of being the queen of the school and my subsequent fall from my throne.

Now, let me set the record straight: I don't consider myself a wimp or a pushover. I consider myself a strong, independent woman who has always figured out a way to forge her own path, even if it meant falling down to get there. I am usually a pedal to the metal speed racer kind of gal. But there was something about this group that rendered me a follower. There were strong personas in our posse, and as easy as it felt to be a part of the group, there was always a part of myself that was hidden, not truly present. As time passed I started to realize that the group resembled more of an incomplete circle, as I was not completely me. At the time, it didn't matter that I felt more like a member of an entourage, because I was happy to take a backseat, just happy to be in the coolest car in town.

Then, in February of 2006, I had a disturbing reading in which my trusted astrologer said that my circle was in for a shift. It wouldn't change totally, but the parts that were no longer working for me would undergo a visible change. I was alarmed. How could it shift? We were all so much in each other's lives. We had a bond that would not break. The results of the reading stuck with me. I would have much preferred hearing, "You are about to come into a large amount of cash."

Soon after that astrological zinger, one of the girls had a birthday. I suggested a group gift in which all of us could participate: we would give her five delicately thin gold rings, each one representing our individual commitment to her and the fifth band representing a commitment to herself. It was a ritual to solidify our circle. The gift was such a hit that we decided we would gift the rings for each of our birthdays that year. It was like I was marrying my friends. At the time, I felt overjoyed and thought, *My astrologer was clearly wrong, thank god.* I couldn't wait for my birthday to arrive, when I would receive my five bands, symbols of our sisterhood. I couldn't wait to *belong* more.

By the time my birthday rolled around, not only did I not receive the bands I had coveted but also, through a series of events, miscommunication, and misunderstanding, one of my tribe unceremoniously ended her friendship with me, and before my very eyes, the circle, as I knew it, was broken. At first it seemed inexplicable, but I was suddenly cast aside by some of these friends with routine antics straight out of a petty high-school playbook. Before this happened, we'd always agreed we would speak the hard truth to each other in the spirit of being open and honest. I got a hefty dose that left me bewildered. And then there was silence. What was once open was now closed, hiding and avoiding resolution. No more sleepovers, just sleepless nights trying to pick up the pieces. The bonds of friendship we'd spent years developing were gone in what seemed like a flash. I cried until I wanted to vomit. It was worse than any

breakup with a lover, because in some strange way I was breaking up with myself, saying good-bye to a version of myself that
was so desperate to belong and define myself through others'
views of me, instead of through my own resolve.

I experienced some of the darkest and hardest moments of
my life, feeling worthless, empty, with nothing left to give, even
to my husband. It was a sense of loss I had never felt. I recall a
night in bed staring at the ceiling. My husband was at my side,
trying to help me make sense of it all, and I suddenly recognized a deep-seated pattern. I relied on other people to feel
good about myself. The harsh truth was crystal clear: I did not
believe in myself enough to be truly authentic in my relationships with these women. My dethroning in high school had victimized me and now this was a different version of a dethroning,
but with the same opportunity to heal. When my body had broken down in high school, it had been humiliation. When some
of my closest friendships broke down in adulthood, it was
heartbreak.

But like that fateful night on the football field, I was at my
lowest point possible. I had to pick myself up and begin to re-
construct my ideas of trust, fault, guilt, and forgiveness. I leaned
on a few notes to self during the healing:

"To be powerful one must go through the crucible" was one.
"Have more faith than fear" was another.

I was fortunate to experience real intimacy with those
friends who stuck around, and I was eventually able to forgive
the ones who couldn't seem to move beyond honest mistakes,
and most important forgave myself for my part in our demise. I
was not without fault, but I needed to let myself off the hook at

some point. This time my friends couldn't do it for me; I had to do it for myself. Through the heartbreak, I learned how to re-commit to myself, to love myself and stand on my own. Afterward, that confidence radiated in all of my other relationships, and I was more authentic with everyone, including my husband and family, and I began to see how I had truly been ignoring a part of me for years. I often see the rings on the fingers of the friends who received them, and I am no longer hurt, but my heart has been fortified with self-reliance: "I am my source of love and security."

My story of heartbreak is not unique. Everyone goes through this sense of getting hurt, getting a raw deal, mistreated, but most important, misguided by one's choices in some form or aspect of their life. Ultimately you have to take responsibility for healing yourself no matter what you face and realize that every interaction is co-created. But when healing clears the way, the truth really does set us free. And we are strengthened by our resolve.

Not long after that breakup, my husband and I moved into our first home. It was a big, ramshackle, turn-of-the-century gem in a transitional neighborhood with taquerias and tire stores on the street corners. Moving into this house, with its sturdy foundation and strong walls, was a beautiful renewal of my commitment to my marriage, and I knew that friendships that were meant to be would follow.

Just as my heart was remodeling itself from the break I

had experienced with some of my friends and I was embracing a new sense of self, unknown to us my husband's heart was breaking down in a much more literal way. A routine trip to the doctor to check up on a congenital condition known as bicuspid aortic valve, or BAV, revealed a time bomb ticking away.

His sweet, strong, thirty-six-year-old heart had an undetected 4.8-centimeter aneurysm growing within. His doctor told him his aorta could rupture at any moment, which would mean game over. This meant that lifting a box or bending the wrong way, or picking up a friend's child, could mean instant death similar to the way the late John Ritter suffered from a catastrophic aneurysm.

My husband was in the prime of his life; he had just completed his first marathon, bought our first house, and was thriving in his career. Yet quietly his genetics were failing him. There was no time to grieve or think about it; we had to take action. While in the midst of moving into our new home, we were thrown into a fast-track preparation for surgery, which meant massive doses of blood pressure medicine to keep him safe and the mental preparation for the "open heart" part of it. We talked to experts from all over the country in this highly specialized field, and, luckily, the best in the world was in our own backyard. Open-heart surgery was in store for my husband, a terrifying concept that defied my ability to grasp, imagine, or even say it. Putting on a good face, I was calm on the outside, but inside I was growing anxious. I had firsthand experience with the body turning on you, but this was an entirely other level than Graves' disease—this was untenable. It was the first time I actually considered what life would be without him. The what-ifs came in, and I quickly chased them out so I could be the rock my husband needed to lean on. He had been there for my heartbreak. I HAD to be there for his.

As I had done so many times in my life, I relied on my friends, but this time it was not for acceptance or popularity—it was for survival. I imagined myself standing atop a mountain and using a ram's horn to make a call throughout the world for people to come and save him. I thought, "If I can gather enough hearts together, I can make sure his won't fail." Our community surrounded us. Literally. My circle never actually broke, it just took on a different shape and size, exactly like the astrologer had said it would. She'd been right all along.

A week before surgery, we hosted an evening at our new house, boxes and all, where twenty of our friends sat in the round, shared stories, and prayed to anyone who would listen. As I sat by my husband's side, holding his hand, I realized I never wanted to let it go. I was one hundred percent completely married to this man, and there was nothing else but that. Love Guaranteed. In the silence of my prayers that evening and with a small piece of jewelry that I gave him symbolizing his courage, I recommitted to him, to my marriage, to seeing the happiness and hardship in relationships, and to standing by his side, through sickness and in health. It was no joke.

One week later, my husband was lying in an ICU in Los Angeles, unconscious. He was hooked up to a heart and lung machine. Only his head was visible. His iPod was still playing, his earbuds in place (the surgeon allowed the iPod in the OR, as I knew it would keep him unconsciously calm), and his body was covered by blankets, which were slowly warming his chilled bones. During the eight-hour, full-circulatory-arrest surgery I'd known all the facts; the human body was chilled down to nearly single digits in temperature to reduce cellular metabolism. With him on ice (think Han Solo frozen in Carbonite), the doctors could shut down his heart, lung, and brain, to replace the faulty pipe with a piece of plastic that would never rupture or break down. I quietly listened to my own heart beat, unwavering in its intention to keep this family together, to love unconditionally all of life's imperfections as they show us the true meaning of triumph.

When he woke up, our lives were all about recovery, which was incredibly painful at first, as well as aggravating and challenging. It was hard. Really hard. Slowly the healing occurred. It took him three months to go back to work and nine months to feel back to "normal" again, although there is nothing "normal" about being slightly bionic.

Nowadays, when I am lying next to him, my head against his chest, I can hear his robust, healthy, safe and sound heart beating. I slip away and burst into tears when I recall his unconscious body, lying entombed in blankets, surviving by machinery. It is a combo of grief and gratitude. During those hours in the waiting room, my entire life flashed before me; high-school humiliation, my circle of heartache and all of my doubts . . . all of it paled in comparison to the possibility of losing him, because he remains the truest extension of myself, in all its forms, old and new. It is a miracle: his broken heart had the strength to heal my wounded one. Love actually does conquer all. So I conclude with a simple note:

"Take nothing for granted, especially the miracles found in love."

Each woman seems to have a private mantra that keeps her going through her darkest hours. And something in our own words brings light out of the shadows, keeps us faithful in ourselves. In each of the stories in this book, you will get a chance to learn about amazing women and their triumphs over humiliation, heartbreak, and hardship. Their triumphs are unique, but the lessons they share, the notes they wrote to themselves, have universal appeal to the female condition. I invite you to consider writing your defining story down, and with the notes that sustain you, remind yourself of how a few words can make miracles happen.

Don't just live it—write it down, make a note, and never forget.

—APB
August 7, 2008

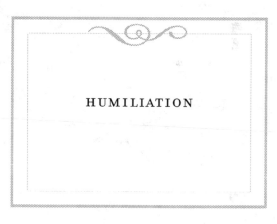

HUMILIATION

When Your Pride's in Jeopardy

CAMRYN MANHEIM

Camryn Manheim is an Emmy Award–winning actress, most notably for her roles as Ellenor Frutt on *The Practice* and Delia Banks on *Ghost Whisperer*. She wrote her first book, *Wake Up, I'm Fat!* in 1999. She lives in Los Angeles with her amazing son, Milo. Her running charade skills are unmatched.

Most of my humiliating and humbling experiences have come not from the moments in which the horrifying incidents occurred but long after, when I put the pieces of the puzzle together and the whole picture became painfully clear. Like the time I wore a pearl jeweled brooch in my hair to a Golden Globes ceremony. At the time I thought I looked so chic and confident, but in retrospect it was truly a fashion faux pas. Lucky for me, the picture only showed up on several thousand websites and hundreds of publications . . . until Tara Reid's boob fell out of her dress on a red carpet and stole my limelight. I should send her a thank-you note.

I'm no stranger to humiliation. Most of the time, though, I'm able to take the punch, put it in its proper place, and find the amusement in the retelling of it. However, there is one moment that lives on in my memory, in my bones. The humiliation can still be felt when I turn the channel to ABC at 7:00 p.m. on any given night. It's humiliating times ten million, because that's about how many people watched me fail, and I failed big.

As the daughter of two Jewish educators who sent their only son to Harvard, there was an underlying pressure that I, too, would follow in their academic footsteps. At the age of ten, when I decided I wanted to be an actor, my parents thought the passing phase was cute. But as ten turned to eighteen, and I decided to seriously pursue being an actress, my parents found it no longer cute but—how shall I say it?—terrifying.

My whole family is a bunch of smarty-pants. And while I think of myself as smart, I guess my strengths would be better described as "differently" smart. For example, I can't spell my way out of a paper bag, but I like to think of myself as a good writer. When my son was born, I began a journal for him. This is an excerpt from my very first entry.

> *Dear Little One, There are a few things you should know about me before we go on this journey. First, you're going to see a few pictures around the house of me on a motorcycle. This does not mean you will ever be able to ride one. Secondly, I'm a terrible speller. I think I'll have you covered through second grade, but when you get into the five-letter words, you're on your own, kid.*

While other new moms were reading first-time parenting manuals, I was leafing through the *Oxford English Dictionary* trying to figure out how to spell *pacifier*. The truth is, I was never able to retain the simple facts you learn in school. Geography? A blur. Social studies? If only it *were* social. Spanish? I was so bad at it, I couldn't even remember the swear words. Oddly enough, I could kick ass at charades and poker, but the decade when Trivial Pursuit was the number one parlor game was slightly traumatic for me. Truth be told, I would rather have a root canal than collect all the plastic wedges required to win that tedious game.

My parents used to quiz us in the car when we would go on long family vacations. How many senators are there for every state? What is the capital of Ethiopia? What kind of number is the square root of eight? Ad nauseam. It always felt like when the genes were passed out among the siblings, they were not equally dispersed. My brother got most of the "fact retention" genes, my sister got all of the "visual art" genes, and I got the "social" genes. I could make friends with a lamppost. That came from my mom. Since my dad was a professor of mathematics, you didn't get the car keys in my household without calculating the wear and tear on the car, the gas mileage, and the increased insurance for having a minor on the policy. Somehow or another, calculating odds and probabilities became my forte. As a result, my reports cards were strangely inconsistent: straight As in math and science, and Cs and sometimes Ds in reading comprehension.

I always wondered why I had so much trouble holding on to bits of information that other people could so easily retain. Because I excelled in so many other areas of my life—math, performing arts, problem solving, public speaking—no one, including me, ever dug deeper to uncover the mystery. I tried to talk about it with my parents and peers, but no one felt it was as important as I did, so I kept my concerns to myself. It was my little secret that I had to read the same sentence three or four times to really understand it but if I read it out loud, I could absorb the information immediately. It never occurred to me that what I was experiencing was a legitimate issue that learning specialists have known about for decades.

But I digress, which is not entirely surprising, considering the fact that I've been asked to talk about my most embarrassing moment. So here goes. It was circa 1998. I had just won an Emmy for best supporting actress on *The Practice.* I was the toast of the town and receiving invites left and right to premieres, charity events, art gallery openings, and talk shows. It was every young actor's dream come true. I was just about to buy a house (and contrary to popular belief, I was not making crazy TV money) when my publicist called and asked if I wanted to be on *Celebrity Jeopardy!* Um, lemme think about that for a second. . . . NO! But then she told me that in lieu of payment, all three celebrity contestants would get ten thousand dollars' worth of Sony electronics. So, although my gut said I probably wouldn't fare that well in a game requiring a knowledge of endless facts, ten thousand dollars' worth of electronics made the idea a little more enticing.

Still, I wasn't sure if I should do it. I tried to discuss it with some friends: Should I? Shouldn't I? Should I? Shouldn't I? But no one really understood my dilemma. Everyone thought I'd be crazy not to go on *Celebrity Jeopardy!* and get a new state-of-the-art TV. "Everybody knows they dumb down the questions for celebrities, right? Besides, you're a fierce game player!" When I tried to explain that I don't retain *Jeopardy!*-like facts and that Trivial Pursuit gave me hives, not one friend believed that I couldn't fill out a United States map or name the landlocked countries in South America. It's not as if they were saying that to be kind or complimentary. They truly believed that I'd go on *Celebrity Jeopardy!* and kick ass. But I knew better. I knew that as the fateful words "Okay, God damn it, I'll do it!" were coming out of my mouth, I'd live to regret them.

When I arrived at Sony Studios in Culver City, I was escorted to the greenroom, where I met Alex Trebek. I don't remember the date. I don't even remember who my celebrity competitors were. I've blocked all of it out, and I have never spoken of it since, until now. It all started out just fine. After meeting Mr. Trebek, I was brought to the *Jeopardy!* soundstage, where we had a practice run, which mostly consisted of getting used to the handheld buzzer and giving our answers in the form of a question. The rehearsal went fine, because they *did* dumb down the questions and I wasn't feeling as hopeless as I thought I would. But when it came time for the real game, the nightmare began.

Thirty minutes never seemed so long. Even recalling it now, all these years later, makes me nauseous. I didn't know the answers to any of the questions, but I kept clicking my buzzer anyway, making my score dip lower and lower into the negative numbers. What evil person thought of docking people for trying to answer a question and getting it wrong? I didn't even know the answer to a question about musical comedy, which made me feel beyond humiliated. In the Final Jeopardy round, the clue had something to do with a bicycle race in Europe. I

thought the answer might be the Tour de France, but because I
had already made such a fool of myself I was sure that anything
my brain had come up with would be wrong—so out of total desperation, I peeked over my opponent's shoulder and copied his
answer. Since I had the fewest points, Alex asked me to reveal
my answer first—and (OH MY GOD, I WANT TO VOMIT) it was
wrong. My only consolation was that contestant number 2 was
also revealed to have the wrong answer. When contestant number 3 turned over the correct answer, which *was* the fucking
Tour de France, the lights started flashing and there was a rain-
storm of confetti and applause. In all my years doing theater, I
have never wanted to get off a stage so desperately. The second
they stopped taping, I quickly slipped out a side door, got in my
car, drove home, and cried.

You can imagine how I felt, knowing that in three weeks my
secret would be aired on national television for millions of people to see—not once, but replayed over and over again for, who
knows, possibly the rest of my life? It didn't matter how many
times Tara Reid flashed her boobs, or that Paris Hilton was in-
carcerated, or that Angelina wore her lover's blood in a vial
around her neck. I was certain that none of these indiscretions
would ever overshadow my *Jeopardy!* debacle.

I considered calling the network to see if I could pay them
not to air my episode, or staging my untimely death so they
would feel bad about airing, but I chose that familiar friend, denial, and did nothing. Three weeks later that *Jeopardy!* episode
aired, after which a strange silence filled my home. I hoped it
was because everyone knew I was about to leave on a big press
tour to promote a book I'd recently written and they wanted to

give me some space, but deep inside, I feared it was because no one knew what to say to me. It was the first time I viscerally understood what the word *dread* felt like.

On my press tour, I traveled to all the major cities. Wouldn't you know it—the same people who read my book also happen to watch *Jeopardy!* So imagine this. For the previous year and a half, I had poured out my heart and soul into an autobiographical book about what it was like to grow up fat in America. It was about my journey traveling from victim to victor, and writing it had been the most empowering feeling I had ever experienced. I was scheduled to appear at seventeen different Barnes & Noble stores across the country, read an excerpt from my book, and have a Q&A afterwards.

The first stop was Seattle, Washington. After reading an excerpt from my book, I spied a sweet-faced young woman with her hand held high. She seemed safe and sincere, so I called on her. Never has my intuition been so wrong. That sweet-faced imposter looked at me and asked, "What happened to you on *Jeopardy!*? You strike me as someone who is extremely smart." I was totally and completely unprepared for that question, and I stood there hoping that lightning would strike the Seattle Space Needle and the city emergency sirens would go off and we'd have to evacuate the building. But no such luck. I just had to try and finesse my way out of it and go on from there—over and over again. It turned out that not only had I humiliated myself in front of millions of television viewers but I also had to relive that humiliation through seventeen cities and three different time zones.

Look, it's my fault. I knew when I said, "Yes, I'll do it," that I would be revealing a carefully covered-up secret. My greed for the coolest new technological gadgets trumped my deepest and darkest fear. And it wasn't until my son was born three years later that my most shameful memory became my most enlightening one.

When Milo was still a baby, I began to read a lot of child development books. There was one book in particular that really resonated with me—*A Mind at a Time*, by Dr. Mel Levine. He wrote, "It's taken for granted in adult society that we cannot all be 'generalists' skilled in every area of learning and mastery. Nevertheless, we apply tremendous pressure to our children to be good at *everything*. They are expected to shine in math, reading, writing, speaking, spelling, memorization, comprehension, problem solving . . . and none of us adults can do all this."

In his book there was a story about a third-grade kid who read a book to his mother every night before he went to bed. But when they tested him at school to place him in the proper reading level, they discovered he could not read at all. Naturally, his mom was extremely confused, because her son read to her every night. After further testing, she learned that her son had memorized the books, which made it seem like he was reading them. The school told her that he had gone to all that effort to cover up the fact that he was not learning how to read like the other kids. And despite the fact that this young boy couldn't read the words, he'd developed an alternative set of memorization and presentation techniques, clever enough to convince his attentive mom. Dr. Levine presented this story to illustrate his belief that one of a child's primary goals, every day of his or her life, is to avoid humiliation, and that a child will go to any length to protect him or herself from it. But as awful as humiliation is, the child's overwhelming need to escape it will often inspire the development of many unique creative and empowering skills and abilities.

As I was reading the story with tears rolling down my face, I realized that I was just like that little boy. I knew early on that I was not learning like the other kids. My strategy was to become the class clown, to excel in other areas, and to develop other skills, all to mask what I could never make sense of. I have always had so many expectations of myself, and this was one area that I couldn't control. Accepting that I had learning limitations has always been the hardest thing for me to do.

It's taken me a long time to forgive myself for it: for not being able to find a way to overcome it. It is such a relief to finally lift the imposter's cloak from over my head and accept that I am "differently" smart and that being intelligent has little to do with whether you know what razor-thin country accounts for more than half of the western coastline of South America, or the temperature at which a gas becomes a liquid.

After studying a few other child development books, I learned a lot about myself, as well as how other people process information. I learned that some people learn visually, others tactilely, and some learn audibly—and that I fit into that last group. Turns out that I learn by hearing information, not by reading it. So basically, I had a learning disability that went undetected for forty years. It was through my work with a psychologist that I finally got the proper diagnosis. What a relief to finally understand why I'd struggled for so long! On the flip side, the harsh reality of having a reading disability meant that unless I reread my textbooks from elementary school *out loud* to myself, I had to continue living life without some of the factual information that others have at their fingertips.

In the end, I choose not to be defined by my humiliating moments but rather by my victories. I choose to see myself as the best of who I am. I am a force of nature, and I refuse to play smaller than that. I live my life out loud, and I count my blessings daily. I may not know about aerospace engineering or the latitude of the Adriatic Sea, but I do know one thing with absolute certainty: you will never see me on *Are You Smarter Than a 5th Grader?*

Note to Self

If somebody treated your best
friend as badly as you treat yourself,
you'd kick their ass.

The Eyes of the Beholder

ANDRÉA BENDEWALD

> Andréa Bendewald is an actress, artist, and writer. She lives in Los Angeles with her husband, Mitch Rouse, and their two-year-old daughter, Tennessee Louise. She has appeared on numerous television shows, most notably *Seinfeld, Friends,* and *Entourage,* and had a series regular role on the hit television series *Suddenly Susan.*

During the week leading up to my thirty-third birthday, I had a hunch that something huge was bound to happen. It was my Christ year, my year of resurrection. This was going to be big, I could feel it. And to kick it off, my six best girlfriends planned a weekend away to celebrate. They wouldn't tell me where we were going, but they promised lots of fun. Now, as a rule, I *hate* surprises. But at the time, I was working with a new therapist on what it means to "trust," which is all about embracing the unknown. And for the past few weeks, I'd been trying to trust that everything would work out, that life unfolds as it should, and that my friends loved me enough to plan something special for my birthday. I just had to trust.

But as the weekend drew near, I didn't hear one specific mention about my birthday plans. What should I pack? When would we leave? Now, I love to plan. Some would call me type A. I call it being prepared. So needless to say, I was pretty annoyed. But I pushed past my anxiety and tried to move on with my daily life. During this time, I received a call from my manager about an audition. We were in the middle of pilot season, so I'd had lots of auditions lately, and I was working really hard to book a job. I hadn't worked in a while, and for a working actress, that's brutal on the ego. Right or wrong, work equals self-worth. But so far, no bites. Needless to say, I was thrilled to pour my energy into prepping for the audition.

The audition material arrived via fax, and I was psyched. It was a one-hour drama, and I was auditioning for the role of a detective on a cop show. I loved it immediately. The character was thirty-three, just like me, and her name was Maggie. Something felt right about it. The script wasn't available—just the audition material, which was two scenes taken from the script—but from what I could tell, this was a great show. The dialogue was seamless. Plus, the show was called *Searching*, and it was produced by Warner Brothers for NBC (two companies I'd worked for previously). The casting director was one of my favorites. The odds really felt in my favor.

That night I ran lines with my sweet husband, Mitch, who's an actor/writer/director, until I knew every word. (He is beyond talented and extremely helpful.) We then started to break down the character: who Maggie was, and what was happening in each scene. I was in a really playful, creative mood.

"Who is Maggie? Who *is* she?" I kept saying.

"She's you," my husband said. "You *are* Maggie."

"Right!" I said. "She is I, and I am she! She is the part of me that could be a cop. She loves justice. I love justice, too!" My husband smiled. I could tell that he was happy that I was enjoying the process, instead of falling apart like a neurotic freak, which is what I usually do.

The next morning I got ready for the audition. I showered and blew my hair straight—with just enough bounce to be pretty on TV, but not look too TV. I applied just enough makeup to hide any signs of being a real thirty-three-year-old detective, and I wore my best black audition suit. I ran my lines, and I knew them all. I felt good.

But driving to the audition, I began to deflate. The old voices of self-doubt grew loud in my head. "Who do you think you are?" I asked myself. "You'll never get the part. You're too old, too blond, not pretty enough . . ." I stopped myself with a pep talk I'd crafted for just these types of moments. "No," I said aloud. "You deserve this. They want you in the room. Be grateful. Loving. You are auditioning. This is your job. Enjoy the process. Don't be attached to the outcome."

By the time I arrived at the Warner Brothers Studio lot, I felt back on track. I signed in at the reception desk, and I was the first one there. I went to the bathroom to apply one last layer of powder, then checked the bathroom stalls to make sure another nervous actress wasn't hiding in one. I looked myself in the mirror, square in the eye, and said, "You can do this. This is what you do. You're an actress. You are a great actress. They would be lucky to have you. Let's do this!"

The casting hallway at the Warner Brothers Studio is famous.

My actor friends and I refer to it as The Versailles of Casting. Framed posters of past and present shows are everywhere, and you always see someone you know—either framed on the walls or waiting in the hall to audition. But this time, the famous hallway was empty, which seemed odd to me. I refocused my attention on the audition. I loved this role; I knew I could really run with it. I felt like this could be the big break that would put me on the map. This could be my *ER*, my *Friends*, my *Searching*.

The casting director came out of her audition room.

"Hi!" I said. I tried my best to be reserved, but I was too excited. "How are you?"

"Great," she answered, deadpan. "You?"

"I'm great. Hey, where is everybody? Am I the only one here?"

The casting director seemed shocked by my question, a little on edge. "Um, I-I don't know?" she stuttered. "You're the first one, I guess. Are you ready?"

"I am, if you are . . ."

I followed her into the room. A young man stood behind a video camera, but there were no producers in sight—which was a bit unusual for a "producer session." Actually, it was totally weird. I must have scrunched my eyebrows, because the casting director spoke as if she'd read my mind.

"I know this was supposed to be a producer session," she said, "but they had to step away for a second, so we will just go ahead and put you on tape."

It only took five seconds for me to sink pretty low. *This tape will be the kiss of death. A live audition is so much more substantial than being put on tape. This is bullshit. I came all this way, prepared their material, and now I'm going to be put on tape?* My insecurities were raging.

"I don't mind waiting," I said.

"No, let's just go ahead." The woman seemed antsy, and more annoyed than before. I wanted to leave the room straightaway, but I needed to act professional. I tried to salvage what was left of my perfect audition composure for my perfect part in this perfect series.

The casting director read with me. I tried to stay focused, but something felt off. What was I doing wrong? I could sense that the audition was going nowhere. How could I take control of the audition, of myself? I finished the torturous scene. I didn't suck, but I wasn't brilliant.

"Wait here," the casting director said. "I want to get the producers. They need to meet you." Hope returned. *Oh, okay, great. I have another shot!*

She left the room, and I smiled at the camera guy to break the awkward silence. But something still didn't seem right. She was going to "get" the producers? That usually doesn't happen. Typically, they call you back for a second audition. I didn't get it, but I decided to go with the flow and trust.

"So, what's your name?" I asked the camera guy. "Do you like working at Warner Brothers? How long have you worked here?" He was midsentence when I noticed the light on the video camera was on. He was recording the conversation. *Why is he . . . ?*

And then it hit me. "Oh, no!"

Just then, the door flew open and in ran my six best friends.

"Surprise!" they shouted. Each one laughed and talked over the next, so pleased with their ability to dupe me.

"We're kidnapping you for your birthday!" they chirped. "Are you soooooo surprised?"

Surprised? I was speechless. I was mortified. And if "surprised" also meant "confused and pissed off," sure, I was that, too. My perfect year, as I'd envisioned it, was no longer. The night before flashed in my head: the perfect script, rehearsing with my husband, my pep talk in the car, my pep talk in the bathroom, making dumb conversation with the video operator . . . *I think I'm dying.*

The girls couldn't stop yammering about how seamlessly they'd pulled off the gag.

"Mitch wrote the sides," one friend laughed. "He was in on it! And so was your manager! Honey, isn't this so brilliant? And now we are taking you away for your birthday weekend!"

My well-intentioned friends, who had no idea what was going on inside my head, squealed and giggled as they dragged me away. I looked over my shoulder at the casting director, who looked mortified as she smiled and waved. "They made me do it," she said.

My husband was waiting in the parking lot, with a bag he'd carefully packed for my birthday weekend. I ran to him for some grounding comfort, meanwhile trying to save face.

"Honey, I knew it all along," I said. "I knew something wasn't right . . ."

"Sweetheart, you just *auditioned* at Warner Brothers," he laughed. "You didn't know anything."

Okay, so he was right. But at the same time, I had smelled a fish. I just hadn't listened to my instincts, and now I felt like a complete idiot. How could I have let this happen to myself? Why hadn't I questioned the casting director? The script? The empty hallway? Had I started to trust too much?

I began to spiral into a pit of self-loathing hell as my friends and I piled into two cars, en route to Santa Barbara. I waved good-bye to my husband from the car window, as if I'd been in the process of being hauled off to jail. I was alone with one of my friends in one car, with my other cohorts in the other. I was in shock. I could barely speak. Everything was happening so fast.

"Honey, are you okay?" my friend asked me.

I answered, but I couldn't look at her. "I feel stupid," I said. "Why would you do that to me in the middle of pilot season? I'm working so hard. Why would you think that's funny? Why couldn't we just go away for a weekend? Oh, and you'd better not show that audition tape to anyone. In fact, give it to me right now." She handed over the evidence with her tail between her legs.

My arms and legs were crossed tightly around my body, as I guarded myself from everyone and everything around me. I stared out the window for most of the drive, though I couldn't enjoy what I saw. I hated the view . . . the stupid ocean, the noisy birds. Even the sunlight was annoying me. I wiped the Kabuki-style makeup off my face with the back of my hand. My black suit felt like a clown outfit.

Meanwhile, my friend who was driving our car was flying solo handling my meltdown. Foundering, she radioed the car ahead for backup. "A little help," she begged. "Not going so well in here . . ."

No response. The girls pretended that nothing was wrong. I silently built my case against them.

We arrived at my friend's beach house, the final destination
for my birthday celebration. Once inside, the group of us gathered around the kitchen table. There, I systematically laid out
why what they had just done was the most horrible surprise they
could ever have thought of; why making light of my "work,"
where I was focusing so much of my energy, was embarrassing,
cruel, and confusing. I had gone after a fake job with my entire
being. And now, reconsidering the audition sides and recogniz-
ing all the clues that my husband had planted in the dialogue, I
felt twice as lame: Maggie was thirty-three. She was "searching."
Her partner's name was Buchwald. (My last name is Bendewald.)
They were "investigating a woman who was abducted at a phony
job interview at Warner Industries." I wanted to disappear.

I thought, *Who are these women with such stunned looks on
their faces? How could they be so clueless? And how could they have
done this to me?*

I turned to a friend, this one a movie producer, and let her
have it. "How would you like it if I arranged a fake meeting between you and a famous director or a studio head?" I questioned
with calm reserve. "You'd have prepared the night before, rehearsed your pitch, and gotten really excited. And then just
when things felt off, the door would have swung open and one of
these yahoos would have shouted, 'Gotcha! Just kidding!'
Wouldn't you be a little upset? Oh, but wait. Then you notice
that not just one yahoo, but all of your closest friends set you up.
Can you imagine how embarrassing that would be? How I felt?
Because if not, we could always watch the videotape!"

I didn't stop there. For each woman in the group, I created a
scenario that would have driven her to tears. Among us were
three actresses, two producers, and one director. I painted a

picture for each, catered specifically to who she was, where she was in her career, and what she yearned for. By the end of my defense, I had each woman wishing she could rewind time and pull the plug on the whole scam. My self-pity was in full effect, and I was taking prisoners.

"But Mitch was in on it, too," one woman pleaded. "Even he thought it was funny!"

"Did he?" I asked. "Like he could say no to you women. He refers to you as 'The Sirens.' He knows your magical powers. He's seen people fall at your heels. You convinced a Warner Brothers casting director to hold a fake audition. Mitch was putty in your hands!"

As I was running low on steam, I stopped to notice that I'd succeeded in making each woman feel as bad as me, if not worse. And then there we were. Six women standing around the kitchen table, staring at the floor, feeling as if a truck had just run us over. One of the brave ones dared to speak.

"We have another surprise," she said. Nervous laughter.

"Okay, great," I huffed. "What else could possibly happen?"

They led me into the living room, where I was handed a pad of paper, a pen, and the telephone.

"There's someone who wants to talk to you."

Who could it possibly be? A relative? An old boyfriend? I didn't want to talk to anyone.

"Just trust us," one of the women said. *She's got to be kidding,* I thought.

One of them handed me the phone. There was a sweet voice on the other end. "Hello there," she said.

"Hi, this is Andréa," I answered back, more than a bit snide. "Who's this?"

"Hi, Andréa. Happy Birthday. It's Byron Katie."

My jaw dropped. I almost fainted. Byron Katie is the author of *Loving What Is*, a self-help book that I'd been obsessed with and had been quoting from for the past month and a half. This was one of my birthday gifts? It again struck me that my friends really could move a mountain if they wanted to. After all, in my mind, talking to Byron Katie was the equivalent of chatting with Oprah, Dr. Phil, or Dan Millman. I idolize this woman and her wisdom. She uses a series of four questions to free yourself of any situation that causes you pain or distress—and then helps you "turn it around." My head felt like it would pop right off my shoulders. In fact, it almost did.

Byron's whole philosophy is that when we "argue with reality," we create turmoil for ourselves. She says that it's our attachment to our thoughts that keeps us in pain, not the actual thought or the reality.

"What do you want to talk about? I'm all yours," she said.

"I don't know," I mumbled.

"Well, what's going on with you right now?"

Really . . . where do I begin?

I told her the whole audition story: the preparation, rehearsal, car ride, self-talk in the mirror, audition, my husband's involvement, the consequent humiliation, the betrayal I felt by my friends. Everything. Byron listened for an hour and a half. And she helped turn it around.

By the end of my conversation with her, I felt like a new person with a better handle on my fears and my friendships. My rage over the faux audition wasn't about what these women had done to me but what I had perceived they'd done. I felt exposed and embarrassed, but my friends had never intended to do any damage. It was my attachment to these negative thoughts about what they had done that was killing me softly.

I hung up the phone with a new perspective and my head held high. And there in the beautiful Santa Barbara sunlight sat my six beautiful best friends, waiting for an update.

"How'd it go?" one asked.

"It was amazing." I told them all about it. "I love you all so much. Thank you. It's all so perfect. The audition, the surprise, the phone call, all of it. I was afraid of being seen, of feeling exposed. I thought you would judge me, but I was simply judging myself. I was embarrassed that you'd see me wanting a job so badly that I'd look like an ass. But that was me judging myself, not you. I love that I wanted the job, that I prepared for it, that I put on the makeup and the black suit. I'm sorry for my reaction and for making you feel bad. I could even watch the videotape right now!"

"Really?" my friends shouted.

"Well," I paused. "Not right now—*right* now."

They still couldn't believe their ears.

The rest of the weekend was filled with even more wonderful surprises. Over those two days I allowed myself to be seen through the eyes of my closest pals, and you know what? I loved what they saw. We talked and danced and ate and laughed throughout the weekend. The whole experience was like four years of psychotherapy, squeezed into a three-hour adventure. And like that controversial psychologist in New York who locked a patient in the trunk of his car and drove him around for hours to cure him of claustrophobia, my girlfriends cured me. They trapped me with my claustrophobic thoughts and fears, drove me to Santa Barbara, and then let me out to deal with my neurosis with a real expert. And it cured me of my fears about being seen.

At the end of our trip, I assured each woman that putting me on the phone with Byron Katie had been the best gift ever. They'd given me more than a well-connected call; they'd forced me to love myself.

Note to Self

Open your eyes to
how your friends view you.
You'll be surprised at what you see.

Too Hip to Be Square

ANNABELLE GURWITCH

Actress and writer Annabelle Gurwitch is a columnist for the *Nation* magazine and a contributing writer and commentator on NPR's *Day to Day*. The *Washington Post* deemed her book, *Fired!*, a comedic look at downsizing in America, "a merry compendium of failure," and her documentary film *10 Ideas That Are Changing the World* earned her a citation in *Time*'s cover story, for bringing attention to the nexus between corporate layoffs and health-care benefits. Her newest documentary series is *WA$TED*, on the Discovery Channel's *Planet Green*. Her writing has appeared in the *Los Angeles Times, Glamour*, and *Child* magazine. Annabelle also works as an actress, known best for hosting *Dinner and a Movie* on TBS. Her last off-Broadway appearance made the *New York Times'* Critics List of Top 10 Performances of the Year in Theater.

When I tell my ten-year-old son that TV used to be in black and white, had only four channels, and no DVR system, he looks at me as though I'd just said you can pee out your ear, sprout wings, and take flight. But I'm old enough to remember watching *I Dream of Jeannie*, *The Beverly Hillbillies*, and *Petticoat Junction*—and that doesn't include the joy that was a 1970s game show. There was *The Joker's Wild*, *High Rollers*, and the Big Kahuna: *Hollywood Squares*.

Without a doubt, *Hollywood Squares* was one of the most memorable. Contestants on the show played a lively game of tic-tac-toe on a gigantic freestanding game cube populated by Hollywood personalities armed with rapier wits. And, unless I'm mistaken, the show's regulars, like Paul Lind, Buddy Hackett, and Rose Marie, actually smoked cigarettes in their squares and downed highballs on the air. It had a distinctly ribald and decadent air. The Squares were bejeweled, dressed with panache, and reveled in their saucy adult and/or insider humor, which is just how I imagined a poker game held in the backroom of a Hollywood nightclub to go down.

It was the year 2000, well into the long run of my interstitial comedy show, *Dinner and a Movie*. The show had acquired something of a following, and I was working steadily when I received a call from the producers of the newly updated Squares. It seemed that one of their regulars, the very appealing comedian Caroline Rae, affectionately referred to on the show as "America's Sweetheart," was leaving to host her now-defunct talk show. They were offering me the chance to occupy her square. Did I want to take her place? the producers asked. Up until that point, I'd never aspired to ever appear on a game show, much less as a recurring guest, but the idea that I, a Jewish gal from Mobile, Alabama, could become "America's (Next)

Sweetheart" was downright exciting. Plus, the gig could prove to be extremely lucrative.

The producers invited me to shoot a week's worth of shows on an upcoming Saturday, their standard shooting regimen, and if the audience was receptive to my persona and banter, I'd join the show, taping episodes at my convenience and at a generous negotiable rate. The only thing the producers required of me in return was charm, a quick wit, and the ability to make the U.S. of A. fall madly in love with me and repeatedly play my square. How hard could that be, really?

On the day of my trial taping, I arrived at the studio with loads of confidence, not to mention my own makeup artist in tow. My dressing room was well appointed with flowers and a hefty basket of gifts. I could get used to this! Also in my room were a stack of cheat sheets, which had been delivered to all our dressing rooms. I, however, took only a cursory glance at these before I broke out the lip gloss. These cards provided us Squares with both the correct answers to all questions and joke answers that staff writers had penned to help us spice up the game. We were told we would bring the cards to our squares with us, so I wasn't too concerned about rehearsing my responses in advance. Instead, I chose to spend my prep time perfecting my hair and makeup. I later learned that while I'd brought a stylist to the dressing room, most of the other stars had brought joke writers to theirs—to punch up the show's material. As we headed toward the stage and the others were still jotting down notes, I had a moment of doubt, but I powdered my nose and it passed quickly. I was shaken, but not stirred. Not yet, anyway.

When I stepped out onto the stage, I was stunned. The set

looked nothing like it appeared on television. The thing looked like a piece of total junk. It felt like meeting Dick Clark or touching the Hollywood sign: up-close and personal, they're much smaller than imagined. The squares also appeared to have had a lot of work done to them and were whiter than I'd reasonably expected. The overall construction was a squat, rickety, metal contraption, and each square was framed in what looked like lightbulbs stolen straight from the makeup room. I couldn't believe all of us B- to C-list celebs, or celebrilites, would willingly climb into this crap—in California no less, home of the earthquake. Was this even up to code? I actually saw a Band-Aid wrapped around a piece of scaffolding as I ascended the spiral staircase to my square. None of this was encouraging.

I should add that when forced to climb up or down a steep staircase, I've often found myself paralyzed with fear. I get very nervous if I'm close to the edge of something without a railing. To be honest, I worry I might jump. Not that I *want* to jump, but for reasons that neither I nor my family would later be able to explain, I have the horrible suspicion I might just be compelled to leap. So as a rule, I avoid ledges and balconies. And when I got to my square and saw that it held a table and chair *but no railings*, I began spiraling into a panic as I imagined a strong breeze that could send me toppling past Whoopi Goldberg, who was seated just below me.

Just before showtime, the lights around my square were brought to their full wattage. It was sweltering hot, and my head began to pound. I heard the producer tell us to smile at all times, because we never knew when the camera might pan to our square. That was when I broke into a sweat. I've never been a happy, shiny person. Although I have been both happy and shiny on one or two occasions whilst performing acts that will never be televised, nothing depresses me more than jocularity on demand, so I said a quick prayer that my square would be hit by lightning. I just wanted it all to stop.

That's when *Hollywood Squares* started.

As the music blared and lights flashed, the set felt more like the *Squares* I remembered watching on TV, though my relief was short-lived. As the other celebrilites sent the audience into fits of laughter wielding their zingy one-liners, I began to suspect that my perfect hair and makeup were not going to garner the same response. I'd planned to wing it and dazzle the audience with my spontaneous delivery and kooky personality. So when Tom Bergeron, the host, asked me my first question, something about Australia and small fruit, instead of referring to the joke cards prepared by the show's writers, I saw an opportunity for a two-minute dissertation about how kiwis resemble testicles. The bit went over like a lead balloon, which is when comedian Super Dave Osborn began chanting, "You suck, Gurwitch!" in the direction of my square. I was instantly transported back to my freshman year of college, when my dorm roommate Stacey Romano, from Teaneck, New Jersey, was cranked up on coke playing David Bowie's "Young Americans" over and over, while I was stoned listening to James Taylor. Clearly, we were just on two totally different wavelengths. And now, once again, I'd smoked when I should have snorted.

Meanwhile, the audience went nuts for Gilbert Gottfried. Positively nuts! And each time the bigger-than-life, baudy co-median and *Hollywood Squares* head writer Bruce Vilanch opened his mouth, the crowd cheered, "Bruce! Bruce! Bruce!" Gray-haired women from Iowa positively swooned at the prospect of picking Bruce's square, and I was so flustered that I became confused about the order of the questions. I also couldn't remember if we were supposed to be helping the contestants or working against them. (The correct answer, I believe, is that we were supposed to be funny.) And each time the contestants pronounced my name wrong, which was often, my answers became laced with sarcasm.

I was not having fun.

That is pretty much how it went for the entire show: *I'll take Annabelle Gartwack to block; Annabelle Ginich, Annabeth Greenwich, Arabella Gatwack to win.* The other celebrities exchanged jokes across their squares, but when I tried to fit in with a quip, they ignored me. By the second game, the audience members caught on to the fact that they should avoid me at all costs. I wasn't called on once during the final game before lunch.

As everyone descended the rickety stairs for our lunch break, my fellow Squares threw pitying glances my way. At the catered lunch, I sat alone and tried to figure out what had just happened. I ate a lot of red meat to ground myself and drank several cups of espresso to boost my energy level. I had two more tapings before I could go home.

Whoopi took the stage after lunch and warmed up the crowd. As I peered nervously over my unsecured perch, I realized that the audience scared me. It was alive with two irresistible teases: a close proximity to celebrilites and the highly intoxicating prospect of winning some money. The audience climbed on stage and participated in a spirited talent contest to win T-shirts and mugs. That's when the thought occurred to me: people wearing cheap cotton T-shirts will do anything to win more cheap cotton T-shirts. The whole time I watched, I couldn't help but think, *Why, why are these people dancing in front of strangers in sweatpants and flip-flops? This is a TV studio, not a locker room.* I know that's not a nice thing to say, but herein was my problem: I'm not a nice person. I am a good person, but nice is another story. Sure, you can count on me in a major emergency. Have you been hit by a car? Caught in a hurricane? You need a tumor removed from your brain? All situations I have faced with honor, but that's basically adrenaline mixed with Jewish guilt. At that moment, I saw my true defective nature. On a day-to-day, minute-by-minute basis, I am not nice at all. And to make matters worse, *Hollywood Squares* only fueled my petty and judgmental fire. *What's wrong with me?* I thought. *Why can't I help these casually dressed Americans win a little extra cash so they can buy more extra-large T-shirts? America's (Next) Sweetheart would be happy to help. Why, she'd be downright thrilled . . .*

That's when I resolved to turn the second half of my day around and tell some damn funny jokes. So when asked by the host, Tom Bergeron, to name the largest indoor entertainment arena in New York, I answered, "My breasts!" Granted, the joke was a gift from head writer Bruce Vilanch. But the fact that I answered "My breasts!" for every answer, for the rest of the day— well, that was my bright idea. I knew I was really bombing when I saw my husband in the back of the theater mouthing the words, "I love you," over and over. My breasts might have been funny the first time, maybe even the second, but by the fourth or fifth time, they just seemed sad. Even Super Dave could feel my pain and ceased his merciless teasing. Eventually, contestants stopped calling on me and started to work any combo to avoid my square, even if it meant sacrificing the win! They hated me, and I hated them, and I hated me for hating them, and I hated them for making me hate me.

After the tapings, not surprisingly, I was not approached by the producer to discuss my next appearance on *Hollywood Squares* or the buckets of cash I would receive for my lifelong contract. In fact, I didn't even hear from those producers until three years later, when we met to discuss another project entirely. Thankfully, nobody ever spoke of my hideous failure and inability to make America love me and play my square. But the memory has stayed with me. Now, when I find myself faced with my own petty nature, I try to push right through it. On those few occasions when I'm able to, even though the cameras aren't rolling, in some small way I feel like America's Sweetheart.

Note to Self

No matter what the circumstance,
(generously) offer everything
you have to give—with a smile on
your face and love in your heart.

Wicked Praise

WINNIE HOLZMAN

Winnie Holzman is an award-winning dramatist and screenwriter. She created the television series *My So-Called Life;* wrote nine episodes of the series *thirtysomething;* and was co-executive producer of the TV series *Once and Again.* In 2003, she wrote the book for the musical *Wicked.* She's as full of complexity, empathy, and humor as the characters she creates.

I'm a full-fledged adult, and I'm still coming to terms with my need for approval and the fear that I'm not good enough.

Growing up, I often felt unattractive as a teenager. That was also hard to come to terms with, because sometimes I privately felt attractive but the messages I was getting—the ones that, for the most part, I believed—said I wasn't attractive, and would never be attractive enough. When I was a child, it was mostly the other girls who did the teasing. The boys got in on it, too, but the girls treated mockery like a full-time job.

But it wasn't just me who didn't fit in. The kids who did the teasing didn't really belong either. I know that now, and I incorporated that realization into *Wicked.* I love how the character Galinda teases Elphaba because of her green skin, bad taste in clothes, and a myriad of other supposed flaws—yet Galinda, in her heart of hearts, doesn't feel she fits in either. She has shame and doubt and all that comes with being human. She's admired for her outward appearance, but being admired doesn't take doubt and shame away. It can actually intensify them.

We all play certain roles—and even in the most mundane scenarios, you're either the mocker or the mockee. I see those particular roles as interchangeable, in a way, because both players in the game are desperate to belong. I was always mocked as a teenager, and it made me see myself as the perpetual outsider. I've often used that perspective in my writing. I let the pain and loneliness of my past surface in my work, so in that way, they become a gift.

I've written ever since I was very small, and I also always wanted to be an actress. Beginning at the age of thirteen, I'd take the Long Island Rail Road into New York City to study acting with a brilliant, somewhat intimidating Russian woman named Sonia Moore, who'd worked at the Moscow Art Theatre. My parents didn't exactly love the idea of me bopping around Greenwich Village by myself, but they never tried to stop me. They paid for the classes and the train tickets.

But when I wanted to continue acting in college, it was a different story. My dad became critical. I got into Princeton, and he thought I should become a lawyer. Today I can understand why he felt that way, but I'd actually been accepted into the Ivy

League because I'd sent in some poetry to the admissions officers, who'd liked it. I hadn't gotten into Princeton because of my great legal mind. I studied English and creative writing, and went on to get an MFA from New York University's musical theater writing program. I got more attention for my writing than for my acting, so I focused on the former. I still consider myself a writer and an actor, but writing is my true calling.

In 1987, my first full-length musical, called *Birds of Paradise*, was produced at an off-Broadway theater called the Promenade. I'd been working on it for nearly seven years with my collaborator, composer David Evans. It began as our thesis project at NYU. The show received only one positive review, from a writer at *The New Yorker*. Otherwise, everyone from the *New York Times* to the *New York Post* to the *Village Voice* termed our musical an unequivocal failure. Audiences went from seeming to enjoy it, to stony silence, to non-attendance. We closed after two months.

My best friend Robin says that bad reviews are a lot like somebody pulling your pants down and spanking you in public. I understood that completely after *Birds of Paradise*. I felt so humiliated that I didn't want to get out of bed. I experienced shame on a cellular level.

Eventually I did get out of bed—but mostly because we had a two-year-old and we were moving our family across the country to California. My husband had been offered a job in Los Angeles, and we hit the road. It felt good to leave the harshness of New York City and the cloud of bad reviews that hung over me there. But at that point, the outsider in me had gone inside, and I thought I might never write again.

I began exploring my actual purpose. I felt like someone had taken me by the hand, back to square one, and I had no answers anymore, only questions—the kind you ask yourself in acting class to work up a motivation to act out but now they had a place in my real life: *Why am I doing this? What am I trying to accomplish? What's my intention?*

In asking myself these questions, I came to see that, once again, I had been desperate for other people's approval. It hit me that I didn't even know the people who had given me the bad reviews, and if I did get to know them, I wasn't even sure if I would respect them—yet I was considering changing the trajectory of my life based on their opinions of me! I was creating my own shame by agreeing with the reviewers—the mockers.

I realized that if I was writing for a good review, I didn't want to write anymore. Don't get me wrong, I love praise. But I couldn't make getting praise the point anymore.

Wicked opened to very mixed reviews, but by the time it came to fruition I'd come to realize that reviews aren't really my business. My job is to express what I set out to express.

I felt blessed by *Wicked* long before it became an international hit, because I knew how hard I'd worked, and how hard everyone involved with it had worked, and that we'd kept at it and not given up. That kind of devotion means a lot to me. In fact, *devotion* is one of my favorite words.

And so I keep going. I'm learning to let go of how other people view me, and even how I view myself. I concentrate on doing my work—taking a plot, and characters, and using them to communicate something that matters to me. This is the fulfillment of my childhood dream, the secret dream of a little girl

who sometimes dared to think she was beautiful. Today, I'm
living it.

> *Note to Self*
>
> Shame is self-generated.
> And it's a choice
> I don't have to make.

HEARTBREAK

Soul Detour

RITA HUNT

Rita Hunt is a community activist and bereavement educator who has taught Death and Dying courses at the University of Hawaii and at Chaminade University. Hunt's advanced studies in education and the nonprofit she founded for people coping with loss and grief, When Is Now, underscore her commitment to helping others deal with death. She believes that grief, and its related journey, needn't be overwhelming. She lives in Hawaii with her husband.

> *Stop, look, and listen,*
> *Before you cross the street!*
> *Use your eyes, use your ears*
> *And then, use your feet!*

This refrain from a children's song haunted me for months after my son Trey's death. I wondered if it had been the one song I should've remembered to include in our nightly rituals of lullabies and bedtime stories. I wondered whether he might still be alive if I had taught him this safety chant. Would he have said to himself, as the other children were playing in the street, *Stop! Don't go out there!?*

Trey was an active nine-year-old, tall for his age. He loved measuring his height against mine. Sometimes I'd ask him, "Who are you?" and Trey would answer, "Mama, I am your sunshine. Don't you know that?" It was our call and answer, I suppose, because Trey knew I loved the sunshine—the rays make me feel alive—and he associated it with happiness.

Trey loved showing off his talents, like swimming and karate, but he could also act silly and make me laugh by singing at the top of his voice and pretending he was speaking another language (he was attempting to speak Spanish). He was somewhat popular in school, but he wasn't always intent on following his teachers' instructions. "He doesn't listen" or "He seems restless," his teachers would say when he didn't have a good day. This seemed like normal behavior for a kid whose parents were splitting up.

Divorce was never part of my grand plan. I'm the oldest of four girls, and for as long as I can remember, I've always felt like the second mother to my younger sisters. Parenting at an early age, having responsibilities, and taking charge came easily to me. When my parents divorced, my mother worked two jobs to support our family. We lived in a great neighborhood and were a financial step above what one might expect from a single-parent home. But Mom was a warrior, and I learned how to "do" by watching her. I also learned that divorce is hard on everyone. I remember thinking that I would never put my own family through anything so traumatic.

By the time I entered high school I was tired of being re-sponsible, and I carefully planned my escape. My plan went like this: graduate from high school early, push through college, and find a husband. Which I did. I was married at twenty-one and couldn't wait to start a family of my own. I wanted to be a mother—a real one, to my own children. In hindsight, I don't think my husband was in the same place as I. I think he was ig-noring his inner voice at the time, which was probably telling him, *You're not ready to be a father.* But his actions spoke much louder.

Not long after we were married, my husband started to act very immature. He'd hang out with his friends and come home late, or not come home at all. Now that I think of it, his behavior wasn't so different from how he'd acted before we were mar-ried; the problem was that I thought he'd grow up and become more of a husband and, eventually, a father. I should have paid attention to the signs all around me that reinforced the old adage "People don't change."

I always expected that my husband would be there for our family—especially for our child. I didn't want him to be a per-fect dad, because I think "perfect" is an unrealistic ideal, but I did want him to be involved. As we neared our son's birth, I began saying things like, "We need to get the baby's room ready." But nothing would happen. I didn't want to buy the stuff myself, because I wanted us to share the experience of getting ready for a baby; it wasn't until our son was born that my hus-band said, "We'd better get a crib." This was definitely not the partner I'd so desperately wanted. We also fought when he'd leave the house with no explanation or good-byes. I grieved a lot in our marriage, wanting something that wasn't there, unable to change my husband into what I wanted him to become, doing my best to not blame myself for the way things were.

Our family was living in Texas, and my parents were in California. My mom could provide moral, but not physical, support. I didn't tell my father about my marriage issues because he'd let my mother down, and I didn't think he'd understand my point of view. Plus, I was ashamed that I had gotten myself into a situation similar to my parents' failed marriage. After ten years of hoping to make it work, my husband and I went our separate ways. I left for California, and he moved to Virginia to be close to his sister and nephews, and we worked out visitation rights for our son. Trey loved his father, and watching us fall apart was really hard on him. It was hard on everyone.

The first summer Trey visited his father in Virginia, he was nine years old. The day he boarded the plane, my maternal instinct told me to keep him safe with me. But my ex had legal rights to time with Trey, and Trey wanted to see his father, so I really had no choice in the matter.

My husband had his friends over for an afternoon barbecue at his place the last week before Trey was to return home. From what his sister told me, a group of kids was playing in front of the house while the adults were out back. Where I'm from, one adult always stays fully alert during such events and checks on the kids. I don't think anybody checked that day. Meanwhile, I was back in California, enjoying a leisurely day of shopping with a friend. For some reason, I'd bought all black clothes that day: a black dress, handbag, and shoes to match. This was odd, since I usually buy bright colors. When I returned home with my friend around 6:00 p.m., there were several messages on my answering machine from my ex-husband, my mom, and my cousin. They'd called around ten o'clock that morning. "Call as soon as possible," the messages said. "Something has happened to Trey." When I returned everyone's calls, they kept repeating, "We lost him. We lost him . . ." Nobody mentioned the word *dead*, so I assumed he'd gone missing.

"Well, where did you last see him?" I asked. "Where do you think Trey could be?"

"No, no, no," they said. Finally, my ex-husband said, "Rita, he died. He's been killed."

Turns out that when the unsupervised kids at the barbecue decided to run across the street, my son didn't make it. He was hit by a car and died upon impact. The driver wasn't drunk, and he wasn't speeding. He simply couldn't avoid Trey, who ran out in front of his car. All my fears about my ex-husband's being an unfit father were confirmed in that moment, and I hated him. My body started shaking violently with the rage and shock that I felt. It felt like I had been left alone, naked, in the snow.

When I put down the phone, my girlfriend who'd been shopping with me said, "What's going on?" I told her, "My son is dead," and then I went into the bathroom, turned on the shower, and ran the water as hot as the knob would allow. I stripped off all my clothes and let the water run down on me for hours. If there had been an ocean, I would have dove right into it. I likely would have drowned myself. Although water can be very healing, the pain was too intense.

When I got out of the shower, I took my new black outfit out of the shopping bag, packed it in a suitcase, and booked a flight to Virginia. I traveled alone, refusing every one of my friends' and family members' offers to go with me. When I boarded the plane, I was in a state of shock, numb to everything around me. It was as if I'd been watching a movie or a play, and I'd merely been a member of the audience and not a participant. In the seats around me, I saw a mother breastfeeding her baby, a high-school girls' soccer team laughing, an elderly couple helping each other get settled. All these lives continued around me. Only I knew my pain, and I've never felt so isolated. I sat in my seat sobbing, afraid of what I would encounter when I landed, wanting to die, and invisible to those around me.

My sister-in-law picked me up from the airport. "I am so sorry," was all she could say. When we got to my ex-husband's apartment, I went directly to my son's room, crawled into his bed, and cried into his pillow. I wanted to yell at my ex-husband. I wanted to scream into his ears with a megaphone and bust his eardrum. *Grow up! Grow up! Grow up!*

Though Trey was supposed to come home to California in just seven days, he'd written me a letter that he hadn't yet sent. It was in his suitcase. "I love you," it read, "and I hope you like this CD that I got for you." It was written in the voice of my sweet nine-year-old. I still keep that letter next to my bed, as a reminder of my son's huge heart and boundless love.

I stayed in Trey's room the whole night, without speaking to anyone. The next day, my mom and aunt arrived; I felt safe to come out. I found my strength, and together, we went to the mortuary to view Trey's body. All I remember thinking was that my son had very long eyelashes. They were enviable, and everyone commented on them. His head was crushed, and I remember looking at him and thinking, *Thank God he's got his eyelashes.*

The day of his memorial service, I kept looking at Trey's eyelashes. They looked like butterfly wings.

When I returned to California, my friends and family offered their support, but nothing seemed to help. When I cleaned out Trey's room two weeks later, giving his things to another nine-year-old in our community, I literally collapsed on the floor. I look back now, and I am not sure how I survived.

One day, a few weeks after the accident, my cousin Tony came to visit. I was still overwhelmed and deeply sad. "You can stay where you are, which is painful," he said, "or you can get up and do something meaningful with what's happened to you. I'm here for you either way." My cousin wasn't judging me. He was simply stating what he saw to be the truth. It was my turning point.

Three months later, I went to my first support group, Compassionate Friends for Parents Coping with the Death of Children. I also bought an Eric Clapton CD and listened to the song "Tears in Heaven" over and over; it made me feel like I wasn't alone. My faith in the power within me—the God within me—helped me eat and take showers. My mother's a very spiritual person, and she's very optimistic; it runs in my blood. Even at my lowest point, I always returned to my higher power—to my belief that I'd get on with my life. I still had faith in the sunshine. Every day I told myself, *You can do this.* If I couldn't convince myself, I'd play music or do anything I could think of to lift myself up and force myself to go on with my life. I would also ask myself, *If I had died before Trey, what would I want him to do?* My answer, of course, was, *I would not want my son to self-destruct.* In a way, Trey is the reason I am alive.

After two years passed, I realized it was time to figure out

how to channel my pain. I decided to heal myself by helping other people manage their grief, too. I knew I needed to
be proactive, and this kept me going. The old cliché says that
time heals, but it's not true. It's what you do with your time that
heals you.

I went back to school and began studying death, dying, and
grief—in our culture and others. I became a madwoman, obsessed with spending days in classrooms and evenings in the
library. I read everything I could get my hands on. I was especially captivated by what I learned about denial. I started to run
support groups and began talking to people about their grief. In
doing this, I began living again.

In my support groups, I try to help people realize that they
have the right to grieve, and that it's natural to feel annoyed by
certain questions or insinuations. For example, the most frus-
trating thing someone could ask a grieving person is "How long
has it been?" This question implies that the person asking is
hoping to attach a time line to your grief. But it's not theirs, it's
yours. Society tries to dictate how many days or years we're allowed to manage something. But grieving has no time line, no
agenda; it has nothing but time on its hands—unabashedly so.
And the longer you grieve, the more people expect you to be-
have a certain way. The whole equation feels unfair, especially
when friends or family tell you, "Okay, it's been a year . . ." or
"She was eighty-two. She lived a good life." As if that erases
your sadness, or helps you stop missing someone. It's a system
of grieving that we learn in an invisible classroom called Life,
and it's inaccurate and flawed.

Through my experience, research, and work, I've also

learned that people don't know what to say to a grieving person. Acquaintances often assumed that "You only had one son, you poor thing" was some kind of consolation. What they didn't know was that I made a choice to have one child, and I wanted him to be a boy. I also know people talk about me behind my back, since, well, I've heard them. They are so uncomfortable because they don't know what to say. Knowing that they're simply without words has helped me handle people's reactions. When others don't know how to deal with someone who's grieving, I suggest they simply ask the griever what he or she needs. Admit you don't know what to do or say. Make no assumptions. Say, "I want to be here for you. If you want to talk about your son or your daughter, I'll listen." Offer *yourself*. Give the gift of a book or a journal. Sometimes it's not the words but the actions of people that help us—a friendly keychain or kind notes, periodically. A friend sent me a card and a book on Trey's tenth birthday that said, "I found this little book and thought about you. You're never alone. Call me anytime." I will never forget that. A year after Trey's death, she sent me a card with a daily meditation book.

Years after my son's death, my ex-husband said to me, "You're right, and I was wrong. Your anger is anger I feel toward myself. Every day and night, I think about that one decision I made." He asked me to forgive him, and I did. It took me a while, but I did. I know my son would want me to. He loved his father, and for that reason alone I had to forgive him. I could almost hear Trey's voice as I came closer to that place in my heart. "Mom," he'd say, "love my daddy." Forgiveness was important to him.

Every September when school starts, I pass kids in the playground, and it's very hard for me to watch. Sometimes I go out of my way to avoid them. I've learned ways to manage my grief, but it doesn't subtract from what I felt for, and still feel for, my son. I also believe that life does not end; the body simply does a disappearing act. The essence, his soul, his being, our memories—these are the things that stay.

Note to Self

Time heals wounds,
but it's your faith and inner strength
that heals your life.

Electric Cowgirl

CAL PEACOCK

Cal Peacock is a folk artist, wilderness tracker, horse whisperer, farmer, ecologist, fairy expert, storyteller, and grandmother, and she never says no to a good time. Her passion for life is contagious.

At fifty-three, I lost my life. Inside and out—my home, my boyfriend, my confidence, my dignity. Everything.

When I met my boyfriend Anthony, I was living in a beautiful little adobe home out in Santa Fe, New Mexico. Our property had fields and streams, and big cottonwood trees stood out in the front yard. I had sixteen horses and every kind of farm animal, including sheep and goats.

I had started this program called Grandma's Farm a few years earlier in which local children could come to my home and learn horsemanship, wilderness skills, and how to take care of farm animals. They also learned how to plant and harvest food and read the weather to tell if a storm was coming in or what to do if a flash flood came. The program was about teaching kids how to take care of themselves. It was a good little business.

Anthony and I dated for about a year, and then I moved in with him on his ranch. We were very happy together, but I held on to Grandma's Farm because I'd had enough breakups in which I'd lost everything. I wasn't going to put all my eggs in this man's basket, and I was going to keep my own sense of security.

Five years into it with Anthony, he started pressuring me to let go of Grandma's Farm and move my operation up to his ranch.

"What are you doing, keeping your back door open or something?" he kept asking me. "You're just not willing to make a commitment."

I wanted his approval desperately, but more important, I wanted a life partner. So I let go of Grandma's Farm. I moved all of my horses and animals up to his ranch. I was able to put all the money I saved into the ranch, and it seemed like our place now instead of just his.

Things went along fine for about a year until June 21, the summer solstice. I'll never forget that day. It was as though a dragon came in and wiped out my life with a breath of fire. I came home unexpectedly and found out that Anthony had another woman on the side.

This wasn't the first time this had happened to me. I was always with tall, dark, handsome guys who couldn't be faithful to me. The last time around it had taken me five years to leave, and by the time I had, I'd been practically suicidal. I'd just kept wondering what was wrong with me, and why I couldn't be unconditionally loved. And why was I so jealous and possessive and narrow-minded? I'd really beaten myself up about it.

This time, when the betrayal happened with Anthony, I did not waste any time. I was out of there by eight o'clock the next morning.

Overnight, my world went away. I lost all my beloved horses, all my animals, my relationship with all these amazing children, my lover, my home. But most of all, I lost my faith, my inspiration, my sense of self. It felt like my spirit was gone. Snatched away by a bird in the big mountain sky.

I cried every day. Even though it was tempting, I didn't want to take any antidepressants or seek conventional therapy because I felt like I needed to face this alone. I realized that in the past I had always grieved a couple of months after a relationship and then fixed myself up and gone to town and found myself another boyfriend. Life seemed easier with a partner. On the practical side, you shared the money and the rent, which just made things easier, and I made sure that I always kept things even-keeled. Rocking the boat was not an option, because then it would end; and every time I left one or was left, I lost everything I had in my life at that moment. I kept gutting myself while the men I had been with went on with their lives and their new lovers. Something had to change. It was bankrupting my soul.

I wound up moving in with my daughter, who has two children. They are the love of my life, and she and I have always been best friends. However, now things were different. I had always been her hero, her cheerleader, and her source of support, someone she'd admired and respected and bragged about;

her mother was a cowgirl. But now I was this dysfunctional basket case, and she couldn't stand to see me that way. So we fought. A lot.

My daughter said to me at one point, "Damn, Mother, there's nothing wrong with you. You're not in a fuckin' wheelchair. Get up and get a job! Get to work, get over it, get over yourself and quit this mopin' around!"

My son, who's a year younger than my daughter, sided with her, too, and started putting the pressure on me. He said, "Mom, do not be a burden to us. You can snap out of this. I don't know what you're pulling on us, but I'm not buying it."

It was rough. It was probably the most painful thing in my life to have my children lose respect for me, but there was nothing I could do about it. I had this terrible fear that I was going to end up a homeless person if I moved out of my daughter's house. I was afraid that I would end up living under a bridge.

I was a complete mess for three and a half years.

At some point, I realized that I was belittling myself all day long and it needed to stop. I started a conscious practice of complimenting myself. I was putting groceries away one day after I had started doing this, and as I put the milk in the refrigerator, I started talking to myself.

"Oh, honey, I'm so proud of you! You are so smart. Look at how you're placing things in a space properly. Look how you figured out just exactly where to put that milk in the refrigerator. You are so good!"

Then I cracked up because I was laying it on pretty thick. It struck me that it was just like talking to children, building their confidence. After that, each time I realized I was putting myself down, I would think, "Oh, honey," and I would switch it to a compliment.

But the crying didn't stop until I met Bobby. Some friends introduced us, and I took one look at him and saw the template was there: tall, dark, handsome. It freaked me out because I literally saw him morph into every man I had ever loved. He was younger, but there was something so deeply soul-connecting about him that it seemed to defy age. I had not even been able to look at a man until now, and I was so excited.

It didn't even last a month—he came to me after a matter of weeks and said that he really loved me "as a friend" but that his old girlfriend had come back into his life and he thought he might settle down for good and marry her. My pattern of failed relationships would have suggested that when the new girl entered the scene, my heart would have broken wide open, but this time it was different. I held it together, and we made an agreement: he allowed me to use him as my "practice boyfriend." I realized that I couldn't work out my issues on a desert island. I needed to talk to somebody, and he agreed—platonically.

Hunting season in the high country commenced, and Bobby introduced me to Mike, who ran hunting camps. One day, Mike was unable to find a wrangler for a group going out, and he asked me to fill in. (I learned later that he would never have asked a woman, but he was desperate and he knew that I was good with horses.)

It was as if I felt the heavens open up! There was nothing in the world that I loved more than riding. I had not been on a horse in nearly three years, and I felt like I didn't even know who I was without riding. I was so excited that it didn't occur to me to ask what the pay was or what exactly I would be doing for him. I would have done it for free. I didn't care. I just wanted to be back in the wilderness, where I felt most comfortable. I agreed on the spot.

Once we got up to the camp in the mountains, Mike told me my job description. I would be waking up at 3:00 a.m. and managing the camp: cooking, fetching water from a nearby stream, making sure the horses and mules were fed and safe, gathering firewood, and cleaning up during the day while the hunters were out shooting elk. Bedtime was around 9:30, so I would be working a seventeen-hour day.

I'm kind of a tough cowgirl in some respects, but you can tell when someone is disrespecting you. It smells like horseshit. The hunters spent their time telling the most foulmouthed, filthy, offensive jokes. I felt like they were trying to do it in front of me because I was a woman, and if I was going to be there, I was going to have to put up with it. They weren't going to change their tone in any way for a lady, and that was the way it was going to be. They wanted to get a rise out of me.

I had been up there two weeks when I realized how fried and tired I was. I was an older woman working my ass off, and I was on the verge of a nervous breakdown! Being treated with disrespect by the hunters and Mike felt familiar to me, but something in me was building, and I didn't know what it was. I was falling into bed exhausted at night, but something was bothering me deep inside that kept me awake. I couldn't name it, but I knew it was there.

Storms were brewing on the outside, too. Thunder and lightning were followed by an arctic chill in the mountains. Sleet was coming down, and it sounded like buckshot hitting the side of my tent. Soon there was no distance between the thunder and lightning strikes. It was happening at the same time. I remember thinking, *Oh, my God, we're going to die. This is it.*

In the distance I heard avalanches and the trees coming down. The whole forest was collapsing under the storm. The aspen trees were snapping in the sixty-miles-per-hour winds. I thought the mules would be crushed for sure by the trees, but they miraculously survived.

The electric storm was over by the dawn's first light. Something about that cold morning made me warm inside, as if I'd been recharged.

As the camp continued, one night before the hunters went to bed, they asked me if I would wake them up the next morning. They had been sleeping through their alarms.

I said, "Sure, no problem."

So at four o'clock the next morning I yelled at the hunters, "Get up, you guys!"

And oh, my God! I heard them in there just cussing at me. They were saying things like, "What the fuck is she doing yelling? What an idiot!" They were really putting me down.

Finally, something snapped in me. I felt it deep inside. It was as if the cold snap outside had whipped me into shape, and I was feeling my nerve. It felt as if I was coming back into my body for the first time in months, and I wasn't going to let anyone kick me around. Until that moment, I had been trying to dodge the way the men had been treating me, but I knew that I had to confront it and stop avoiding what I was most afraid of. The cold snap saved me.

That day, I started talking back to the hunters and to Mike. If they said something I didn't like, I told them so. If Mike was too hard on me, I told him to back off. All of a sudden, things shifted in the camp. All of those men were looking at me as if they didn't recognize me, and they started showing me some respect. They began making me a little food in the morning and treating me as if I was part of the group.

I had some gumption, and I was shooting from the hip and cleaning up the blood later. All of a sudden, I was the boss of the camp.

I got paid seventy dollars a day for that job, by the way. That comes out to just over four dollars an hour. That was how little self-respect I had when I started working at that camp. It was never going to happen again.

At the end of the hunt, when we went back down from the mountains, all of the hunters gave me big hugs and told me to keep in touch. They invited me to their homes and asked me if I was ever going to come up to the camp with them again. I just smiled and told them I might see them around. I was amazed at how their attitudes about me had changed just as a result of my standing up for myself.

I moved to California not long after the hunt, and since then I've been thriving. I'm sending money home to my kids and I bought myself a new car, a fast little thing that gets thirty miles to the gallon. I've been doing art commissions and I'm giving workshops. I am alive and well, and I haven't had one bad day.

I have come to embrace the wisdom of being older. I believe that wisdom is finally having lived long enough to recognize a pattern. There's no way you can see something repeat itself until you have lived long enough to stand at a distance from it.

Note to Self

If you stand just an inch away
from the edge of a tapestry,
you can't see the whole pattern.

The Will to Leave

MICHELLE ROTH

Michelle Roth is a happy mother of four who lives in Newport Beach, California. She is active in her community and is involved in various charities, both locally and nationally. She loves sports, traveling, and renovating homes, but mostly she loves her children.

There's no way I could march out the door. Anyone who hasn't been cheated on and struggled with the confusing feelings it brings on would say that they would leave in a second. They think they'd just say, "I'm out" and walk away. But it's not that easy. You're hurt, your whole world is shattered, and you're scared. I wouldn't wish the pain or confusion on my worst enemy—even if she turned out to be, say, my best friend.

I married Byron when I was twenty-five, and I had my first child, Chelsea, three years later. Life was great until we moved from Pasadena to Newport Beach, California. Byron interviewed at some of the top investment firms in the area, but he didn't have much luck finding a job. At the time, we were heading into an economic recession, so I worked in the fashion industry to make ends meet. Then my dad introduced Byron to a gentleman who owned a small firm in Newport, where my dad had done some business. Byron was hired, and soon enough, with some loans from my father to buy into the firm, Byron was named president. Thus began the demise of his character, family values, and morals.

I got pregnant a second time but miscarried. We had to wait eight months to try again, and when I finally conceived, I was extremely careful. I took it very easy. I was busy with Chelsea, acquainting myself with this new community, making new friends, and helping Byron with his business. And that's when Byron started having an affair with his hairdresser—when I was pregnant with our second child.

I had absolutely no idea what was going on behind my back. Byron was staying out later and later, but never in a million years did I think he was having an affair. I was young. I didn't get it. I just figured that he was out with the guys.

After Madeline was born, my best friend, Susan, godparent to Maddie, threw me a baby shower. I will never forget the night before the party: Byron didn't come home until 7:00 the next morning. I was up all night with the kids, but the next day, I put on a smile and went to my baby shower with Madeline in tow, praying it would get better but knowing deep down inside I really didn't know what to do. The last thing I wanted was my friends speculating on my marriage.

But I did talk to one friend about Byron's all-nighter. I told Susan. From the moment we met, Susan and I knew we would be in each other's lives forever. People used to ask if we were sisters. She was as disgusted as I was, if not more, by what Byron had done. She promised to keep my secret safe.

As soon as the gathering was over, I checked into a nearby hotel. Within twenty-four hours, Byron begged me to come back, and the next thing we knew we were moving into our dream home . . . truly, just like that. But an affair continued with me not having a clue. At the time Byron signed the papers on the house, he said he felt awful for spending so much time with "his friends" and staying out so late. We moved into the house; about six weeks later, I was pregnant with our third, a boy, and we were thrilled. Byron kept things even-keeled enough that I thought our life together was going according to our plan to have a beautiful family.

But I should have known better.

From the outside looking in, Susan was married to a wonderful man named Steve, who had grown up in the same town as me. Steve was very successful at a young age. He met Susan and married her months later. She was attracted to his success, to say the least. The two of them were forming a great life together. They also had four children, a beautiful home, and many friends. We all became very close friends, traveling together, joining the same organizations.

In the meantime, Byron and I were getting counseling. Byron told me he wanted very much to work through our problems and would do anything to win back my trust. We even went so far as to promise our therapist that if he ever had contact with this hairstylist again or had another affair, our marriage was over. That would be it. Despite agreeing to all of this, I remember thinking that I could not leave him if I had to . . . I was blindly devoted to him. That sounds so pitiful to me now, but again I had let Byron take my life away. I felt like I was nothing without him. Considering our past and Byron's wandering eye, he probably doubted his ability to stay faithful and my ability to punish him.

After a good year of couples therapy, Byron convinced me he "was healed." We stopped the sessions, and I rededicated my life to him . . . thinking that must be the answer. Don't rock the boat! I became the "perfect" wife and mother. I made our home more beautiful than ever, I participated and headed up many charities, I played the Stepford Wife to a tee. I also continued to look over my shoulder and grew to suspect any woman who would flirt with Byron in any way. I walked on eggshells constantly, for fear that if I rocked the boat, Byron would have another affair.

The trouble was I had been living with a form of abuse for years that sucked the pride, self-confidence, and any kind of strength right out of my soul. It was mental abuse that clouded my ability to see things clearly for what they were.

When your husband is unfaithful, this is how you begin to live. Infidelity thrives on insecurities . . . and I hoped that if our close inner circle of friends saw me as the perfect wife, then my husband would view me this same way, too, and appreciate it.

Over the years, Susan was showing signs of breaking her promise to me and exposing things about my private life. She started talking. People who were closest to me would ask me why I was friends with Susan. I would look at them and think, *Why not?* I really loved her and was loyal to her. I'd reached a point in my life when I realized that nobody's friends are perfect, but you don't dump your friends over harmless flaws. Eventually over the years I did start backing away from our friendship. Her behavior was making me increasingly uncomfortable. There was something in our friendship that I was outgrowing. But it was difficult to distance myself, because the minute I would pull away, she was right in my face asking why. Then I noticed her flirting with Byron. At the time I would have felt like a fool confronting her about my husband, and my insecurities, and besides, I thought of the scene she would have caused around the community. We had a lot of friends in common.

One night we had dinner with Steve and Susan. Byron and I had just thrown a political party for a California gubernatorial candidate (which meant I busted my ass to throw a great event). Susan was invited. She was mildly confrontational with me and made some nasty comments. I just laughed it off, and Byron and I went to dinner with her and Steve after the party. While waiting for our table at the restaurant bar, Susan became enraged by how attentive Byron acted toward me. I thought it was odd, since no one had said anything to make her upset. By the time we sat down for dinner, Susan had drunk way too much. Suddenly, she jumped up and went to the bathroom. Steve didn't follow her in, but Byron did. For a while after they left, neither Steve nor I said anything. I was confused, but I didn't want to embarrass anyone, and I didn't want to jump to conclusions. But I thought, *Not again.* After an awkward silence, I suggested that Steve check on Susan. When he returned to the table, he was white as a ghost. I asked him what was wrong, and he said, "Nothing. Susan's just drunk."

As Byron and I were getting into the car, I told him how weird it had looked that he'd responded so quickly to Susan's outburst. "You know, it's not right that you jumped up at dinner to follow her," I said. "Why would you do that? Let Steve handle it. Why do you care?"

Byron didn't say a word, which was a warning sign. But I was still in denial about him. Susan was another story, so I said to myself, *You know what? I am done with Susan.* I reassured my conscience that she wasn't acting like a good friend, had issues with Steve, and I didn't have time to deal with her drama. Unfortunately, we'd made plans with Susan and Steve to visit Napa a few days later. I didn't want to go after that night, but Byron really wanted to go, and he encouraged Susan and Steve to beg me. Susan even apologized for acting so strange earlier that week. "Michelle, please come," she said. "It's going to be so much fun. I am really sorry about the other night. I've just been having some issues lately. I'm okay." Finally, I agreed to go—more for Byron than for me. That was a mistake. When we met Susan and Steve at a midway point on the highway, Susan hopped out of the car in a plaid miniskirt, boots with six-inch heels, and her shirt tied under her boobs. I assumed she was simply going through a midlife crisis. In fact, I felt guilty that I hadn't been there for her as a friend when clearly she was going through something.

That night at dinner, Steve looked visibly upset, but I couldn't figure out why. After a few drinks, he turned to me and said, "I need to tell you what I heard the other night at the restaurant." I felt socked in the stomach as I anticipated what he was about to say. Then he turned to Susan and said, "I'm going to tell Michelle." Susan said, "I don't care."

I looked at Byron and said, as if he hadn't heard, "Steve has something to tell me." Byron was very silent (again).

As it turns out, Steve had overheard Susan yell at Byron in the bathroom, "Why are you so into your wife if you're so into me?" The question didn't register immediately, but once it did, I blamed my friend for anything that might or might not have been going on between them. *Susan's after him,* I thought. *Byron hasn't done anything to bring this about.* Talk about denial. When we got back to our hotel room, I grilled Byron for hours. He denied everything, of course, but in the end I knew one thing for sure: my friendship with Susan was over.

A few days later Byron was on his way home from a business trip. That night I did something I rarely did: I checked his voice mail at work. I had the password—I'd known it for seven years—and once in a while, I'd check it. I was suspicious after the hairdresser affair, and I made sure I was aware of who he was talking to. I know it was horrible, but I did it. So that night, I checked it and discovered that Susan had just left him a message on the machine—two, in fact—and in both she went on about how much she loved him. I remember her voice saying the opening sentence, "Hi, my love."

I was paralyzed as Susan went on about how much she'd loved seeing Byron the day before, and how she couldn't wait to see him again the next day, and how she wanted to be with him forever, and how they were going to work through her pregnancy! Then I hung up the phone and called her house. She answered and said she was doing homework with her daughter.

"You fucking bitch. You've been having an affair with Byron."

"What are you talking about?" she asked.

"I know everything," I said. "I cannot believe, after the pain you've watched me go through, that you would do this to me."

"I don't know what you're talking about," she said again.

"You have been having an affair with Byron," I repeated.

"Talk to your husband," Susan said and slammed down the phone.

I found out later on that her poor child had sat up every night over the summer listening to her mother talk to Byron. She'd known about this affair before any of us had and had kept it a secret.

As devastated as I was, I had a fight in me. While he was getting on the airplane to come home, I called him and told him I knew about Susan. He denied it and called me crazy. In the meantime, I called Steve and gave him the password to the messages so he could hear them for himself.

When Byron arrived home, I was curled up in bed. The reality had hit, the evidence was numbing, and the realization that my life was about to change forever was gut wrenching. He sat down in a chair beside me, and I said, "I know about Susan." Byron still denied it. He always denied something until he knew I had absolute proof in my hands. I did have proof. Susan was busy cleaning up the mess on her end.

Steve later told me that after he heard the evidence, he sat down in front of the fire and downed a huge glass of vodka. Then he looked at Susan and said, "You've got to fucking be kidding me." "I'm sorry, I'm sorry, I'm sorry," Susan said. I think Susan apologized so profusely because if it didn't work out with Byron, she didn't want to be left out in the cold.

For the next forty-eight hours, all I did was interrogate Byron. The pieces of their affair fit together with my unhappy marriage like a perfectly unsettling puzzle. Like something out of a movie, Susan had left my baby shower early that day. I asked Byron if they'd had sex. "Yeah," he said, "we did." I asked Byron if he'd actually screwed her when I was in the hospital with

Hudson. He didn't say yes, but he didn't say no. He said, "Michelle, let's not go there."

I replayed it in my mind, like slow motion: that day in the hospital when Hudson was born, Byron and I were overjoyed. The next night, Susan brought me dinner. She held Hudson. I told her how happy Byron and I were, how we planned to have another child. "I just can't tell you how much good has come out of something bad that happened so long ago," I said. Minutes later, her phone rang and she said it was her son asking for help with his homework. I think that was the night she got pregnant with Byron's child—if not then, then at least during the next several days.

The discovery of the Susan-affair happened in November. Byron stayed in the house until February. During that time, I became emotionally stronger. In November I started going through options in my head. I could kick Byron out of the house, but then I would spend every day wondering when he was sleeping with that woman. I had to force myself to fall out of love with him. But I wasn't ready to walk away. I didn't know how.

So I waited. Sometimes Byron would come home and be so sweet, and at other times, he'd walk through the door so arrogantly, such an asshole, that it took my breath away. It was obvious to me that when he was a jerk, he'd just gotten off the phone with Susan and felt trapped. The more I found out about how often they saw each other, or spoke to each other, the more strength I gained. He would walk in and be horrible, and my resolve would expand. He was pushing me closer to accepting that I'd soon be a divorcée with four kids—and that this would be better than the situation I was in.

I also promised myself that no matter how things played out, I wouldn't become bitter. I'd rely on friends and family to carry me through. For years, I thought people liked me because of who I'd married, but as I became more independent from Byron, I learned that not one person in Newport Beach admired my husband. My sister advised me to see every lawyer in the area about making our divorce official, so I met with thirteen divorce attorneys. I felt empowered now that I was doing something about my unhappiness. Our split was a long time coming, but I had to manage it on my own clock, or else I knew I'd fail.

Toward the end of December, Steve called. It was the first time we'd talked since I'd made him listen to the voice mails Susan had left Byron. We talked for two hours, during which we realized that we needed to act as one another's detectives, for the sake of our families and our futures. By then I knew our marriages were getting close to the end. Nonetheless, Byron, the kids, and I spent a Christmas together. But by New Year's, I was in tears. I kept thinking back to all the years we'd spent together and all we'd been through. Sometimes you do that on New Year's Eve.

On New Year's Day, when Byron's family came to visit, his brother said to me, "I really can see a change for the good in Byron. Michelle, I think it is going to be okay. He is over her."

What his brothers did not know, but what I knew, was that Byron had set up a new voice mail so he and Susan could communicate. I told his brother, "Honest to God, he is out of here. I am tired of the lack of respect and deceit he brings into this house."

After the family left, Byron was in one of his loving,

it's-all-working kind of moods, but I sat him down. I confronted him about the phone calls. "You have been walking in and out of this house long enough," I told him. "Your continued actions are very disrespectful to our kids and to me, and I want you to leave. Now!" I was finally in my power.

By February, I gave myself a birthday gift: a divorce. Byron spent the day chasing me around begging me not to do it. I had fallen out of love the hardest way I had ever known. I had seen such an ugly person before me. It would be impossible for him to ever regain the love and respect I once had for him. I have never truly been able to look in his eyes again.

Seven years later, I now fully understand that I was living with a man whose actions throughout his life really did speak louder than his words. It was so difficult at the time to see that simple truth. To this day, my stomach turns when I look at Susan. The two of them turned me into a fighter. Fortunately for me, Susan has now inherited all the affairs and indiscretions in Byron's life, and the enormous weight has now been lifted from me.

Telling the kids that Mom and Dad were divorcing was one of the most heartbreaking moments of my life. They were all so young. Chelsea was the one who truly understood, and she was crushed. Only time will tell how it plays out in their adult lives.

I did date Steve for a brief period of time after the fact. I think we both needed a shoulder to lean on to get through the tragedy; in fact, I don't think I could have made it without his friendship. Unfortunately, this gave Susan and Byron the excuse to run around accusing us of having an affair, which is so far from the truth.

And recently, there has been a man in my life who is the first to make me laugh from my heart again, which I thought would be impossible. We are planning on getting married. He is honest, cares for my children as if they were his own, and thinks I am the most beautiful woman in the world (it is sure nice to hear that every day).

Byron and Susan got married and live in chaos with eight children.

I mourn once in a while the loss of this family dream for everyone involved, but at the same time I really believe in not selling yourself short or settling for less than you deserve; in moving at your own pace toward recognition; and in taking the time you need to gather strength before walking out of a bad situation. Sometimes you have to come to terms with the ugly before you can figure out how to deal with it. This way, there are no regrets.

Note to Self

Don't punish yourself for moving
at your own pace toward
an informed decision.
The only thing that comes
from making a rash decision
is prolonged self-doubt.

Love, Interrupted

BEVERLY LONDON

Beverly London is a retired teacher of English as a second language, a mother of three children, a grandmother of ten, and a great-grandmother of one. She converted to Judaism and lived in Israel for six years. Her passions include opera, playing the piano, cooking, her family, and friends.

I am the happiest seventy-year-old woman I know, but my life hasn't been without its challenges. Before I arrived at this beautiful place, I fought the AIDS virus long and hard—not to mention the shame, secrecy, pain, and confusion that come with it—both for me and the man I loved.

My AIDS saga began when I fell in love with a man named Perry London, a well-known, highly respected, and extremely complex college professor. I was thirty-nine years old at the time, and I stretched and grew in Perry's dazzling world of professional psychology. We created a relationship of love, laughter, travel, opera, and debates that felt bigger than life, and we dated for only one year before marrying. Our home was filled with the whirlwind energy of combined families and interests:

seven children, Russian and Israeli relatives, intense colleagues, creative students, hosts of friends, and a madcap schedule. Perry's career included a few hours of teaching each week and a lot of time to read, write, study, attend conferences, listen to classical music, and hang out with me. If that wasn't enough, his professorial lectures took us all over the globe. We lived in Israel for six years, and when we traveled, we mingled with world-renowned behavioral psychologists like B. F. Skinner, Jack Comfort, and Rollo May. After meeting Simon Wiesenthal, a Nazi hunter and humanitarian, in Jerusalem, we were invited to his home in Vienna, Austria. I had tears in my eyes the night I met Erik Erikson at the Harvard University Faculty Club, because his essays had changed my life in college. It was a remarkable lifestyle that suited us both well.

Perry, however, wasn't my first love. At twenty-two I married a successful businessman, and for seventeen years, I stayed at home like a good suburban wife and mother. After high school, and with much difficulty, I'd left an ultraconservative and devout community of born-again Christians, the type that didn't condone movies or dancing. I grew into a beautiful '50s female stereotype. I was a devoted caretaker and great cook; we owned a huge house next to a lake, with a forty-foot swimming pool, a new car, cashmere sweaters, and gowns to burn. My husband and I attended socially prominent parties when we weren't spending summers and holidays on our 435-acre ranch with horses, cattle, motorcycles, dogs, and my three healthy and happy children. Some might say I had it all, but I always itched for more. I divorced my husband after nearly two decades together, and I encountered a whole new world soon after.

Perry began courting me when he was an esteemed professor

of psychology, psychiatry, and behavioral science at USC. Meanwhile, I was almost forty and fresh from a broken marriage. I didn't have the breadth and depth of Perry's experience and education, but we fell for each other nonetheless. At the start of our relationship, I wondered why he was so interested in me, especially since he worked among pretty young graduate students in their sexual prime, some unmarried. I often joked that college professors sexually lived off the fat of the land! But Perry reassured me that he liked how I brought stability, a quiet resolve, and a deep intimacy with my friends and kids to our manic life. I would have eagerly grown old with him. Not only was I hooked on the enormity of my life by his side but I was also able to use every God-given talent I had during our years together. I had no fantasies of wanting more, as I'd had with my first husband. Even when Perry got sick, I never wished for the stability and riches of a suburban marriage. What I didn't know then was how differently our lives would play out, together and apart.

After USC, we moved to Israel, where he taught at Tel Aviv University. Even though I was a recent convert to Judaism, and not yet fluent in Hebrew, I became absorbed into the Israeli culture. However, Perry, a born Jew, a graduate of Yeshiva University in New York, and fluent in both Yiddish and Hebrew, did not adjust to life there, and, sadly for me, we left when he was offered a professorship at Harvard University. We'd been in Boston for several years when the doorbell unexpectedly rang on December 28, 1988. I remember that I was sitting in my kitchen, sipping my morning coffee, and working on a paper about second-language acquisition when the bell broke my concentration. The mailman needed me to sign for a registered letter from our insurance company that was addressed to Perry.

He was driving cross-country for a sabbatical at UCLA, and, knowing that he had applied for additional life insurance, I opened the letter, assuming it just concerned family business. Instead, what I discovered would change my life forever. The letter stated that Perry was denied further life insurance because he was HIV-positive.

I called my doctor at the Harvard Medical Center, who told me to get tested for the virus as soon as I joined my husband in California a month later. Until then, I focused on completing my final paper for a master's degree in English as a second language from the University of Massachusetts. It was a fine distraction, indeed.

I did not tell Perry about his infection until I was alone with him in Beverly Hills in January. When I delivered the crushing news, his eyes darted furtively around the room. Imploding with fear and panic, he begged me to keep his infection a secret. He said he had not wanted to tell his family because he had "enough trouble" and that he had not wanted to tell his colleagues because he had not wanted "to be disgraced." I vowed to keep his disease a secret, but my promise became a fool's bargain. Perry cautiously explained that his infection must have come from a hooker with whom he'd had sex on frequent trips to the West Coast. I believed him and chose not to address his infidelity. I also was accustomed to choosing my battles, and I knew that AIDS had already won. My job now was to live my life as well as I could with HIV in my household; I had yet to learn that the secrets would become my most difficult problem.

A few weeks after Perry learned he had HIV, I tested negative for the virus. Four months later, after assuming I'd successfully dodged the plague, I tested positive. It was a devastating moment for obvious reasons, but it didn't help that our marriage had also changed since Perry's diagnosis. We looked like the same couple to outsiders, but our private lives were ruled by the virus. Our joie de vivre was gone—and with it, the intimacy of our sexuality and conversation. Perry's secret had now become mine, and it governed our every thought. We lied constantly. The open, casual, honest, joyful conversations we'd typically had with others became a façade to our grief.

Our lives were also controlled by fear. Had anyone learned of my deadly infection, I certainly would have lost my teaching job in L.A. Surely, Perry's job would have been in jeopardy, too. We rented an apartment in Beverly Hills during his sabbatical, and we could have been forced to move. In 1989, the HIV-positive community lived in a war zone. Landlords evicted us, caregivers feared us, strangers recoiled from us, physicians refused to treat us, preachers condemned us, the government ignored us, families disowned us, spouses left us, insurance companies bilked us, schools refused to teach us, employers fired us, and morticians refused to bury us. People are less afraid of those with HIV infections now, but back then it was very scary to even peripherally associate oneself with AIDS.

While in Beverly Hills, we decided to move Perry away from the competitive and likely judgmental environment at Harvard University, which could have ruined his reputation had anyone discovered his personal battle. He applied for and was offered the deanship of the Graduate School of Applied and Professional Psychology at Rutgers University in New Jersey. Rutgers offered him not only a new beginning but also more money and a spiffy title. Yet when I picked him up at the L.A. airport after his interview in New Jersey, Perry was surly about the post. He'd always been a complainer, but being sick seemed to give him permission to gripe even more.

During my years with Perry, I perfected a valuable trait: I learned not to speak in times of stress until I knew what to say, or to blurt out hurtful thoughts that made difficult situations worse. So the morning after grumpy Perry came home from his meeting in New Jersey, I told him that Rutgers was the only good thing to happen to us since we became HIV-positive. I told him that if he did not stop complaining, he'd have to go to New Jersey without me. "I am HIV-positive and struggling for my life, too," I reminded him. "I've been happy during our eleven years together, but now life is really hard for me. I love you and I will leave you sadly, but I *will* leave you if you don't stop complaining." Perhaps it was my levelheaded reproach, or possibly even his guilt for inflicting me with HIV, but Perry changed his attitude. We moved to New Jersey within weeks.

While Perry was ill, I learned the true significance of ". . . in sickness and in health, until death do us part"—and the power of unconditional love. His cranky attitude aside, I can't explain how tender I felt toward Perry and how deeply I wanted to relieve his pain. I protected him from his grown children, who would have confronted him and treated him unkindly. I took care of him, which allowed him to continue working at the job he grew to love. I rubbed his feet at night, I held his head when he cried, and I held his body when he slept. I went with him to see his doctors and stayed with him during his chemotherapy treatments. I got his pain medication for him at all hours. Most important, I kept his secret and did not betray him. My love for

Perry helped me be with a man whose actions led to my illness and, at the time, certain death. In some ways, his final years were some of our best.

Perry died three and a half years after we moved to New Jersey, and, of the hundreds of people who attended the four memorial services that were held for him on two continents, only a handful of people knew he died of AIDS: my children and oldest grandson, who'd helped me care for him during the final weeks of his hospitalization, his children, whom I'd told two weeks before he died, our doctors and pharmacists, and seven old and trusted friends. I did not tell my kids about *my* infection for eight more years. In New Jersey, I took seven prescription drugs, as my doctors insisted I'd die two years after my husband. But when Perry was in the hospital, I read a book about a macrobiotic diet that had a great effect on me. Elaine Nussbaum's *Recovery from Cancer* encouraged me to ease up on the meds (which angered the doctors) and follow a macrobiotic diet (which angered them even more). Sure enough, my immune system got stronger, and my spirit and body soon followed. The only thing I focused on was the task of living well.

Although my doctors, culture, and symptoms insisted I was destined for an early grave, I tried hard to have a full life after Perry died. I taught English as a second language to the foreign graduate students at Rutgers, and my home was brimming with students at the kitchen table or lying on the living room floor. They ate my cooking, spoke English, met my family, and learned what life is like in an American home. Now the house was filled with my students, not my husband's; it felt unexpectedly good to come out from behind Perry's shadow.

My only remaining problem, then, was that someone might learn that Perry had died of AIDS. So I taught one last year at Rutgers and then moved back to California to escape the community with whom I was most dishonest. I had no idea how long I'd live, but in California I saw a chance to feel healthy, make new friends, and continue teaching. For the next six years, macrobiotics consumed my schedule; I spent four hours a day cooking, and I lied to my neighbors about why I did it. I also lied about how Perry had died. I lied about why I didn't go out on dates, about everything really, and I realized that these lies were no better than those I'd told in New Jersey on Perry's behalf. Thus, I decided it was time to "come out." One day while walking my dog with my neighbors, I spilled the whole story. (Later, this marvelous couple encouraged me to tell my children about my infection.) I joined a macrobiotic support group for people who treated various illnesses with this diet, and I told them about my infection during our first session. It scared me to death to utter the words "I am HIV-positive" to a group of strangers. I had no idea what they'd say, or if anyone would even sit next to me, but they accepted me as if I'd been a sister.

Talking about my virus to strangers was one thing, but telling my family was something else. Instead, during a writing course, I read aloud a story I had written about what it was like for me to live in tandem with the gay community, hold the hands of young people dying of AIDS, and attend AIDS funerals where parents were ashamed of their deceased children. I read aloud about suicides, fear, and bravery—and all the tears shed by the victims and their families while the world at large hated us. My teachers insisted that my stories could help others. Soon, I found myself in a Melrose Street coffeehouse, reading to a new audience on a regular basis. But I still couldn't tell these stories to the people I loved most.

I completed a first draft of a memoir and returned to Rutgers to tell my old friends about Perry and me. It was an honest start. They embraced me, and I began witnessing the art of forgiveness. Soon afterward, I told my born-again sister and her family and, lastly, my children. The born-agains, even now, never say the word "AIDS" or mention my illness. My children, however, accepted the news with the same attitude I'd had with Perry: unconditional love and a willingness to help me. However, a word they cannot utter without contempt is *Perry*. All three of my children have removed pictures of him from their homes, his books are hidden away on the back of their bookshelves, and he has become persona non grata in their minds. I contracted a painful case of shingles not long after I revealed my secret, and began taking the antiviral drugs for AIDS. It was then that the doctors announced I'd live a normal life span. I should have been thrilled at the news, but instead I was in intense and chronic pain with shingles. What's more, the medical community was giving me ghastly nerve blocks and throwing pain pills at me, the antiviral drugs made me nauseous, and I was unable to work or write. I began slipping into a depression. Slowly I began admitting to my family and friends that I was lonely and unhappy. Admitting and accepting despair was a low point for me. Little did I realize that by hitting the bottom the way I did, I had begun the process of reclaiming my life and the ability to look for a life I wanted.

I saw a psychotherapist to talk about living with AIDS. This is when I came undone, but believe me, it had been a long time coming. I lay on his floor and screamed about my infection. I cried about my loneliness, and the burden of so many untruths that had been ruling my life for too long. I even found an editor to help me with my third attempt at a book. And just when I began to make some real psychological progress, I received an unexpected blow. I learned from a longtime mutual friend of Perry's that Perry had not gotten AIDS from a hooker, as he'd told me. Instead, he'd been part of an ongoing tryst with a man since before we were married; and even after, he'd continued to have unprotected sex with him and then come home to me. Perry's lover had died of AIDS in 1986, and yet we'd continued to have unprotected sex. My shame with this new secret seemed worse than anything that had come before. I felt so hurt by this that it was overwhelming. I'd been so naïve.

Until then, I'd not been angry with Perry about giving me AIDS; after all, I'd felt he'd loved me and would never have intentionally hurt me. I'd simply considered AIDS, in the context of our marriage, to have been a tragic accident. But Perry's long-term relationship with a man changed all that, and it just broke my heart. To think he'd sworn me to secrecy and then abandoned me to live alone with his secret—and then carry on his legacy in my sick body. . . . Loving Perry had been a transforming experience for me, but for him? I wouldn't have harmed a hair on my husband's head, but he'd repeatedly exposed me to AIDS. I'd cared tirelessly for him during his illness, and he'd deceived me. From the minute I'd met him, I'd worn my heart on my sleeve, and now I wasn't sure if I could ever trust the memory of Perry's love. We had been each other's foundation, and he'd betrayed me.

It only took a few months before I began telling people about

Perry's homosexual behavior. I had no more room for grim secrets in my heart, and if others were offended by the truth, so be it. With the help of my therapist and editor, I gradually understood that Perry's fear of disclosure had been greater than his love for me. It was a hurtful realization, to say the least. Writer Elie Wiesel, a Holocaust survivor, says the opposite of love is indifference. No one has ever treated me with more indifference than Perry did. But his shame had crippled him, and I still feel sorry for him. In this way, he'd died in disgrace. It's ironic, because that's what he—no, *we*—had tried to avoid for so long.

Until I lived with HIV, in the form of both my own disease and my husband's, nothing of great effort or worth had been required of me. But in its wake came a series of well-learned lessons. Without AIDS, I wouldn't have known some of my dearest friends or how brave and kind the gay community is. I wouldn't have had a clue about my own strength, or the goodness and strength of my children. I wouldn't have known how to confront doctors whose treatments are harmful to me, or how to laugh and love so freely. I would have continued being the person I was when I was thirty-nine, the one who lived a colorless life in an upper-middle-class suburb. The most important thing I've learned, however, is the power of love—and that my finest hour was when I first learned I was HIV-positive and didn't hate Perry for it. When we lived in New Jersey, I channeled my energy into my work, home, and sick husband. I learned to be tough on the inside, and gentle on the outside. Love became the chief motivator of my life. In our marriage, Perry taught me how to win a loving bond and accept its consolation prizes.

I've learned how to accept forgiveness, and to shake myself

of the shame I felt for lying to so many people for so many years. I've also learned that people will trust you again if you ask them to. I wish I could take a pill to make my virus go away so I wouldn't have to spend so much time with doctors, or suffer the side effects of so much medication. But I chose Perry, and I wouldn't have missed a minute of him or his flaws. In many ways, he brought out all my best traits. I don't know one person who's enjoyed a better or more fulfilled life than I. I've been a wife, mother, lover, teacher, and friend, who got the chance to grow and become a nicer person. I was dying and learned that life happens a day at a time, so make the best of each day. I learned that it's possible to remain in love even when the unspeakable happens.

I'm grateful for my journey and the course it's taken. In fact, I recently met and married the nicest man in the world—and my macrobiotic support group even threw me a reception! I keep in touch with the exceptional people that AIDS brought into my life, and I have the health to read, write, teach, and attend the opera on both the East Coast and the West Coast, and in several cities in between. At each opera, I hold the hand of a man who loves me. I've lived a marvelous life. I would not have missed a moment of it.

Note to Self

Love conquers all,
especially when you least expect it.
(Love conquers all, PERIOD.)

Fastening a Life for Myself

SHARYN SPILLMAN

Sharyn Spillman lives in Scottsdale, Arizona with her two Malteses. Her life's journey has taken her through several careers, and she is currently president and CEO of a successful aerospace fastener company. She believes her greatest accomplishment is her daughter, who is mother to her two wonderful grandsons.

I had been dating Howard for three months before he asked me to marry him. Well, actually, he told me that we were going to get married. It was more of a mandate than a proposal. I was eighteen at the time, and I married Howard for his financial potential. Back in the early 1960s I was like most girls I knew and got married for all the wrong reasons—namely, a false sense of security.

At nineteen, I sensed trouble literally as I was walking down the aisle during my wedding. I turned to my father and said,

"Daddy, I don't think I want to do this." He said, "Don't be silly. Let's get you married."

Growing up I was very sheltered by my parents, and I always assumed that I was going to marry somebody who would take care of me for the rest of my life. Those were the expectations set in my household. I thought I was marrying my white knight! I honestly didn't think I would ever have to worry about anything, because I hadn't been raised to work in business or take care of myself.

When I married Howard, he was only four years older than me but twenty years older emotionally. Howard was more of a parent to me than a husband, and he continued to shelter me much as my parents had. Consequently, our unbalanced relationship became my picture of what love was supposed to be, of what a husband and wife should look like. Three months into it, I knew that I had made a terrible mistake. I had become very attracted to somebody else, and though I eventually got over it, I thought to myself, *If I was really in love with Howard, would I have experienced this crush?* Something was wrong with this picture.

Howard worked at an investment group with my father. Howard was a very smart man who could put a deal together better than anyone around, and he knew the ins and outs of money and finance. After we got married, I went to work for him. I started out as clerk, and then I became his bookkeeper. Life was pretty uneventful for a while. I'd go to the office, do my job, and go home with him. Our daughter was born in 1968, but I went back to work part-time when she was just three months old. This was the closest I got to "settling down," but inside I felt completely unsettled. I wanted to do something more with my life.

I had to find an outlet, something to express myself more fully. Life with Howard was getting boring fast. One night we were in a nightclub with a girlfriend. She knew the vocalist, and he invited her up to sing. She invited me up, too, and I ended up doing a solo. My friend's husband had told the club manager that my family and friends alone would fill the house, so he hired me on the spot. My repertoire consisted of only three songs, but they were enough to get me noticed. I sang in various nightclubs in the Valley for five years, and Howard would come every time and watch the audience watching me, which was a little strange. Again, it was like he was more of a second father figure rather than a husband. Despite this dysfunction, singing at clubs felt like New Year's Eve every night. My musical delivery was much better than my voice, which wasn't all that great, but boy, could I sell a song.

After five years of dazzling nightclub audiences, it occurred to me that if I could sell a song, I could sell anything. I could sell a house. One day I said to my musical arranger, "I'm going into real estate."

He said, "You'll be back."

He was wrong. I never went back. And I continued to run into people who underestimated me. Ironically, the man who ran my real estate school pulled me aside while we were preparing for the state exam and said, "Sharyn, save your money. You're never going to pass the test."

Well, I passed that test with flying colors and went on to have a nice stint in real estate. But Howard continued to shelter me, and it made sense to work closer to home rather than to join a big real estate firm. Our daughter was now eight years old, and the demands of motherhood were growing, but in 1982 I started my own little brokerage company. Howard encouraged me to do this because he had a hidden agenda: it was a perfect way to save the commissions on his own real estate acquisitions. This put my first professional venture in a difficult position. It made matters at home even worse.

While my professional life was blossoming, my personal life was deteriorating. Howard and I weren't having sex—we had stopped being intimate after our eighth anniversary. He barely patted me on the back anymore. Instead, he would tell me that he wasn't interested, or that he had health problems, or complain that I was bothering him. My self-esteem was in the toilet. I needed someone to break into my life and steal me away and set me free.

Then out of the blue, when I was thirty-seven, we had a bizarre home invasion, a full-scale home robbery. I can still remember looking up and seeing the intruder standing in the hallway with a blue bandana over his face. He had wild eyes, and he was holding a hammer in one hand and a gun in the other. I thought, *I'm going to be shot and pummeled with a hammer, I never thought I'd go like this.* Howard was in the bedroom watching TV, and I screamed several times, "Howard, there's somebody in the house!" I got no response. As I was yelling, the intruder told me to shut up, then fired his weapon! At that point, despite the intense fear, something inside me took over. I charged at him with a large book and forced him into the bedroom. He then approached Howard.

"Put the book down, Sharyn," Howard said to me. "I've got this under control."

Unable to calm down, I yelled, "Tell us what you want and get the hell out!"

"I want cash and credit cards and I want your diamonds," the intruder said.

I felt something running down my leg, and I pulled up my robe to look. The shock had numbed the pain of the bullet wound.

"You son of a bitch! You shot me!" I was so angry. "Take what you want and get the hell out of here!" Gathering our valuables, the intruder disappeared.

That night, at around 4:00 a.m., after we had been to the hospital (thankfully the bullet had not hit any bones), Howard and I arrived back at the house and crawled into our king-sized bed. We always slept on opposite sides, but on this night I tried to cuddle with him, to feel safe after one of the most disturbing nights of my life.

Howard looked at me like I was crazy. "What are you doing?"

"I'm so scared," I said.

"Don't be silly," he said. "The alarm is on now. You'll be fine. Nobody's going to come back here."

That's when it hit me: if Howard no longer wanted to protect me, and it was the one and only thing he offered in our marriage, then there was no reason to stay together. It was time for me to be strong and protect myself. And it was time for Howard to go.

Living in his shadow no longer did me any good. Sometime

during the next year, Howard moved out of our bedroom and began sleeping in the guest room. Our daughter Julie's bat mitzvah was planned for February of 1982, and we decided that we would separate when it was over.

As it turned out, I didn't get a chance to properly and legally divorce him. Howard was indicted for racketeering the day the invites for the bat mitzvah went out, and it was no longer a decision I had to make. The law took him away for me.

Howard's indictment centered around working for a publicly traded company based in Chicago. He was managing four offices and seventy-eight employees. At some point, the company was computerized, and it was discovered that someone had been misappropriating a great deal of money. Everything pointed to Howard.

Around the time litigation started, I was having breakfast with a girlfriend in a restaurant. She looked up at one point and said, "Oh! Here comes my neighbor!"

I said, "Cute neighbor!"

His name was Jack, and he sat down with us just as my friend had to leave to pick up her son. Jack said, "I have time to stay a little longer. Do you?"

He told me that he didn't have much to say, and that he was a pretty quiet person.

"Don't worry," I said. "I talk enough for two people."

Three and a half hours later, we stood up and left the restaurant. I have always felt that we fell in love with each other that day. Although we were both married, he was as unhappy as I was, and we began our storybook love affair. I had met a new white knight, but this one loved, respected, and adored me.

Meanwhile, Howard had been begging me to stay with him for purely business reasons. "If you stay with me, we can save the properties and you'll have some money." He tried to entice me with all the trappings of our inflated lifestyle. We were living in a 5,000-square-foot home in the best neighborhood in Phoenix. I drove a Mercedes and shopped regularly at Saks Fifth Avenue. He had spoiled me for sure, but Howard, the great protector, had put our family in a really vulnerable position. I had to get out even if it meant losing it all, but with all of his legal troubles, there seemed to be little space to conduct a separation or divorce proceeding.

Howard was fined $1.8 million and sentenced to six years in prison. The day he was to report to prison, he asked me to pick up our daughter from school and then meet him for lunch. He told me that he was terrified of prison, and since I had Jack in my life, he was skipping town. He deposited two thousand dollars in my checking account and disappeared. To this day I have no idea where he went or how he survived, but almost five years later the police found him at his mother's house. I don't think he'd been there long. He served almost four years in prison, and when he died in 1999, at age fifty-nine, he claimed he was innocent.

The $1.8 million in Howard's plea bargain was considered taxable income. As his spouse, the taxes became my responsibility. This meant that I owed approximately $900,000 of federal income tax and $350,000 of state tax to the government!

I was not going to let his mistakes screw me over. Howard had left me with a financial mess. The first thing I had to do was find the best tax attorney in Phoenix, and that meant the most expensive! My father flew in from Texas with a check for half the retainer, and Jack, now divorced himself, came up with the other half. In the end, I was given "innocent spouse" status, but I lost our houses—including our primary residence—when I declared bankruptcy. Julie and I moved into Jack's small town house. My daughter was sixteen, and she handled the entire situation with maturity and dignity. She was just amazing through this awkward transition.

I was forty-two years old, and my life was suddenly and radically changed. Until Howard left, I had never seen a bill, let alone paid one. Life was very different with Jack. We shared everything—the good, the bad, and especially the passion. For the first time in my life, I felt truly loved, and I loved him equally in return! Divorcing someone who couldn't be served papers wasn't an easy task, but one and a half years after Howard disappeared, my divorce was final. I did not waste any time—in fact, trying to make up for lost time, I married Jack in 1986.

As a newlywed, Jack took a sales position with an aerospace fastener company. Six months later, I said to him, "I think this business is something that we could do together." He agreed, so I went to my mother for a start-up loan. My father had passed away, but he would never have agreed to lend me the money. He'd thought that businesses should be run by men. He'd raised his daughter to be a wife and a mother. That's it. In his book, signing and selling real estate was a far cry from running a business. Thankfully, my mother believed in me, in Jack, and in the idea.

Jack and I bought a franchise with the funding. We did a great job with it at first, but unfortunately, seven months after we bought the franchise, the company we'd bought it from went Chapter 11. My cousin Jim had also bought a similar franchise with the same company, and he was also in the red. One morning, the three of us put our heads together over breakfast and talked about what to do next.

In May 1989, through the help of another family cousin, Ben, we started an Arizona-based fastener company called Aerofast, Ltd. When we were still growing the business, I worked at a trade school to make money, and Jack did drywall repairs at night. We took no salary and lived hand to mouth for a year and a half. Jack and I even rolled quarters, and we occasionally went out to eat, indulging in tuna salad sandwiches with a basket of fries, washing it all down with water, not wine, so we'd have enough money for a tip. Once in a while, we went out to a movie. It was such a simple life compared to what I had had with Howard, but I had never been happier. Being in love conquered being broke.

But then the unthinkable happened. Two months after we drew our first real salary checks, Jack died of a brain aneurysm.

Life was dealing me a hand of cards that seemed completely unfair. I tried to make sense of it all, but I was devastated and unsure of how to go on.

I had always felt that Jack was on loan to me from God, and I really believe he was sent on a mission to teach me unconditional love. He protected me better than anyone I knew, because he guarded my independence. He changed me from a sheltered woman to a capable businessperson, but most of all, he helped me live up to my highest self. But those shitty cards kept coming.

Four months after Jack died, I was diagnosed with breast cancer. I completed my chemotherapy a year later and was blessed with a clean bill of health. For the first time in a long time I felt like I was turning a corner. My cousin begged me to return to work at Aerofast. He wanted my help because the company was suffering. In my heart, I knew that staying in business with my cousin ultimately wouldn't work. I feared that I would be under his thumb, the same way I had been under the thumbs of Howard and my dad.

I needed money and an opportunity, and I needed the wisdom to recognize when both arrived. In July of 1995, one of my customers offered to support a small business of my own. On a handshake, I went into business with him and his brothers. I would own 55 percent, and the three brothers would share 45 percent. Later, they told me that the money they had put up for me to start the company was the best investment they'd ever made!

I walked out the door of Aerofast, Ltd. on July 16, 1995, and on the morning of July 17, 1995, with only a phone, a fax machine, a Rolodex of vendors, and my knowledge of the industry, I started Millipart Fasteners in my spare bedroom. Four and a half years later, my business was shipping two and a half million dollars a year with 37 percent gross profit margin, and I was having the time of my life. I had a knack for business that men like Howard and my father never acknowledged or encouraged.

Four and a half years later, my business was more profitable than my cousin's. In June of 1999, I was approached by the owners of WG Henschen Co., a distributor of Ring-Lock products. They wanted me to buy the company. Financially, I knew I could do the deal and sales would be a slam dunk for me. I also knew that my cousin and Aerofast, Ltd. had the quality certifications I needed to really move the company forward. I called my cousin and said, "We went into this business together, let's buy this company, merge the three, and go out of it together!"

Today, WG Henschen Co. has thirty-two employees, grosses thirteen million dollars a year in sales, and has offices in two states. We specialize in aerospace fittings, fasteners, nuts, bolts, and rivets. When I first got into this business, people would say to me, "Sharyn, it's not a very glamorous industry." I would always tell those people, "You know what? I find a two-hundred-dollar twelve-point nut very glamorous. In fact, I find it sexy as hell."

I'm nearly sixty-five now, and what started out as a life predicated on relying on others has turned into a life of self-reliance. I taught myself how to be strong, how to support my family, and how to protect myself and my businesses at all costs. One truth I learned along the way: men fail, die, leave, and disappoint; I am my sole protector.

Note to Self

Things change.
Make each change work for you.

Sole to Soul

CAROL LEIFER

Carol Leifer is a stand-up comedienne, writer, producer, and actor. Her stand-up credits include opening for Frank Sinatra, who was later heard saying, "Carol Leifer is one funny broad." She is funny, compassionate, and will go to the ends of the earth for animal rights and women's rights. Her first book, published by Random House, is entitled *When You Lie About Your Age, The Terrorists Win*. She lives with her partner, their son, and seven rescue dogs in Santa Monica, California.

Everyone had told me what to expect when a parent dies: shock, disbelief, sadness, denial. What they neglected to mention was that when they go after eighty-six years, they forget to take all their stuff.

So what to do with all of it? My dad's home office was a cinch to pack up. It was an optician's office, crafted forty years ago from our family's former garage, so that after working a full-time day job in New York City, he returned home every evening to treat patients in the neighborhood. My mother, sister, brother, and I decided to donate Dad's leftover frames to charity—that was a no-brainer. Dad was one optometrist who had an overwhelming love and commitment to eyewear—he was so committed, in fact, that he never even sold contact lenses in his private practice. "Why would any person wear contact lenses," he'd demand, "when there are so many attractive frames out there to choose from?"

Dad prided himself on being a one-stop shop when it came to prescribing glasses. My siblings and I grew up with *whiz* and *screech* sounds coming from the other end of the house, where his behemoth lens-cutting machines smoothed out the rough edges of delicate glass. So we donated his equipment to charity, too, knowing that my father would be pleased to know that some newbies were learning their trade on his broken-in machines. I could almost hear him saying, "Kid, if you've got a business, know it from start to finish, inside and out, and upside down. *That's* when you know your field."

Optometry was my father's passion for sixty years. How could it not be when he had been named "Seymour" (you know, SEE-MORE?). And optometry affected the way he looked at the world. He had an optical explanation for practically everything he encountered in life. This was never more apparent than when the O. J. Simpson case erupted. On the evening of her death, Nicole Simpson arrived safely at home after eating dinner at the restaurant where Ron Goldman worked; but she'd left her glasses behind. Goldman returned them to her nearby townhouse, and everyone knows how the rest of the grisly story devolved. What was my father's solution for how the entire tragedy could have been avoided? "It's a testament to having two pairs of glasses. If she'd had a second pair at home, the two of them might both be alive today!"

Once we'd dealt with Dad's professional goods, his personal effects were fairly easy for us sibs to split up. (Our mother wanted us to have them all. His things now were too much of a painful reminder of his absence.) These included a few objects he'd kept in a glass bowl on top of the living room credenza that were part of his everyday existence:

A class ring from Columbia, which he never removed. My sister took that. His Seiko watch, which he was forever praising ("Who'd buy an expensive watch when the Japanese make such a superior product? The Swiss can kiss their ass!") What were the odds that the Seiko would fit my brother's wrist perfectly?

His wallet, which was a tricky item for us to assign.

How strange to have someone's wallet, but not the person. You feel like calling the police and reporting yourself. My father's driver's license, AAA, Social Security, credit, and insurance cards—all so important to him in his day-to-day life—were rendered, in a flash, meaningless. Then, we found the Holy Grail: a piece of paper, still in his wallet, that we'd all heard of countless times. It was a list of jokes that he always kept with him.

The list came about after he had accompanied my mother to one of her psychology conferences. The scheduled entertainment for the night had canceled at the last minute. Aware that my dad knew his way around a joke or two, the attending PhDs asked if my dad would mind stepping in and telling a few jokes to the crowd.

Mind stepping in?

For a man who dreamed of becoming a stand-up comedian (but happily settled for watching his daughter become one), this was easily one of the highlights of his life. And, as it was reported back to us, Pop slayed that crowd of shrinks. And if he were ever asked to perform a second time, Dad planned on being better prepared for his next show; hence, the list he kept in his wallet. Now I keep that little piece of paper in my wallet. And don't think I won't pull it out the next time I'm stuck at a show.

But then there were the clothes. For someone who wore the same six outfits his whole life, I don't know where all these items suddenly came from. I had the hardest time with the sweaters. My dad loved wearing sweaters. Any time we ever wanted to raise the heat in the house, it was only a matter of seconds before we'd hear his standard rebuttal: "Just throw a good sweater on and save some oil!"

While rummaging through my father's sweaters, I couldn't help but give them a good sniff and—voila—there it was: his smell. That only made me want to get them out of the house as soon as possible. Because if they stayed too long, the Daddy Smell would soon be replaced by the smell of must and moth-balls, and that wasn't him.

So off Dad's clothing went to Goodwill, another destination for his stuff that he would've appreciated. He grew up during the Depression (as we were so often reminded), and those Depression-era folks are very familiar with the concept of re-cycling, though their version has less to do with the environ-ment and more to do with survival. Plus, Sy Leifer would definitely get a kick out of the fact that a leisure suit he bought thirty years ago from Syms in Roslyn, Long Island, would be discovered and described as "vintage cool" by some hipster doofus one day soon.

And as I taped up the last sweater box, congratulating myself for appreciating Dad's things without getting too emotionally attached, I looked down in the closet and felt like I'd had the wind knocked out of me. I'd found the one thing I couldn't bring myself to put in the Goodwill box: the brown shoes, the ones with the rubber soles. The slip-ons he always wore.

They were all-purpose—for around the house, for going out, for when we took our three-mile walk around the neighborhood together. ("Dad, why don't you put on a pair of sneakers?" "Sneakers? Who needs sneakers?")

I was constantly on Dad's back to get rid of them, they were so comically old. In fact, I can't even say what brand they were because the lettering inside had long worn away. So old that they were from a shoe store that went belly-up ages ago, Miles Shoes. I pestered Dad all the time to spring for a new pair, but he would always say, "Why should I get a new pair when these work just fine?"

No wonder the concept of fashion does not compute with fathers. How can it when clothing is reduced to either "working" or not?

The brown shoes . . . they just couldn't seem to add themselves to the Goodwill box. Instead, they sent a change of address card from the back of Mom's closet. Nobody could decide what to do with them, and, when in doubt, do nothing, right? Isn't that the code of every procrastinator?

As I continued to pack up Dad's things, I asked myself—out

of everything, why the shoes? Why were they so hard to get rid of? Was it because they once held him, like they were kind of the trunk to his tree? Because his soul somehow seemed to stay in their soles? Was not getting rid of them some version of denial? Like, how can he be that far away if his shoes are still here?

There does come a point when you cry "uncle"—and finally have to admit that someone really is not coming back. For me, this happened at a specific moment during the week after my dad died.

As Jewish as my father was deep down, he and my mother had not belonged to a synagogue for a long time. So to perform the funeral, we hired what our tribe calls a "Rent-A-Rabbi": a rabbi you don't know, but who officiates at a burial. But our Rent-A-Rabbi turned out to be quite different from what we had expected. Usually, they just show up, ask a few routine questions, and get on with the task at hand, but ours seemed genuinely compassionate and engaged. After the ceremony, he gathered us all together and said, "If there's anything I can do to help you through this difficult time, please don't hesitate to ask. I am here for you 100 percent. I will call you in a few days and check in."

"Sure," my mother said sarcastically after he left. "Once the check clears, adios!"

Yet lo and behold, three days later, he did call. I answered the phone.

"Hello, this is your rabbi from the funeral," he said. "I'm just calling to see how your family's doing."

I was touched. "Thank you for calling, Rabbi!"

"How are you doing, sweetheart?"

"Right at this moment, I'm doing okay. But honestly, Rabbi, two seconds from now, I could be a total wreck. My feelings change from moment to moment."

"Sweetheart, that is completely normal. Losing a parent is one of the most difficult life passages. It's a roller coaster of emotions."

I nodded thoughtfully.

"Do you have any other concerns, darling?" he asked.

Feeling very safe and secure due to the rabbi's unexpected kindness, I decided to ask him the one question I'd been wrestling with for the previous seventy-two hours. "Rabbi, I do have a question. Where is my father now? I know he's not here, but he must be somewhere."

The rabbi sighed deeply and said. "Where is your father now? Oy, sweetheart, I'll be here all day! Can you put your sister on now, please?"

And did we laugh.

That Rent-A-Rabbi story quickly became running joke one million and one to the Leifer family, and the next time someone said something curt, impatient, or insensitive, one of us would race to be the first to say, "Yeah, now can you put your sister on please?" The problem was, this was the first joke Dad wasn't there to share with us. And this reminded us—if we hadn't been 100 percent aware of it before—that Dad was really gone.

I'd always thought that when someone died, your relationship with that person was over. The end. Kaput. But it's not like that. Your relationship goes on, even though the other person isn't physically there. My dad's there when I hear Stevie Wonder's "I Just Called to Say I Love You," a song he had a kooky kind of attachment to and whistled as he did crossword puzzles in the living room. He's with me when someone mentions disco, and I remember him valiantly trying to learn this new dance called The Hustle with me in 1974 as we listened to KC and the Sunshine Band. He's there when I buy a six-pack of individual orange juice containers. ("Carol, what a waste. You're paying for the packaging with those small things! Do me a favor, and buy the quart or the gallon size next time.") And he's there when I get a whiff of Jergens lotion, the cream he would put on his hands after doing the dishes. (And then you start to think things you never even thought when they were alive. Like, "Gee, that's an awfully femmie hand lotion for a man to use.")

And we still have discussions. I have not made one important decision yet without talking it over with the old man first. I know he'd be happy with some choices I've made since his departure, others not so much. For instance, my recent decision to become a vegan would've inspired a lively discourse: "So you're deciding to give up meat completely? And dairy, too? Well, what the hell are you gonna eat? Nothing's left! All right, look, if that's what makes you happy, knock yourself out." (He said this last sentence countless times. It was his eventual response to almost everything.)

As the fourth anniversary of Dad's passing approaches, I've decided that the next time I'm back home on Long Island, I'm going to finally drive over to Goodwill and donate the brown shoes. The shoes are now wedged between a pair of too-fancy slingbacks and Moroccan espadrilles, ridiculously out of place in my mother's closet. They're like the only guy you see sitting in a gynecologist's waiting room.

It's what Pop would want, anyway. "Carol, why deny some-one the pleasure of these shoes? Who knows how long they can go?" he'd ask.

We are not our things—and my father was not his brown shoes. But I think I finally understand why I had a hard time letting them go. Putting the shoes to rest meant ultimately put-ting Dad to rest, too. And I'm okay with that now. Dad liked a good rest. And I can say that now I understand—you don't have to be here when you're still everywhere.

Note to Self

A man is not his loafers,
but more the places he goes and
the lives he touches and the
mark he makes on the world.

The Love Pot

RUTH ANDREW ELLENSON

Ruth Andrew Ellenson received the National Jewish Book Award for her bestselling anthology, *The Modern Jewish Girl's Guide to Guilt* (Plume, 2006). She is a journalist whose work appears in the *New York Times, Los Angeles Times,* and other publications.

Smash it," Orit said, the vast expanse of the Pacific Ocean reflecting off her sunglasses. As she commanded me to do what my heart stubbornly resisted, all I could see was a sea of blue.

"You have to destroy the Love Pot. It's the final step. We're not leaving here till you do."

The Love Pot had been her idea. When I'd received it, I'd thought it was a silly name, but that she should have trade-marked the idea, it had been so clever. Inside a blue ceramic vase scattered with bursts of crystallized metallic gray paint that looked like exploding stars, Orit had sealed two letters under a thick layer of white wax.

The letters had been written by my then-future husband Robert, and me, to each other on the occasion of our wedding. They'd been sealed in the vase and were to be opened on our twenty-fifth anniversary. Everyone had cooed at the romance of the idea, at Orit's creativity, at our certain future and happiness contained within the pot. After we were married, the pot had sat reassuringly on the mantel, stout and strong, amid the willowy crystal vases we'd received for wedding gifts. It had been, as they say, a conversation piece—we would smile, and Robert would touch my arm when we'd told people we couldn't wait to read the letters. After all, the pot could only be opened when we'd reached twenty-five years.

That was in August of 1999. As I write this in August of 2008, Robert and I are heading into the final stages of our divorce. Very soon, our marriage will be dissolved, as if it never was, and our bonds to each other will be cut. The person who had been in my heart since I was nineteen, who was the emotional center of my life, will be somebody I never have to see again.

There are some people who are relieved at a divorce, and some people who are furious about it. I am neither. I fall into a third category—deep sadness. There was no dramatic act of betrayal, no direct act of cruelty, but rather an emotional abandonment that took place slowly, over years.

I fought the divorce as much as I could. As the child of parents who'd divorced when I was six, I was determined not to suffer the same fate. I knew marriage was hard work. I made us go to three different therapists. I asserted myself, diminished myself, apologized, stopped apologizing—all the while haunted by a sinking feeling I was negotiating myself into oblivion.

My stepmother, Jackie, who is as practical about love as she is committed to it, created a family with my father that developed over twenty-eight years and nurtured five children. She offered me pearls of wisdom at the commencement of my marriage.

"You can be right, or you can be married." "Marriage isn't fifty/fifty percent compromise, it's one hundred/one hundred percent compromise." "There's not constant happiness in a good marriage, there's contentment."

My father would add the rather witty observation, "The only problem with relationships is that they involve other people."

At first I'd dismiss their words as the advice of a couple who'd been married too long. But the longer I was married, the more I saw how right they were. Robert and I would engage in what I jokingly called The Stubborn Olympics. It got to the point where rationality didn't count; neither did listening. All that mattered was the defeat of the other person's point.

It hadn't started off that way. I'd met Robert in a religion class in college and had liked him immediately. I'd liked his beard, his blue eyes. I'd liked how serious he'd been while still being kind. He'd essentially been introverted, but the depth I'd sensed in him had compelled me toward him.

When we fell in love, during the spring in New York City, it felt like something bigger than both of us. Something the fates were commanding us to do despite any judgment we might have had otherwise. We had, as he later said, "fallen" in love—we'd been intoxicated with each other. We'd been drunk on the magic between us.

With the wisdom of hindsight I can see that when you fall in love as a young adult, it is enough to simply be in love: worldly matters are of no consequence. If you're lucky enough to find love, it feels as if the movie romances you dismiss in your cynical days are actually documentaries. The bliss a person is capable of feeling in being totally and utterly adored, and adoring in turn, is transformative. When we married I felt confident that Robert knew my lightness and accepted my darkness, and I his.

Then things changed. Our mutual unhappiness began like a slow leak—easy to ignore if you didn't look at the water stain too hard. After eight years of marriage it became glaringly apparent, as much as I tried to deny it, that we were incapable of making each other happy and wanted totally different lives. I wanted children, he did not. I wanted the complex embrace of community and friends; he wanted solitude and quiet to pursue his studies.

I felt utterly alone. It is terrifying to feel alone in a marriage. There is no hope; you are shut off from even the opportunity for happiness. When a marriage begins its final stages of disintegration, it is agonizing. My divorce was not the ripping off of a Band-Aid; it was the festering of a wound.

In late July, nearly a year since we'd separated, I was sitting in the living room of the apartment we'd once shared. I now lived there alone, and the silence could still scare me. To distract myself, I was chatting with Jackie on the phone.

We were dissecting the minutiae of a date I'd recently gone on. Dating was surreal for me. I'd never done it as an adult, and it felt more like sociological research than anything romantic. I was used to the dailiness of marriage—doing the budget together, preparing food, running errands, and sneaking out for the occasional movie. The public relations event which is dating was totally foreign to me.

"Be sure to fall in love with your head as much as your heart this time," Jackie warned me kindly. She was right. But since I had experienced the intoxication, the overwhelming certainty of true love, I was holding out for it again. I had experienced that, I told myself again and again, even if it had died. My marriage had been real, but it had clearly not been with the man I was meant to be with.

Orit came by later that day. My friend since we were fourteen, she had stood under the *chuppah*, the Jewish wedding canopy, when Robert and I had taken our vows. What would have been our ninth anniversary was approaching in a few weeks.

"What are you doing with the Love Pot?" she asked.

"Ignoring it," I said.

I glanced up at the top bookshelf. When Robert had moved out nearly a year earlier, I had placed it in a far corner and had pretty much disregarded it. When he had packed his boxes, we'd told ourselves it was only a break, a time to collect our thoughts. We'd still been in therapy, trying to work it out. We would still be together. I believed it, too.

"On your anniversary we're going to take it and throw it into the sea," she declared firmly. The daughter of Israelis, there was a toughness to her that belied her delicate looks. For someone who'd invented something called "The Love Pot," she could be a total hard-ass.

I sighed. I had wondered what I would do with the thing,

and it seemed fitting to mark the day with some kind of rite of passage. There's no secular ritual for divorce; it's just a cyclical wrenching of the soul. I didn't want to hate Robert. I wanted to stop caring. All other life events, those that bring us joy, are celebrated, and even the finality of death is marked, but there is no common social custom to mourn the death of a marriage.

"Okay," I finally agreed. "But I want to open it up first and read the letters."

The morning of what would have been our ninth anniversary was 8/8/8. The start of the Olympics. A day the Chinese associated with good luck. And for me, the last time I would mark the passing of my marriage and the life I had shared with Robert for twelve years.

Orit picked me up and gestured with a wicked smile at the implements of destruction she had loaded into the backseat: a hammer, a lighter, and a knife. I put the Love Pot next to them, a lamb to the slaughter. It sat silent, round, and innocent of its impending doom, its gray stars glinting in the sunlight.

We got to the beach and parked. Walking to the water's edge, we sat in the sand and Orit handed me a knife.

"Cut it open," she commanded. I held the knife in my hand lamely, unsure which side of the blade was sharper and could cut through the thick layer of wax that sealed the pot.

"You'll have to stab it in to get through to the other side," Orit said.

I took the knife up in my hand like a dagger and plunged it into the snowy white center of the pot. It barely budged. I raised my hand, stabbing again and again until finally it yielded, cracking itself open despite all of its resistance. The wax fell into the sand with a dull thud. Orit took out the letters.

My stomach flipped as I saw them. My elongated cursive on the pink letter, Robert's tight writing on the blue one. I reached for mine first. I was stunned to see that it read like an obnoxious teenager's love note—flip and attempting to be witty with no sense of the solemnity of the occasion. Clearly, I'd thought I was being hilarious. I hadn't been. It shocked me to see what a child I had been. Despite all my martyrdom at the end of our marriage, I'd just been a dumb kid when it had begun.

And then I read Robert's letter. It was beautiful, full of emotions and declarations of passion, deeply mature and moving. The letter was proof. He had loved me utterly and completely. I cried as I read it. Once Robert had loved me like this. Our marriage had been real. And the sadness that marked its death on this, the day of its birth, was overwhelming.

"I want to keep the letter," I told Orit. "I need to remember how much Robert loved me, that our marriage wasn't a lie."

"You can't," she said calmly. "Your marriage wasn't a lie, but whether it was or not doesn't matter anymore. It's over."

I wanted to smack her. She was nine years into her own marriage. She had a four-year-old son. All I had was this fucking letter.

"Ruthie, you have to burn it," she said and held my hand. "If you don't get rid of it, you'll obsess over it and it will haunt you. You have to let it go."

"I'm not burning it. We can burn my letter. I'm keeping Robert's," I declared, the blue paper contrasting with my white knuckles as I clenched it tightly. I folded it to put into the pocket of my jean jacket. The wind was blowing off the cliffs. "Besides, it's too windy up here for anything to catch fire."

"We'll put it inside the pot and burn it there. Let's do your letter first."

Without asking permission, she took my letter, lit the corner on fire with a lighter, and dropped it into the pot. I watched the paper transform from a smooth soft blush into a crinkly transparent black as the fire consumed it. The letter smoldered and did not stop burning. It lit up the inside of the pot and created such heat that the remaining wax around the opening began to melt and run down its sides in thin white lines.

"They look like tears," she said and pulled out her camera to take a picture.

"Okay. Now Robert's letter," she said gently, putting her hand on my back. "I love you and I know you don't want to do this, but it is the best thing for you. Your marriage is over, Ruthie. It was a real marriage and your life was better for having married him, but it's over. It's dead. You have to bury the ashes."

I glared at her, full of resentment. How dare she? She'd never gone through this, never experienced the betrayal of having someone who'd declared loudly and publicly to love you forever change his mind. Her marriage, as any marriage does, had its own complications, but when she and her husband grew apart they found a way to come back together. For them it was a cycle, for me a dead halt.

"I'm not doing it," I said and stuck my hand into my pocket, holding the letter protectively.

"Oh, yes, you are," she said. "You have to. The letter isn't real anymore. Your marriage is over. You are going to move on now, and you can't do that while you're still holding on to that piece of paper."

I knew she was right. I could see myself placing it into the back of my wedding album, reading it over and over again at 2:00 a.m. to torture myself with regret. I should burn it. Keeping the letter would be punishing myself.

She put her hand out, and I took the letter from my pocket and placed it in her palm. She took it and gave me a small squeeze; she lit the corner on fire and placed it in the pot. For a minute I thought about sticking my hand in to rescue it.

The wax melted even more, running down the sides in clear rivulets, pooling on the bottom edge. Orit handed me the hammer.

"Smash it," she said.

"There's no way it's going to break," I complained. "It's too thick, it's too solid."

"Try, honey, try," Orit said gently.

I lifted the hammer above my head and swung it down. The pot exploded into dozens of pieces. Even if I wanted to, there was no way to put it back together. Our marriage was symbolically broken, just as the stomping of a glass in a Jewish wedding marks the moment the marriage has officially begun.

The shards from the pot flew all over. One sliced my hand, drawing a long line of blood, which began to run, bright red, down my index finger. It didn't hurt, and I was struck by the beauty of it, the vivid, almost cheery, redness. Orit took a picture of my bloody finger held up against the sea. I decided I would frame it to prove to myself what I could survive: the blood, sweat, and tears of my marriage perhaps had been in vain, and the Love Pot was broken, but at least now I had an opportunity to heal, and maybe, even, to hope.

Orit and I got into the car. She looked at me for a good long minute and gave me a tight hug. She started the engine, and we took off along the highway, rolled down the windows, and screamed at the top of our lungs until I didn't know if it was our voices or the wind that howled in my ears, and I didn't care.

Note to Self

**Set fire to what you thought
you knew and find yourself
in the ashes.**

Recall

MARGARET NAGLE

Margaret Nagle is a screenwriter living in Los Angeles. Her movie about FDR and his struggle with polio, *Warm Springs*, won the Emmy for Best Television Movie. Her brother Charles is a successful Outsider Artist and still cared for by their mother. Margaret's son responded to multiple therapies and is considered recovered from autism. He is starting college in the fall.

My mother called for me to come into the room. Her voice was unnaturally calm and sounded almost rehearsed. Hanging limply in her arms is what looked like a rag doll. Suddenly, it moved. It was alive. It was a little boy who couldn't hold up his head. Gently, my mother laid him on the carpeted floor. I toddled over and stared at him. His arms and legs were tight against his body. Water streamed from his mouth. The gaze of his eyes wandered everywhere. He could not move his limbs in a purposeful way. He could not talk, but he could smile, and his smile was huge and inviting. My mother said, "This is your big brother . . . Charlie." I loved him right away.

When Charlie came home from the hospital, he had been there for so long I did not know who he was. I was an infant when his brain stem was partially severed in a car accident. He was two. He had been in what the medical experts had thought was an irreversible coma for many months. My parents had kept a round-the-clock vigil at his bedside, trying to coax him from his deep sleep with favorite sounds, stories, songs, even smells (our milkman would come to the hospital in his milk truck and bring coffee ice cream to Charlie's bedside and hold it under his nose). But nothing had been able to rouse Charlie, and he'd been wasting away to nothingness. The doctors had recommended moving him to a facility where he could die; there had been nothing more the hospital could do. My parents had reluctantly signed the paperwork.

While sitting with my brother in his hospital room, my bereft mother had blown up a balloon. It had been a last-ditch effort to make contact with Charlie before he was removed to an institutional facility far away. Her exhausted hands had been shaking as she'd tried to tie a knot in the neck of the balloon. Suddenly it had slipped from her grasp and flown crazily around the room, the air expelling itself in a farting sound. My mother had heard laughter. It had come from Charlie. He'd been laughing in his coma. My mother had grabbed the balloon off the floor and blown it up again, letting it go to make the farting sound. Charlie had laughed harder. She'd run down the hall to find a nurse to witness what she had seen. He'd laughed again, as if on cue. Soon doctors had gathered around the bed, blowing up balloons and letting them go as my brother had laughed himself into consciousness.

By late that night Charlie was awake and tasting coffee ice cream on his dangling tongue. My mother had her child back. Not the child she began with, but another version of him.

When Charlie came home to live with us, he could not swallow, blink, or even roll over. He was like someone with cerebral palsy. In fact, that is what his condition would be medically termed—acquired cerebral palsy. And now the hard work would start.

My mother worked with fervor day and night to push my brother beyond where he was. There was so much damage to undo—to him and to us. In many ways, our damage was more complex and more terrifying. In Charlie we could see what the problem was. My parents didn't believe any discussion was necessary about my brother's accident or their changed life. In fact, they were adamant that it never, ever be discussed or acknowledged, yet, unlike so many other parents of their generation, they did not hide my brother from the world. He was not sent off to an institution. He was not kept with a nurse in his bedroom. He was front and center in everything we did, which was unnerving and progressive. Unnerving because the average person wasn't used to seeing or relating to a child like my brother, and progressive because my mother wanted him to be mainstreamed before the word existed. This was actually a function of her deep denial, which she'd developed in an effort to keep her enormous grief at bay. Denial, I have learned, can be an equally wonderful, as well as destructive, coping mechanism. It is brilliant in life-and-death situations, but when applied to daily life it arrests internal growth.

This tremendous wall of denial allowed my mom to devote herself day and night to my brother, teaching him to swallow and talk and even walk and eventually feed himself without ever giving up. And she became the ideal mother for a disabled child. But there was me—this other child, who was a reminder of what her son could and would have been if not for a fateful day. I didn't understand why my being alive could cause so much pain to the people I loved most.

Living at arm's length from your family is a very strange orientation to the world. I was destined to become a deeply destructive fill-in-the-blank (drug addict, anorexic, alcoholic), but somehow I didn't. I think I lived in fear of doing damage to myself because my life was defined by this damage to another person's body. My brother's accident made me self-preserving. And I refused to be bound by my guilt or duty to him. I didn't want my life to be limited or defined by someone else's limits.

So I married very young and found myself pregnant within weeks. I needed to create emotional ties that made me feel safe, and this was how I did it. I was young to be pregnant, but I also knew that it increased my odds of having a healthy baby. And I did. Over nine pounds of boy. He was utterly remarkable. He was healthy and normal. And the minute I held him in my arms I realized everything my mother had lost. I recognized the power of her grief, and I was able to understand what she couldn't give me and to find forgiveness.

Eighteen months later I was in a hospital with my son surrounded by doctors. He had stopped speaking or making eye contact. He recoiled and screamed at loud sounds. He was retreating into a world of ritual. He was autistic.

Autism cannot be seen on the body of an autistic person. It

is an internal disease. Somewhere deep inside the brain there is a misfire or an overabundance of a chemical or too little. At this time autism was not on the cover of *Newsweek* or in the *New York Times Magazine.* Years later, a well-meaning show business friend said, "You are such a trendsetter. You were into autism before it was fashionable."

I was now my mother in more ways than I cared to imagine. The life I had never wanted was coming true. It was like a bad dream I could not wake up from. It was the end of any happiness I could ever hope for. I was cursed. How could I ever make sense of this? My life would now be a revolving door of doctors and therapists, just like my mother's. My daughter, who was soon to be born, was going to be me, the little sister being dragged to doctors' offices while her brother was seen by the latest specialist, and who knows? maybe she, too, would be autistic. I had never known such fear. Just as I had come close to the life I had wanted, it was being snatched from me. At the time I was beside myself with despair that my son would never have a relationship with the world around him. I was devastated, and I felt victimized.

One of the coldest doctors I met with, a woman who was a neurological and behavioral pediatrician and was considered unbearably mean but chillingly accurate in her diagnosis, surprisingly gave me the best words of any doctor my son saw. When I asked her if he would be all right, she looked at me and said, "Yes. Ultimately, I believe he will." I was shocked to hear something hopeful come out of her mouth. I asked why she believed that. And she replied simply, "Because you're his mother."

When she said this, it was like being sucker punched in the gut. Of course, it was so clear. The woman who I didn't want to be was who I had to become to save my son. It was all laid out in my tortured past. The footsteps already existed for me to follow into my present to give my son a future. This was a huge canyon to step over, and I had already done it.

I went from Clark Kent to Superman in an afternoon. I decided to blaze a trail with my son's intervention and treatment. I had no idea what therapies he might respond to, but I was going to try everything, even if it meant going into huge debt. And like my mother before me, I would do everything that was humanly possible to discover the key to undo this strange spell that had overtaken my child in the form of this invisible disease. "No" would not be a suitable answer.

I also knew I was in a desperate race against time and that the clock had already started ticking away. Real change in the brain is possible if therapies are begun early; a child's brain can recover in certain areas while it is supple and still growing. It is much harder to effect change at a later age. So I had a window of opportunity to help my son, and I needed to drop everything and do it.

My son will be okay because I am his mother. That simple statement was the key to me. My life was not wasted. My brother's accident would save my son. Far from having the wrong mother, I had the right mother. By example, she taught me to dive into the mess of rehabilitation and be creative and forthright and unflinching. My son's autism brought my life into new focus and made my purpose seem clear. Instead of being a victim of circumstance, I was on exactly the path I was supposed to be on.

I was empowered by my life and the people in it. I had the perfect mother, the perfect brother, the perfect son. My greatest tragedy would be my greatest friend. Now the hard work could start.

Note to Self

The worst thing that ever happened to you can be the best thing that ever happened to you if you only let it.

Skinless

MELINDA McGRAW

Melinda McGraw grew up in Massachusetts. She was classi-
cally trained as an actress at the Royal Academy of Dramatic
Arts in London, where she remained for several years, performing in theater and television before returning to the States
in 1990. Some of her most notable roles include Melissa Scully
in *The X-Files*, Larry's deviant girlfriend, Alex, in *The Larry
Sanders Show*, Barbara Gordon in *The Dark Knight*, and Bobbie
Barrett in *Mad Men*. She lives in Los Angeles with her husband, Steve Pierson, a composer, and her courageous daughter, Lucy Grace.

They must be able to stitch you up or something . . .
right?" Steve, my husband, says. He's driving, and I have a towel
between my legs, and all I can think is, *I did everything right. Why
didn't anybody ever warn me that things like this can happen? That
things can still go very, very wrong, even well into the second trimester?* We are scheduled to start Lamaze class later this week.
Rushing to the hospital three and a half months before I'm due

is not on my WHAT TO EXPECT WHEN YOU'RE EXPECTING calendar.

"I think you better call my parents," I say, trying to breathe.

"No," he says. "Let's not worry anybody, let's make sure that there's something really wrong first." All I can do is blink at him, embryonic fluid dripping down my leg. And this is when I realize that nobody's ever warned him, either. The blind is driving the blind to the maternity ward.

Thank God it is Sunday morning at seven o'clock, so there is no traffic. When we arrive at the hospital I tell the lady at the front desk that I'm worried that my water's broken. I am rushed right into the maternity ward. My knees are clenched, and when a blond, intense resident OB-GYN asks to examine me, I make a joke about putting a giant rubber band around my ankles and stringing my legs over my head. He doesn't chortle appreciatively like I want him to. In fact, he fails completely to acknowledge how charming and brave I am being in the face of such catastrophe. *What lousy bedside manner,* I think. *I'm just trying to quell my panic, for God's sake. Help me out here, that grave face of yours is terrifying me.* Once I reluctantly open my legs, what feels like a gallon of water rushes out. "Well, yes, your membranes have definitely ruptured," he says.

Now I know for sure. I have not merely sprung a little leak. The whole dam has broken.

"But it's too soon," I say.

The resident looks away, and my husband says, for the second time this morning, "You must be able to stitch her back up or . . . something?"

Nothing but silence from the resident. I look at my husband's stricken face. "Honey, I don't think they can."

The resident says, "You will be here until the baby comes."

Her due date is December 1. It is August 17.

"I'll call your parents now." My husband starts to shuffle out into the hall. "I'll call everyone."

Now everyone will know we are in trouble, and that she is in danger. Now it is official. This is really happening. Oh, God. Please, please do something.

As I am lying there alone, the hollow realization that this could all end here, any minute now, dawns on me. I call a nurse over. "Nurse? Have you ever seen someone keep a baby in after their water broke?"

"Yes, sometimes it can mend itself, I've seen that happen." She has a gentle voice and a crooked smile that I find very reassuring.

Stay here till the baby comes. Okay, I can do that. I will keep her in, they will put supplemental fluid in me or something. I mean, I'm not sure if I can manage sixteen weeks, but I will roll up my sleeves and try. I will try to keep her in until October, Halloween. That's a doable goal, something to sink my teeth into.

The maternity ward is over capacity, all the rooms are full, so they basically put me in a supply closet. Are they fucking kidding me?

"It's a full moon, this always happens," all the nurses say. But . . . really? Isn't this kind of an emergency? There are no windows in my closet, and it is dark. Am I going to have to stay in here until my daughter is born?

They set up monitors and put an IV in my arm. They are giving me what they tell me is a very high dose of magnesium sulfate (which is basically Epsom salts) to relax my body so much that the contractions stop, and—oh, shit—it feels like acid going up my arm, and the migraines that plagued my first trimester slam into my skull. I am, shockingly, denied pain reliever, because the doctors worry it might mask an infection. I am also denied food and water so I won't vomit. Despite this, I vomit roughly twenty-seven times in quick succession, and every time I feel more of my little baby girl's embryonic fluid gushing out from where she needs it.

Wait a second. In what scenario could I keep my little precious baby girl inside me for much longer? Do they intend to keep pumping this sodium compound into me day after day after day, with this aching head and these bleeding lips? My poor little girl, my poor little dream. I was going to have a midwife in a water suite down the hall from here, a real room three and a half months from now. She would be born into a bath of warm water with gorgeous African lullabies or gospel choirs playing, in the soft light of candles and with the smell of grapefruit in the air. It was supposed to be so joyous and so delicate. I try to whisper something to her but can't, so I just drag my fingers across my belly and hum.

My husband rubs my head and neck and tells me who's picking up my mother at the airport when she arrives, and then ultrasound techs and my lovely OB-GYN visit. "I'm so sorry," she says, and I assure her it will be okay, I will keep this baby in for eight more weeks.

She says, "Well, two more weeks would be ideal, but you absolutely have got to try for three days. We can get steroids into you during that time to help her lungs."

I stare at her. "Do I have to keep taking this mag sulfate?" I

say. She nods. "Do you guys always use this stuff to stop labor?"
I ask.

"Now we do. They used to use pure grain alcohol to basically
knock you out. Not pretty."

I don't want to give up my October goal, but I just do not see
surviving two months of this. It's time to call an audible. "Okay.
I can do it. I will keep her in for at least two more weeks."

When the neonatologist comes to see us to explain what our
baby's prognosis is, he speaks as if we already fully understand
what a neonatal intensive care unit is designed for (as if everyone should be prepared for this perfectly plausible scenario).
We don't understand, and there is nothing plausible about it.
He has a thick German accent, and listening to him is like
watching a slow-motion sequence in a German film as he
drones on, my relentless migraine stomping, and I start to hear
just snippets of his lines: *extreme prematurity, maybe a 50/50
chance, danger, cerebral palsy, imperative to keep her in the womb
until she is at twenty-eight weeks, risk, deafness, retardation, mor-
tality rate.* It will be a marathon ahead in the NICU, a roller-
coaster ride throughout her stay, and the outcome a crapshoot.
I keep turning my head to try to see my husband's face—is this
man really talking to us?

The sleepless hours grind on into days, and I pass them by
turning the wind-up mechanism on the white musical teddy
bear with the blue gingham bow that my husband brings me
from the hospital gift shop. It calms me and Baby down. I want
to be calm for her. *Lullaby, and good night* . . . my pillow is soggy
with sweat and tear puddles, my poor husband is begging the
nurses for ice chips to trace onto my cracked mouth and rub-

bing, rubbing, always rubbing my neck and head to try to chase
away the assault of pain. *Lullaby, and good night.* He whispers to
me that he has called everyone we know and asked them to pray
for our baby girl, even if they never have prayed in their lives.
He puts his forehead on mine as he rubs my neck, and I believe
him when he tells me he wishes he could swap places with me. I
can feel his hot tears rolling down into my ears. He sings his
song to my belly, "I'm just waiting on your smile . . ." as he has
every night since he wrote it, since we found out at week twelve
we are having a girl. A girl! My dream, my baby girl.

One glorious moment the next day my mother finally appears at the foot of my bed, here at last from the East Coast. I
gurgle with relief and she starts rubbing, rubbing, giving my
husband's sore hands a rest at last. Everyone keeps telling me I
should sleep, as if I am choosing not to. I wish I could. I am in
too much pain. I am too concerned for Baby's future as the neonatologist's statistics start to sink in. But we're doing everything we can, we are. The baby is not in distress, and there's
still some water up there. I'm giving my womb time to knit back
together. Maybe they can ease up on the mag sulfate, maybe the
pain will stop then, and she will be safe again. A kind nurse
sneaks me a lemon Popsicle from the pediatrics ward. It's the
best fucking thing I have ever tasted.

On the fourth morning, after an ultrasound, they tell me it is
time. She has run out of water, and we have been able to get her
three days' worth of steroids to help her little lungs mature, and
now she is safer out than in. They are putting in the epidural, it
will be a caesarean because she is so early she is still upright, of
course. They promise that as soon as she is delivered, they will
give me pain reliever for the migraine, but I am pissed. I look at

my OB-GYN. "You said two weeks at least. The neonatologist said we have to get to twenty-eight weeks. It's only twenty-six and one day. We have to wait a little while longer."

She gets it. She speaks to me softly. "You've done it, Melinda. She's gotten all the steroids. You did all you can do, the cord is wrapped around her feet and there is no water up there at all. She has to come out now, it's better for her."

As we roll to the OR, with my husband looking scared but TV-doctor handsome in his scrubs, my OB-GYN tries to prepare us for how it will go. There will be several people there with an isolette (which I guess is a modern word for incubator), seven specialists ready to take her up to the neonatal ICU. She will be unconscious, and they will have to revive her, get her to start breathing and put her on a respirator. She will be about two and a half pounds. It will be nothing like we've come to expect. She will be completely silent because she will have no breath to cry. No midwife, no grapefruit candles, no water birth, no cry. How did it go this wrong? *Hang on, Baby, hang on. They will take care of you.*

Steve kisses me and talks to me the whole way through. When my OB finds her, she says, "Oh, she's a tiny little peanut! But she's gorgeous!" And there, in the glare of that hospital operating room, there comes the most indescribably beautiful sound: a teeny, tiny, reedy cry. And another. There is nothing but a hush, and her cry, her cry and gasps all around us—the team of seven, the nurses, my doctors, all gasping, "She's crying! She's breathing on her own!" I catch a glimpse of her as they carry her from my womb to the examining table way across the room, and I see her dark pink, waxy body and her face—she looks just like him, how is that possible already?—and she's

crying, and someone says, "Hello, Beautiful!" and I am grinning. They shout, "Her APGAR scores are nine!" and then they
have to take her up to the NICU, but first they bring her over all
wrapped up and I get to see her little perfect face. She is the
size of a tiny doll, and her eyes are fused shut like a newborn
kitten's, and she cries her tiny cry. "She is only a pound and a
half," they say. My husband offers to stay with me and I tell him
no, go with her! And they take her.

They take her away.

The morphine floods my IV and the migraine dissolves
away. I wait in recovery, trying to count blessings and stave off
panic. My husband arrives with the very first pictures ever taken
of her, and he describes as best he can her new home, floors
above.

He wants to know if we can name her now. Upstairs they are
asking him what her name is. "Not yet," I say. "Not yet." We had
settled on the perfect name, and we both know, now that we
have heard that cry they told us wouldn't come, that it is unmis-
takably the perfect name for her. I do not tell my husband this,
but I do not want to give it to her. Because if she dies . . . we can
never use that name again. We will bury it with her. I want a
do-over. Maybe we should give her our second-favorite name.
I know I am being horrible, and weak. For the very first time,
my mind contains no optimism. My courage has folded up its
tent, and I am desperate to find cover. Her arrival in the world
is a shadow. I can't feel her, she is elsewhere. I am told I must
wait twenty-four hours to see her, an interminable wait, and a
secret relief. I am terrified to see her again. It is unbearable,
her complete tiny-ness, her fetus-ness.

While he is up with her, I stare at the picture he's brought me. She is so red, so transparent. She looks like she has no skin. "My skinless baby," I whisper to her, and I try to send thoughts to her while I weep. "I am so sorry. So sorry I couldn't hold you in. I know your body is not ready to be here. If you can't stay, if you need to go, we will understand."

Once the twenty-four hours pass, I am rolled in a wheelchair up to the NICU. We have to scrub our hands furiously and douse ourselves in Purell every time we enter the ward, my husband tells me. She is lying in the last incubator, in Bay One, reserved for the very sickest babies. All I see is monitors and machines. I am rolled to her little plastic igloo, and there she is, eyes tight shut, IVs attached, with a blood pressure cuff around her leg that is the size of a Band-Aid I'd use for a paper cut. She looks different, not all shiny like yesterday, and I can see her ribs. What does that mean? She is down to a pound and two ounces, they say, but they reassure me, "Oh, that's normal, don't worry. The babies dehydrate." They smile at me. "What have you named her?" they ask. I do not answer.

She is my very own Thumbelina. Her head is the size of a small plum. She weighs less than the last package of hamburger meat I bought at Ralph's. I am unabashedly overcome, and I lower my head onto the top of her isolette. "I'm sorry. I'm sorry, Baby. Please forgive me." I stand silently, swallowing hard, with tears dropping on the floor for almost two hours, at which point Steve and my mother insist I go back to my room to rest. I can come back later and say good night, they say. I relent and collapse into my wheelchair. I return to my room and lie staring at the ceiling.

I am taught how to pump by the lactation team—thank God, something I can do for her. But with plastic cups at my breasts instead of her tiny mouth, I am struggling with the surrealism of it all. *Why? Why did this happen?* My husband and mother try to keep me focused. I try to cheer up for them. But whenever I am alone, in the throbbing stillness of the room, I lie there and stare.

I know this is somehow my fault, though everyone keeps saying it is a "fluke." My husband and I had a terrible fight last week, and stress is bad. I walked into the edge of that car door. Maybe we shouldn't have taken that trip to Europe when I was five months pregnant. I am broken. My body is broken and I couldn't keep her safe. I have failed her.

Over the next two days, between pumping sessions, I am at her isolette, my head leaning on it, murmuring. I'm sure I must look like something out of *Girl, Interrupted,* "Please, Baby, please stay. It's okay if you want to go, but I'd like you to stay. I need you to stay with me. Now I am skinless, too."

"You've gotta give this beautiful baby a name," announces a woman, suddenly standing next to me. "I'm Natalie. I'm the nurse practitioner. C'mon, what are you waiting for?" She smiles a huge smile at me even though I have snot and tears cascading down my face.

I look over at my husband. This is it. I am going to give this baby my favorite name. I have decided that even if she dies, she deserves this name. It will always be hers, no matter what. "Her name is Lucy." They make a pretty name plate and hang it on her little home. I stare at it, trying to find comfort in it, but I can't.

It is her fourth day of life. They are discharging me tomorrow. Around dinnertime I feel a strange tightness under my chest, in my diaphragm. I stand up to relieve the tightness and suddenly, terribly, someone is ripping into the base of my skull with an axe—the single most excruciating pain I have ever even imagined. I manage to whisper to my husband to call the doctor. "I think I am having a stroke." Suddenly I begin vomiting . . . repeatedly, violently, just like I did on our first day here, over and over. At fifty times I stop counting. They take my blood pressure, and it reads 160 over 220—how is that possible? I see glimpses of the panic in my nurse's movements, my mother's ashen face, and my husband's viselike grip. Now what? What is happening? We don't have time for this shit, there is a baby upstairs clinging to her life! Now I am, too?

They rush me up to the cardiac ICU, where all the other patients look jaundiced and over eighty. The on-call cardiologist informs us that I have had a heart attack. Doctors tell us it is in no way related to the extremely premature birth of our baby, and my husband and I actually both laugh. "Of course it is," I say. "My heart is broken." My husband runs his hand over my tangled hair, and my mother stands at the foot of the bed and holds my feet. I am blessed.

A parade of medical students and residents begins to pass through my room in a steady stream, as I hear my story retold ad nauseam. I am some kind of cardio-mystery, which makes me a celebrity in this teaching hospital. The head cardiologist insists that I have an angiogram to rule out any overt heart disease, and the neurologist tells me it's possible I had a stroke and suggests a brain MRI.

I opt for the angiogram first, and, with the catheter still in, the cardiologist tells me I have the heart of a marathon runner. I say, "Good, can I go see my baby now?" It has been almost twenty-four hours, I am out of danger, I must see her, and I am not taking no for an answer. With a portable heart monitor and IV, I am wheeled up from my ICU to hers. I am all scrubbed clean and in front of her isolette and damn it, I am no braver, I am no stronger, I am bereft and wracked with grief. There is nothing I can do here, why did I think there was? She is just lying there, all wires and tubes, and they have been poking her and hurting her and I can do nothing to stop it. A woman comes up behind me. "Would you like to hold her?" It's Natalie again.

"They told me we have to leave her in for two weeks before we are allowed to touch her."

"Not while I'm here," she murmurs with a wink. I realize she feels sorry for me, and is probably worried for my health. I must look gray and haggard. She probably figures she should let me hold the baby now, in case I kick the bucket.

It takes almost half an hour to arrange all the wires right, between my monitors and hers, so that her tiny body can safely reach my wheelchair. I watch Natalie and the nurses busying about, alongside the blue glare of the monitors, and the sounds of constant beeping, the hollow chorus of ventilators, the whispers of parents over their babies' incubators. What will she feel like? Will she be like a bird, or a languishing little doll? What if I bruise her? What if I drop her? How can I caress her without breaking a little rib? I'm starting to change my mind. I don't want to hold her! What if she dies right here, right here in my arms? I start to panic. I begin to tremble, to whimper. My wet eyes stare ahead, and I do not dare speak. Natalie picks her up and coos, "Hello, gorgeous, this is your very one and only Mommy." And she places her into my two hands.

And here she is. She is here. Finally, I am touching her again.

I stop crying immediately. She feels like she is a solid ten pounds. Her body is actually vibrating like some big baby battery. She is IN there! Her soul is not somewhere looking down, wondering if she wants to stick around, wondering what her odds are, deciding if this body is a good enough vessel to enter, waiting for this body to decide for her. That was me doing all that. Her soul is in that impossibly tiny little baby body. She is committed, she is here, she is fighting.

And right now, in this very moment, I become a mother. In this very moment I grow all the way up. Pacing, waiting, analyzing, measuring, regretting, rationalizing, hiding, denying, grieving, procrastinating, blaming, parsing, deconstructing—all these distractions collapse and wisp away in this instant because there is no longer a doubt in my mind that she has decided! She is alive, she is here, she is all in. It is a miracle. She is a miracle. What have I been waiting for? I climb out of my foxhole and I laugh with the relief of it, relax into her strength. I sing to her, and I hold and caress her with utter expertise. Fear melts away from me as gratitude flows in. I know that I am now suddenly, wonderfully, and inexplicably qualified to be the most loving possible Mother to her. I lay her on my chest, right over my heart, and brush my lips in circles on the top of her fuzzy, gorgeous little head.

There will be unforgettable days ahead of us, some full of horror, but I am newly fortified by her superhuman strength. She will, amazingly, continue to breathe on her own until her tenth day, when her tiny body becomes too exhausted and they will put her on a ventilator. Day after day for the next four months we will navigate the grave dangers of her many conditions, my knees will grow raw from praying on the cold linoleum floor of the NICU, we will grow weary from pacing during her eventual twenty-seven blood transfusions, weak from comforting fellow parents whose babies weren't so lucky. Natalie will save her life, more than once. Ahead, there will be years of therapies and surgeries for Lucy. Her unflinching, raw courage is what will propel us through. One day I will finally discover what was behind her early birth and my heart attack: I have an extremely rare form of HELLP disorder (hemolytic anemia, elevated liver enzymes, and low platelet count) that makes it deathly dangerous for me to carry a baby.

And years from now, as I watch her chubby, healthy legs wobble around the house as she's singing, "Tippy-toes, tippy-toes" to a melody her daddy has written for her, I will remember the moment I first held her, and I will tingle even then with the glory of it. We will give her the middle name of Grace. She is here because of it. She sprinkles the world with it. And she has given it to me.

Note to Self

Childbirth requires courage;
motherhood requires Grace.

HARDSHIP

Kicking My Demons

KATIE HNIDA

Katie Hnida made history as the first woman to play in and score points in an NCAA Division I-A college football game while at the University of New Mexico. Her book *Still Kicking* is about her groundbreaking experience as a woman playing a man's sport and includes her experiences at the University of Colorado and the harassment she endured there as the only woman on the team, plus the rape she survived soon after. She continues to play football, kicking for the minor league Colorado Cobras, and is a frequent public speaker on sexual assault and violence against women.

My life has always included sports. My two brothers, sister, and I spent all our free time playing some kind of game, whether it was shooting hoops in the driveway or playing two-on-two soccer in the yard. Our family picked our lotto numbers by the jersey numbers of baseball greats: Sevens for Mickey Mantle and nines for Ted Williams. Every fall weekend, our family TV would stay tuned to sports stations for nonstop action: Saturdays were devoted to college ball, and Sundays were all about the NFL. We lived in Denver, so I was raised a die-hard Broncos and University of Colorado Buffaloes fan.

I always assumed that due to my size and gender, I'd be forever stuck enjoying the game from the stands. That didn't stop me from daydreaming, though. My football fantasies started in elementary school, when I wrote a short story about a girl who played the game. She was a quarterback and had to hide her hair under her helmet so no one would discover her true identity. She led her team to the championship, and at the end of the event, she took off her helmet and shook down her long hair. Everyone was shocked to learn that she was a girl, but they were happy for the win.

Soccer became my main focus as I went into junior high, but when I was thirteen, an injury to my quadriceps muscle interrupted my soccer career. Ironically, that's what led me to the football field. I had been rehabilitating my leg for about a year when one night I was tossing the football around the backyard with one of my brothers and my dad. On one particular play, the ball hit the ground. On a whim, I propped the ball up and kicked it back to my dad. It flew about twenty yards over his head.

"Holy smokes, Kate!" my dad cried. "Can you do that again?"

"I don't know, probably," I shrugged. It hadn't been a big deal to me; I had just kicked the ball.

"Hang on a sec." My dad grabbed the ball and crouched into a holding position. "Go ahead. Kick another."

I gave this one an even harder and more concentrated kick,

and the ball landed in our neighbor's yard over thirty-five yards away. My dad chuckled as he shook his head. "Well, kiddo!" he laughed, "if you can't play soccer, maybe you can make a career out of kicking footballs!" I laughed, too, but after a second I began to seriously wonder if I could actually become the girl in my short story.

A few weeks later, I noticed a sign in my middle school about a meeting for athletes interested in playing for the high-school football team. I gathered every ounce of courage I had in my thirteen-year-old self and went to the meeting. As I walked in, all the guys stared at me. The coach even asked if I was looking for the girls' lacrosse meeting. My parents were incredibly supportive behind the scenes. "If the football thing doesn't work," they said, "at least you can say you tried." Mom and Dad always encouraged me and my siblings to take risks and follow our dreams.

That fall, I attended my first football practice. I started out with the freshman squad but was soon kicking well enough that I was asked to kick for the varsity team as well. As far as my coaches and teammates were concerned, as long as I could kick the football, they could care less about me being female. They treated me just like one of the guys. I'd found a home on the football field, and never in my life had I felt as connected to the world or as in sync as I did when I was out kicking.

The next four years were great. I led the state in points my senior year, and I got national media attention when I was crowned homecoming queen during halftime. All of the other girls were dressed up in high heels and dresses, and I had on my sweaty jersey and shoulder pads. My kicking and the media attention brought interest from colleges. I received recruiting letters from colleges and universities across the nation, but I wanted to go to the University of Colorado because I had grown up idolizing their football team. The head coach of CU, Rick Neuheisel, had been following my career since my freshman year, and he invited me to join the team when my high-school career ended. Although I knew the jump to major college football was going to be huge, I was comfortable with Coach Neuheisel and was excited that he wanted me to play for his team.

Then the unexpected happened. Coach Neuheisel took a job at another university, and a new coach, Gary Barnett, took over. He watched a tape of me kicking and said that he would extend Coach Neuheisel's invitation to join the team, but I wasn't sure where the change left me. Would the new coach be comfortable with a female player? It was too late for me to apply to other schools, so I stuck with my plan to attend CU.

I began summer conditioning up in Boulder with my new college team, the Buffaloes. On my second day, I had my first negative encounter. I was on a break from doing sprints when one of my teammates asked in a snide, mocking voice, "So, are *you* the kicker?"

"That would be me," I answered, a little on guard due to his sour tone.

The guy made a face. "Weren't you the prom queen or something like that?"

"Something like that," I said.

"Well, go home. You're not a football player, you're a girl."

"What?" I wasn't sure I'd heard him right.

"I said, GO HOME, PROM QUEEN!"

I couldn't believe some guy had said that. In my four years of playing, no teammate had ever said anything negative to me. Luckily, the whistle blew and I had to start running again. I didn't know what to think.

That encounter was the beginning of things to come. When the season started, I found myself in living hell; every day with my new team seemed to bring new forms of harassment. Verbal abuse occurred on a daily basis. I would come off the field and get called a "cunt" to my face. I had never even heard the word before! The physical and sexual harassment were never ending, too. Players grabbed my buttocks when we were in huddles, and another teammate launched footballs as hard as he could at my head as I tried to kick. I'd duck to get out of the way and hear chuckles from the other players. I was so confused, and it was so humiliating, because so many other guys, the ones who never bothered me, stood around but did nothing to stop these things from happening. Not all the guys on my team were bad guys, but it seemed as if they all accepted using me as a whipping post, even by their inaction. A lot of players, and even the coach, knew that I was having a rough time, but nothing changed.

One afternoon after practice, I took the footballs into the equipment room, which was located near the men's locker room. As I came around a stairwell, a player was standing there. He said, "How do such big shoulder pads fit a little girl like you?" He cornered me up against a wall and started to try to feel my breasts. I was paralyzed with fear, and I couldn't get any words to come out of my mouth. I jerked away, and he backed away, laughing. I ran to the safety of my locker room and started to cry.

I didn't know what to do about any of this. I was eighteen years old, living on my own for the first time, and trying to figure out how to be a college student and athlete. I had obviously entered a world that I wasn't prepared for and couldn't understand. Football, the thing I loved more than anything in the world, was becoming something I dreaded, and nothing seemed to make sense any more. I didn't know who to talk to about what was happening. Coach Barnett was out of the question. He wasn't friendly to begin with, and I got the feeling that he felt like having me around was a nuisance. I was afraid that he would tell me to leave the team, and despite everything I was going through, I didn't want to give up on my dream. And while I have always been close with my family, I couldn't bear to tell them what was happening. I knew it would hurt them, too, and I was particularly afraid of my dad's reaction. If he knew how some of the guys treated me, I thought he might physically hurt someone.

So I decided I would push on. I told myself that I could handle it, and that no matter what, I wouldn't give up on playing just because that's what these guys wanted me to do.

I went into survival mode to get through my classes, practices, and workouts. I became the first woman to dress for a Division I college football game, and the first woman to go to a postseason bowl game. I made it through my freshman year by being tough and staying focused, but in the summer before my sophomore year, my dream truly became my worst nightmare.

It was June, and one of the few teammates I trusted invited me over to his place to watch a basketball game. I had been there a number of times before, just to watch games or movies and hang out and shoot the breeze. This guy was one of my closest friends on the team, and we talked easily and a lot. I considered him a confidant and a big brother to me, and I even talked to him about the harassment I faced from the team, and problems I had with my kicking. "You're a strong woman," he would tell me. "Stay strong. Those guys are morons." When he knew I was having a bad day at practice, he would try to make me smile by joking around. I felt completely safe with him.

On that particular summer night, everything changed. I was sitting next to him on the couch, like I'd done so many times before, when he slid his arm around me.

"You are so pretty," he said.

What? That was strange, I thought.

"Really," he said. "You're beautiful." He began to kiss my neck.

"Hey!" I exclaimed. "What are you doing?" I was caught completely off-guard. One of his hands had found its way to my thigh, while the other snuck behind my neck and pulled my face toward his. He started to kiss me. I flinched and pulled back.

"Come on, babe . . . ," he whispered. "You know you want me, too."

No way, I thought. *What is going on?*

Now he was on top of me, his hand on my thigh.

"Stop!" I was really beginning to panic.

He ignored me and shoved his tongue into my mouth. He put one hand on my shoulder and felt around under my skirt with the other.

"I don't want to do this," I pleaded, trying to maneuver out from under him. I couldn't move, though. He outweighed me by more than a hundred pounds and was much stronger. I was stuck.

Then his hand was inside me. *Oh God*, I thought. *Not this.*

"I don't . . . no . . ." I tried to form words.

"Shhhh . . . ," he said, shoving his finger onto my lips. "You're old enough for this now."

He hovered over me and pulled down his shorts. He lowered himself down, and I feebly tried to free one of my arms to push on his shoulder. I squeezed my eyes shut as he forced himself inside me. It hurt like hell for a minute, but then all feeling stopped. My body went limp and lifeless. I could vaguely feel his cheek rubbing against mine and smell his cologne and sweat, but I felt like I had disconnected from my own body. I felt like I was watching this happen to someone else.

Suddenly, a buzzing sound came from the other side of the room. His cell phone was ringing. He muttered something and pushed himself off me. For a second I didn't move, and then I blinked. Slowly, I pulled myself up. I was completely disoriented, and I stared at him as he picked up his cell and began to talk. My instincts told me to get out of there as fast as I could. I grabbed my keys, bolted out the door, and ran to my car. By now, I was shaking so violently that I couldn't get my keys into the ignition, and it took me several tries to get my truck started and whip the transmission into reverse. I stomped the pedal so hard that I slammed into a light pole behind me and smashed my bumper, then I shoved the car into drive and peeled out of the parking lot.

My mind and body were numb, and I vaguely remember getting back to my apartment and fumbling to get the door unlocked. I was still shaking. Inside, I locked each of the door's three locks and didn't turn on any lights. I stumbled to the couch and sat in the dark trying to comprehend what had just happened. Hours went by, I don't know how many. Finally, I picked up the phone and called my roommate, Libby, who was back home in Wisconsin for summer break. Not knowing what I'd say to her, I dialed her house. It was 2:30 in the morning there, and her dad answered. I apologized for calling so late and asked if Libby was around. She was out. I assured her father that everything was fine and apologized again for calling at such an ungodly hour. I hung up. That's when I totally shut down. I spent the night on the couch, drifting in and out of consciousness.

Toward daybreak, questions began to float in and out of my head. *What happened to me? Where did this come from? What should I do? Was I raped?* He'd been a good friend and a teammate. Rape is what happens when you walk somewhere alone at night and a stranger tackles you with a weapon. This had to have been a mistake. This wasn't happening. It couldn't be.

When the sun came up, I was still in a daze, and I began having horrible waves of nausea. I finally changed my clothes, mechanically taking off each item and shoving them into the hamper one at a time. I went back to the couch. Tears sprang to my eyes for the first time since the assault. I still didn't know what to do. I felt disgusting and ashamed, and I didn't want to tell my parents, let alone my coach. My thoughts were blurred by the groping, and the sexual and physical intimidation and harassment I had been experiencing since I had joined the team. No one had seemed particularly bothered by that behavior, so what would they think about what had happened now?

In the days that followed, I didn't tell anyone about that night. I knew that what had happened was wrong, but I didn't know who to turn to. I felt responsible for what had happened, and the effects of the past year caught up with me. I was mentally, emotionally, and physically drained. My health began to suffer. I had constant bouts of tonsillitis, complete with fever and chills. In the fall I had tonsils and an abscess in my throat removed, and I didn't return to the team after my surgery.

I decided that I needed to get out of Boulder, away from the memories, and get a fresh start someplace where no one knew me. Despite all the hell I had gone through, I didn't want to give up on my dream of playing football, so I decided that going to a junior college would be my best option. I transferred to Santa Barbara City College in California.

I was still struggling with the memories of CU, but I just shoved them down any time they came up. The moment I stepped onto the field in Santa Barbara for my first football practice, I was flooded with flashbacks that I couldn't control. Images of my rape and other harassment flashed through my head like scenes out of a movie. At that moment, I realized that I needed to get help for everything I'd gone through. I knew that if I didn't deal with these experiences, I was never going to be the football player or the person I wanted to be. I decided not to play football that fall, and to take part-time classes. Even though I didn't tell my parents about the rape, I did talk to them about some of the other harassment I'd experienced. They told me to do whatever I needed to do, and they would be there to support me.

The next few months were difficult, even though I knew I'd

made the right decision. I started seeing a school counselor, but I wasn't ready to talk about the extent of the harassment I'd endured—or the rape. However, I was finally able to admit to myself that I had been raped. To me, *rape* is the most vile four-letter word on the planet. And although I'd admitted to myself that I was a rape victim, I was still plagued with shame, fear, and self-blame.

I fell into a deep depression while I was still in Santa Barbara. I was tired all the time, yet I rarely slept. Instead, I'd stay up all night, haunted by the incidents at CU. Some days I couldn't even get out of bed. I had no motivation to go out or do anything besides go to therapy. I would let the phone ring, and emails went unanswered. I just didn't care.

Then one day, I slowly began to pick myself up. I can't point to anything specific that happened except a voice inside of me that whispered, "You're a fighter." I knew I wanted my life back, so I began doing volunteer work again, something that had always been a huge part of my life. I mentored a little girl and helped her with homework and doing art projects for a few hours once a week. I slowly started to work out again and finally started kicking footballs. As I gained strength, I reconnected with my core self and realized that I wanted to keep playing football. That little voice had been right. I was a fighter, and I wasn't going to let anyone take away my passion. I also told my family and friends about the rape and the harassment I had faced. Even though it was hard, a huge weight was lifted. I wasn't carrying around this huge secret anymore, and I had people to help me as I continued to heal.

In 2002, I transferred to the University of New Mexico and

joined a new football team. It was one of the scariest experiences of my life. What if it was CU all over again? My fears turned out to be unfounded. On the first day of class, I ran into one of my giant offensive linemen on campus. When he found out we were headed in the same direction, he scooped me up and gave me a piggyback ride. That ride was indicative of how my teammates were with me. New Mexico was better than I ever could have hoped, and during my second season with the team I kicked two extra points, becoming the first woman to play and score in a major college football game.

Meanwhile, while I was at New Mexico, news was coming out of Boulder. Two women came forward and said that football players had raped them at an off-campus party. The women decided to sue the university on the grounds that the football program was fostering a climate that allowed this kind of behavior toward women. CU denied the charges, stating there weren't, and never had been, problems with football players misbehaving around women.

I was stunned. I knew firsthand about the environment of the football program and was horrified to hear that other women had been abused. I also knew that there were people in the athletic department who were aware of the fact that I had been harassed, including Coach Barnett and the athletic director. I had met with both of them when I hadn't returned to the team. My parents and I decided that the best course of action was to get in touch with the university's chancellor and talk to him about my experience on the team. The chancellor told us not to worry, and that he would take the new allegations seriously.

Shortly thereafter, another woman came forward and said that she, too, had been raped by a football player. She had worked in the athletic department, and she'd gone there for help after being assaulted. She claimed that the department had told her to keep quiet about the assault and they would handle it internally. Once again, the university, including the chancellor, came out with strong denials that there were problems within the football program. Needless to say, I was frustrated at the university's response and felt that I needed to do something.

I decided that I wanted to let someone in law enforcement know what had happened to me. I didn't know if I'd want to press charges in my own case, but I knew that I wanted to let someone in law enforcement know what had happened. As I waited to meet with the prosecutor, I thought I was going to throw up while I stood in the lobby, trembling.

Luckily, the DA helped put me at ease. She was very straightforward about my chances of winning a case if I decided to pursue one. I didn't have any physical evidence, and I hadn't reported the rape immediately to the police, but it turned out that neither was as uncommon as I'd thought. The DA explained that even if I did have physical evidence and an immediate police report, the defense's tactic would likely be the same: that it had been consensual sex, not rape. I also learned that fewer than 30 percent of the rape cases that are reported in the first place get prosecuted. That was discouraging, but the next thing I heard was even worse: many rapists don't get jail time, even when they're convicted. The DA told me that even if my rapist was convicted, he likely wouldn't see the inside of a prison.

How could he not go to jail if he was found guilty? I didn't understand.

I thanked the prosecutor and left with a lot on my mind. I didn't feel like I was ready to press charges. I was still scared of my rapist, and I wasn't sure if I was ready for the toll that a trial would take on my life. I was finally feeling like I had gotten a bit of my life back; I was busy playing football and going to New Mexico, and I would have to give up both in order to truly pursue a case. I struggled with what I should do.

As the weeks went on, media coverage of CU's football program and the rape and assault allegations increased. CU issued statement after statement denying any wrongdoing.

Finally, I knew I couldn't just listen anymore. With the support of my family and New Mexico teammates and coaches, I decided it was time to speak up. Nearly four years after I was raped, I spoke publicly to *Sports Illustrated* about my experiences at CU. I never could have predicted what would follow next: there was a media firestorm, and everyone had an opinion. People took the most awful experience of my life and attached their own judgments to it. I was criticized for various decisions I'd made: why hadn't I gone to the police? Why was I talking about this now? Some even inferred that I was lying as a way to get back at the football program, since I'd had a bad experience there.

I wish I could say that I just blew off whatever was written about me, but that wasn't the case. What some members of the press wrote and said is still painful for me to think about to this day. In the wake of my public announcement, I began to have severe nightmares and flashbacks about my experiences at CU.

There were times when I felt as if I was being raped all over again.

Despite all the agony, I'm glad I spoke up. In the days following my interview, five more women came forward saying that they, too, had been raped or assaulted by members of the CU football team. This prompted the governor of Colorado to order a grand-jury investigation into the allegations. Though no charges were filed (mostly at the victims' request), new rules were put in place for the CU football program. It was a much-needed win in a long, drawn-out battle.

I now spend a lot of time speaking about sexual assault to women all over America. After learning more about it, I feel like it is part of my life's mission to help people understand the reality of this trauma. It's so important for me to reach out to the many women who are suffering in silence, and let them know that they are not alone. I remember how lost and confused I felt after being raped, and I want other women to know that it's okay to feel that way—that rape doesn't have a blueprint, and neither does healing from it. I also want them to know that there is help out there, and there are more people who understand what we're going through than we know.

The subject of sexual violence is still somewhat taboo, and the secrecy that surrounds the subject only makes the situation worse. As we continue to address the issue, I hope more women will find the courage to speak up and report violent acts. I also pray that someday sexual violence will end altogether, because no one should ever have to go through the feelings of powerlessness, shame, and dehumanization that come from assault.

A reporter once asked me what it was like to be "America's

most famous rape victim." I said that I was glad to put a face to the epidemic, and I went on to explain that I wasn't ashamed of being a victim. More important, I was proud to be a survivor, football player, sister, writer, friend, and teammate. Maybe I was defined by rape in the media, but I'm not defined by it in my life.

I still have hard days, nightmares, flashbacks, and moments when I feel nauseous over the memories of my assault. This is okay. I might never "get over" being raped, but I don't have to. My life is affected by what happened, but it's not controlled by it. It is a part of me that I have integrated into myself and my life, just like every other experience I've had. I will continue to fight through the tough spots, and I know that between my faith and support from my family, I'll make it.

Note to Self

Only you can determine
the moments that define you.

Bring Tenacity to a Boil, Then Serve

ADRIENNE KANE

Adrienne Kane is a food writer living in New Haven, Connecticut. Her memoir, including recipes, is entitled *Cooking and Screaming* and will be released in February 2009 by Simon Spotlight Entertainment.

I am cooking again. Alone in the kitchen, I let my senses take over. My ears pique from the rhythmic rumble of vegetables being pushed from side to side by my wooden spoon in the pan. I watch as the zucchini change color from a bright, verdant green to a subtle, buttery hue when the heat takes effect. The smell is comforting as it wafts past my nostrils in puffs of warm steam. On the cutting board, the grater stands squarely near the green vegetables, like an army general presiding over his soldiers. Moments ago I'd placed my right hand on top of the handle, grasping the grater with a tight fist, holding the tool firmly and steadily; this enabled my left hand to do most of the work, which helps make up-and-down motions to create shaggy piles of zucchini.

I am a lefty now.

I love being alone in the kitchen. I seldom notice how many hours pass. Instead, my thoughts are consumed by what could be perceived as the petty business of the kitchen: the simmering pot of pea soup, the jumbled tossing of a salad, the naked cupcakes enrobed in pools of rich chocolate ganache. My appreciation for the kitchen didn't develop with ease or rapidity. It developed over time, and the discovery was a gradual one, like peeling apart the layers of a pomegranate, slow and finger-staining. Before I discovered that cooking gave me purpose, I had a lot of time to think about it.

In May 2000, I suffered an AVM (a cerebral arteriovenous malformation), which led to a strokelike hemorrhage in the brain. This left me in a coma, paralyzed on the right side of my body. An AVM is a rare birth defect that affects 0.5 to 0.8 percent of the population. AVMs alter the capillaries of the brain; instead of tiny, smooth conduits, an AVM produces large, misshapen passageways that have a heightened potential for rupturing at any time. AVMs show no preference—if you're male or female, young or old, they are equal opportunity offenders and go largely undetected until they strike. Like a stroke, the effects vary, depending on exactly where the bleeding is located in the labyrinthine recesses of the brain. I bled in the basal-ganglion region of the left side of my brain, an area that controls the motor skills of the right side of my body.

There's never an ideal time for life-changing events, but mine couldn't have happened at a worse one. I was twenty-one, just finishing college, and I, like so many of my peers, wasn't sure what to do with the rest of my life. In school I was a modern dancer, and I filled my days with hours in the studio, examining each muscle of my body, toiling in front of a mirror, watching my reflection mimic the motions of the choreographer. I loved it, but knowing a dancer's career is a finite one, I'd majored in English. But suddenly, school was coming to an end, as was my dance career, and while my peers were packing up their lives to begin anew, my life as I knew it was suddenly on hold.

My AVM ruptured on a bright spring day. Bare-shouldered college kids were busy studying for finals or meeting friends for coffee. I'd planned to meet my best friend near campus to talk about her careful edits to my senior thesis. The AVM came quickly. My surroundings began to spin, I had waves of nausea, and my vision blurred. Suddenly the ground, littered with cigarette butts and candy wrappers—detritus from a college town— looked pretty, a kaleidoscope of color. I sat down on the cement, and the pavement felt comforting and cool. My friend called 911. The ambulance came, and for a moment I became the object of rubberneckers' attraction. And then, everything went from crystal clear to a hazy shade of gray.

Weeks later, I woke up in the intensive-care unit of the hospital surrounded by my family and notes from well-wishers. I was reclined in bed, and the entire right side of my body felt as if it had been struggling under a tremendous weight. As I gazed down toward the foot of the bed, seeing the gentle slope of my feet beneath the sheets, I thought about wiggling my toes. The left side responded to my brain's command, but the right side remained still. I wished my nerves to remain as placid as my body. Terror and frustration would have to wait; I sensed how much work would have to be done in order to make me whole again.

My body had now become a spoiled child, with little regard for what I asked it to do. After a month my doctor lifted me from my hospital bed and placed me in a wheelchair. This was not my preferred mode of transportation. At twenty-one, I was not ready to bid farewell to my legs, the legs that only months ago had been pliéing and jetéing in the dance rehearsal room. Over the following months, physical therapists guided me in learning to walk again. But this walk was different. My graceful dancer's stride was now a slow and labored gait.

When I was released from the hospital after a three-month stay, I went home with my parents to recuperate. After long days of being shuttled to various therapists, each night I'd exhaustedly tumble into my childhood bed. But eventually, exhaustion gave way to fitful nights of restless sleep. I'd lie in bed, surrounded by mementos from the past: postcards from travels to foreign cities tacked helter-skelter to a bulletin board, piles of mix tapes that hadn't been listened to since the advent of the CD player, and a closet full of clothes for the skinnier me. My right arm rested across my stomach as I tried, with little success, to move the fingers on my right hand.

I would wake up in the mornings creaky and sore. My muscles would remain tense through the night, and as I would set my feet on the ground, it would take a minute to get my physical bearings. Brushing my teeth became a one-armed dance. Stabbing the toothbrush into my clenched right hand to ready it for the toothpaste, then switching it to my left hand to make the action of brushing was a lesson in patience. Having to call my mom to pull my hair back into a neat ponytail and away from my face reminded me of mornings spent kneeling on the bathroom floor as a child so she could tie a bow in my hair. But slowly I became adept, and eventually I was not so much a one-armed girl as a one-and-a-half-armed girl. I could steady my toast with my right arm while I carefully smoothed on a slick of butter with my left.

Some people talk about having a calling, an interest that beckons to them like a dinner bell to the table. This wasn't the case for me: my food calling was more like a whisper that over time became a yell. However, food had always had a prominent place in my family. I'd heard stories about my maternal grandmother rising at dawn to cook breakfasts of eggs, biscuits, sausage, and hash brown potatoes for dozens of farmhands in South Dakota. For my uncle, food *was* a calling; after years of training, he cooked in restaurants and then catered cocktail spreads of blini with caviar, stuffed mushroom caps, and filo-wrapped shrimp for clients in the Silicon Valley. And my mother is a wonderful home chef, who prepares healthy meals of beef stew, or roast chicken with caramelized green beans, for my family.

But when I moved away from home for college, my life had become consumed with dance, friends, school, papers, rehearsals, and ramen noodles. The days of homemade soups percolating on the stove, the aromas thick and the broth hearty, had become a distant memory. After my AVM, however, cooking became therapy for me, an excuse to practice my dexterity. And it all started with a stir. One evening, while preparing dinner for my father and me, my mother placed a wooden spoon in my sleeping right hand and implored me to just try. "You can stir with the left arm, but at least hold the spoon with your right," she said. My mother had become my harshest critic, as well as my strongest supporter. She always believed, as many parents do, that her child could do anything she put her mind to. The offering of the wooden spoon was not so much a gentle coaxing as it was a necessary command. This command was met with eye-rolling, but I complied. Little did my mother know that her nagging encouragement would be met with eventual joy. Stirring, which is such a simple action, soon grew into an all-consuming passion. I began assisting my mother with daily meal preparation. My stump of a right hand, once so mobile and vital, was happy to be used once again in a decisive way.

Like a child, I had filled my Saturday mornings with the routine of television. But now, instead of cartoons, I'd plop myself in front of the TV to watch Saturday morning cooking shows on PBS. Julia Child would cluck about stewing a chicken with an entire bulb of garlic; Jacques Pepin was deft with not only his knife skills but also a rolling pin; and Rick Bayless blackened yet another tomatillo over an open flame. What started as entertainment grew into a learning experience and an obsession. The cooking shows made me think about food all the time; I grew anxious to attempt pommes dauphinoise, or a leek and Swiss chard frittata.

My mother was an avid cookbook collector and had a small bookshelf in the kitchen almost entirely dedicated to her cookbooks. Every day I'd hobble to the shelf, eager to thumb through the books and decide which recipes to try. These cookbooks demystified the cooking process for me and inspired me to cook my own recipes to feed my loved ones. My friends and family became my guinea pigs, sampling elaborate meals and simple pairings alike. With no professors, instructors, or, for a few precious hours a day, therapists to guide me, my education was continuing in an informal way in the kitchen. This uncharted territory was as personal as it was exciting. Recipes became research, research became food, and my taste buds became my guide. My pastime began asserting itself, calling to me from the recesses of the pantry.

Like a soufflé rising in the oven, my desire to be in the kitchen expanded. And my new passion was fueled by the appreciation of friends and family who sat around my dining table. Each was eager to eat the latest dish I'd cooked: the toasty, roasted butternut squash from Alice Waters, the lamb chops sprinkled with crumbled feta cheese from Nigel Slater, or Mario Batali's rich meat ragu. I loved to watch my guests' faces as they ate. Seeing others enjoy my food became *my* sustenance. I would forget about my disabilities because there were people that needed to be fed!

Having a disability can be an isolating experience. I was no longer comfortable with my body now that I was brutally aware of the difficulties it caused me—and I knew other people were, too. Plus, I no longer had an arsenal of easy answers to the questions people usually ask when they first meet someone; this made me feel even more uncomfortable in social situations. I have never loved a party, and now they were tiny minefields filled with explosive yet seemingly innocuous questions like, So, what do you do? Standing with a glass of wine, I never had a good answer. Dinner parties were slightly better. The table-cloth covered my right leg, and as I sat with my right hand calmly in my lap, it just looked like I had stellar manners. I became an expert at disguising my disability. If I was still, no one would have the chance to see and to judge.

But it was food that forced me out into the open when, in 2003, I decided to start a small catering business. At first I was nervous about advertising the image of a one-armed chef, limping around the kitchen. I anxiously anticipated what I'd say should someone inevitably ask, "So what happened to you?" But as soon as I got my first job, a small cocktail party at the Berkeley Art Museum, I realized my issue was a nonissue for partygoers. I watched guests pose, flirt, and eat, and as easy as it was for me to become self-absorbed in the trials of being a newly disabled person, I saw that each person at the cocktail party was equally (and thankfully) self-absorbed, too. They were consumed with talk, with each other, and with eating from the crudités platter with warm bagna cauda dip I'd prepared. I desired this feeling of normalcy on a regular basis; this was what I wanted to do with my life. Now I had food to hide behind. But more important, I had food to push me forward.

Note to Self

**Success may taste sweet,
but fortitude is to be relished.**

Now, Back to Me

RENÉ SYLER

René Syler has been a broadcast journalist for twenty years. She coanchored the CBS *Early Show* for four years and published her first book, *Good-Enough Mother,* in March 2007. She lives in New York with her husband and two children.

Once you stop the bleeding, then you can start the healing. That's the theory behind triage, and it was my mantra for four long months. I'm not a doctor, but it seemed a fitting metaphor for what I was going through. In December 2006, I was fired from my job as coanchor for the CBS *Early Show.* Two weeks later, on January 9, I underwent my first round of surgery for my prophylactic double mastectomy. My last and final operation occurred on March 8, 2007. Losing both my breasts was bad enough, but coupling this physical loss with the professional and psychological loss of being fired doubled not only my pain but also the trauma that I felt. I'd lost my job, one of the symbols of femininity as a woman, and my dignity—three attributes that had taken a lifetime to build and five months to destroy—temporarily, at least.

I've always been an information junkie. In a roundabout way, this tendency led me to my career in journalism. When I was in my early twenties and studying for my master's degree in psychology, I worked the nightshift at a suicide prevention hotline, a requirement for my degree. On a quiet night (which, considering my workplace, was a good thing), I was biding my time thumbing through a stack of magazines, and I came across an article about Liz Walker. She was the highest-paid black anchorwoman in the country at the time. She was also pregnant and unmarried, and the NAACP was up in arms, claiming that she was setting a bad example. I remember thinking, *Here is a woman making well into six figures; I think she can support her own kid.* In that instant, I realized that I wanted to be a journalist and be on the front lines of information.

I didn't complete my master's program. I'd devoted years to studying psychology, and to just walk away from it was not easy, but I knew in my gut that TV was for me. I went back to school and took a few journalism classes, and then I just started knocking on doors and looking for an internship. I was like a dog with a bone. I ended up at the Fox affiliate in Sacramento, which had one newscast a day. I made friends with the cameramen and would cover stories with the reporters. It took me a while to get the hang of it, but eventually I learned how to put a story together.

After about a year of shadowing the experts, I had a resumé and tape, and in 1988, I landed my first real job at a CBS affiliate in Reno, Nevada. I was the weekend reporter. After reporting in the field for nine months, I got a call from the news director. The main anchor was out sick, so the weekend anchor was filling in for her during the week. This left the weekend show anchorless, so she asked me to step in.

That weekend, I sat down in the anchor chair and never got up. I went from CBS Reno to the ABC affiliate in Birmingham, Alabama. And then I landed a job in Dallas at WFAA-ABC affiliate as morning and noon anchor. I spent ten years in Dallas at two different stations, and I loved every minute of it. Dallas is where I built a fan base, a community, and, most important, my family. When I met my husband, Buff Parham, he was forty-three and the station manager where I worked. I was twenty-nine. I wasn't looking for a relationship, much less a marriage, and he was in the process of ending his. But after months of working together, we struck up a friendship that turned romantic. We fell in love. Once Buff finalized his divorce, we jetted off to the Bahamas to get hitched. Fifteen years later, we're still together with two kids. It's not a perfect marriage by any stretch (I don't know a marriage that is), but it's one that's full of respect, admiration, and space to grow.

Dallas was good to me. I was working at the CBS affiliate doing a noon and 6:00 p.m. show. As a team, we brought in nice viewership, and I loved my colleagues and my work. I never aspired to do a network show and was very happy as a local news anchor. I liked being part of a local community, and my ego wasn't so big that it needed to be fed on a national level. Plus, Buff and I were busy building our life together—not to mention our dream home. We weren't going anywhere (or so we thought), so we bought a plot of land in an up-and-coming area, hired a builder, and designed our future house. When we moved in, we joked that we'd never move again and that we'd have to be dragged out of there kicking and screaming.

What's that famous saying, "God laughs hardest when you try and make plans"? Well, I could hear Him chuckling from my Dallas living room on a Friday afternoon in September 2002. I'd just finished ordering and installing window treatments when my agent called. "CBS is revamping its morning show," he said, "and I told them they should take a look at you." The first thing that sprang to mind wasn't that this was an unbeliev-able opportunity, or potentially a lot of money, or that it might yield national fame. The first thing I thought about was my house. I'd spent the last two years building it and had just moved in two months prior to this phone call.

"HENRY!" I said. "I just built a *house*!" As if that should have stopped me from the chance of a lifetime.

"Oh, René," he said. "Don't be ridiculous. Just go talk to them, and let's see what happens." So I flew to New York, had a couple of meetings, and before I knew it, the job was mine.

CBS's producers wanted me in New York right away; the next few months were a total blur. My daughter was in kindergarten, my son was in a Montessori school, and my husband was well established in Dallas. I couldn't just uproot everyone, so for a year I commuted from Dallas to New York. I hopped on a plane every weekend, lugging my tired body between cities, and it was both physically and emotionally exhausting. Prior to my sur-gery and losing my job, it was the most difficult time of my life. Being away from my family and home, while trying to adjust to a new job and all its magnitude, was a huge test of strength. Strength that I would need tenfold later on.

During the first few months at CBS, I discovered that you can live in Manhattan, surrounded by twenty million people, and still feel deeply alone. I had no friends, so I'd go to work and then return home to my rented apartment, kick off my shoes, talk to my family in Dallas, and stare at my four walls. Then I'd wake up at 3:00 a.m. the next day and do it all over again. It was brutal at first, but once I became acclimated to the routine, I started to really love the job.

It helped that I was doing the kind of television I loved to do. The show was a nice balance between hard news and feature stories. I interviewed government officials and first ladies, jumped out of airplanes, and swam with beluga whales. No other job on the planet is like this, and I loved it. It was an amazing time, and with the arrival of my family one year later, I could finally feel the pieces fall into place. We moved into our house in Westchester, New York, and I really started to love every aspect of my life.

In mid-2005, CBS brought in a new president, Sean McManus, to the news division. He made it clear he was going to shake up everything, including *The Early Show.* His words were deeply unsettling, to say the least. I knew that an adjustment was in the works, but I had no idea what the change would be. Were they going to keep all the anchors but change the format? It was anybody's guess. Closed-door meetings kept everyone but the top brass in the dark.

During the first week of December, my alarm went off at the ungodly hour of 3:30 a.m. so I could make it to the studio by

5:00 a.m. I'd been told the day before that McManus wanted to meet with me. That morning, I knew in my gut that I was going to be fired, because Buff was never up with me at that hour. As we stood in the kitchen, I told Buff what fate awaited me.

"There's no way in hell they're going to fire you," he said. "Don't be ridiculous."

I shrugged. "They don't call meetings for no reason."

He kissed me in the dark and sent me on my way. He tried to reassure me. "You're fine. You add spark, and spark will add light to that show."

I climbed into the backseat of my Lincoln Town Car, greeted Ernie the driver, and we headed into the city. It was the longest drive from Westchester to Manhattan that I've ever experienced.

When I arrived on set, I immediately went into hair and makeup and became caught up in the whirlwind of our morning routine. We were heading into the holidays, and the mood was festive and frenzied. After the show, I completely forgot about the meeting for a brief moment, but then I got a call to come on over to the executive offices on Fifty-seventh Street, two blocks away from the studio. Suddenly, I was back in slow motion. The four-minute cab ride might as well have taken forty minutes. I arrived to find both the executive in charge of morning broadcasts and Sean McManus, president of CBS News and Sports, sitting side by side. My antennae went up, and my stomach dropped. I looked at the clock. It was 12:32 p.m. Sean said, "I'll be right back," and disappeared. "What's going on?" I mouthed to Steve. "You'll have to wait until Sean gets back," he said. I knew that was not a good sign.

I could feel my heart beating fast and practically out of my chest. When Sean returned, he was very matter-of-fact. "Look," he said. "You know that we want to go in another direction." I was able to piece together that this direction didn't include me, and that I was being let go.

"How do you want to handle it?" Sean asked.

"How do you guys want to handle it?" I said. "It doesn't matter to me."

"Why don't you talk to your agent and work it out," McManus suggested. And that was that. My career at the CBS *Early Show* was over.

I willed myself not to cry as I got up, shook both men's hands, and said, "Thank you for the opportunity you gave me." They nodded, and I left. It was 12:41 p.m. as I walked out the door. I'd given them four years of my life—2,628,000 minutes—and it had taken CBS nine minutes to fire me. I was humiliated and sad. As I turned the corner into the hallway, I felt like the walls were closing in on me. All I could think was that I had to get out of the building and call my husband.

I left the building, hailed a cab back to the studio, and called Buff. "Guess what?" I said. "I got fired." He was floored. He didn't believe me. I didn't feel much of anything during that cab ride. I was trying to process everything mentally, and the feeling part of me needed time to catch up. I just kept thinking, *What did I do wrong? What is wrong with me? Was I somehow inadequate?*

When I got back to the studio, I told two people: my coanchor Harry Smith and my assistant, Jahayra. I finally cried when I told Harry. I'd seen him on the way to the meeting and announced, "I'm on my way to get fired"—to which he'd said, "Don't be ridiculous." Then I finally lost it: the heaving, the sobbing, the uncontrollable "Why me?" questions just came pouring out. I'd never been fired from anything before. I'd had no idea what this would feel like. I was surprised that hurt was my number-one emotion. Not anger, just hurt and deep sadness.

I'd become good friends with a lot of the people I worked with, but I knew I'd lose touch with them, just because of the fact that we would no longer go to the same place to work every day. I hated the thought of losing friends. I was so sad about that. I was also worried about what this was going to mean for my family and my future. And I worried about what this was going to mean for my health. I was about to undergo a major operation, and I didn't want to be completely stressed and worn out.

In the summer of 2006 I'd made the very difficult, but very necessary, decision to have a prophylactic double mastectomy. Those three words strung together sound intimidating, and rightly so. Choosing to electively remove both my breasts had been an unbelievably hard decision to make, but not making it had become harder than making it. My mother had been diagnosed with breast cancer when she was sixty-five, and my father had also had breast cancer. There are about seventeen hundred cases a year of men who get breast cancer, which made my risk for developing the disease much higher. In 2003, I'd been diagnosed with atypical hyperplasia, considered by many to be the stage before cancer. The cells had been growing abnormally and fast, but they hadn't been cancerous yet. So every year, for four years, I'd gone in for a mammogram, and the long-faced radiologist had come back and said I needed a biopsy. So we'd scheduled the biopsy, and then waited three days to find out if I had cancer. Plus, I'd had to cope with recovering from the biopsy. I'd had four biopsies in four years, and the last one, in 2006, had been so disfiguring that afterward, the affected breast had been a half cup smaller than the other. When the swelling had gone down, I'd taken a good look at my breast and seen places where there was no breast tissue between the chest wall and the area in which the doctors had repeatedly pulled out tissue cells. I'd looked in the mirror and cried.

It had felt so unfair. I work hard, I watch what I eat, and I exercise. I don't smoke. I don't drink excessively. I do all the things you're supposed to do to be in good health, and here I was with bad luck of the draw. There had been nothing I could have done except be hypervigilant. I'd had mammograms every year, and in between the mammograms, I'd had sonograms, MRIs, and seen my doctor multiple times. But after staring at my deflated breast that day, I'd gone to my doctor and asked how we could fix it. "If we fix it," he'd said, "we'd have to use an implant, and if you have an implant, we can no longer do the less invasive biopsy." This meant that I'd have to have had a surgical biopsy each time I'd had a suspicious mammogram, and the procedure was painful and hard to recover from. I remember thinking, *What am I doing? If I put an implant in here, I'm gonna be back in the hospital next year, on that table I hate, with the doctors cutting me open. They'll have to work around the implant, so they can pull out more and more of these suspicious calcifications. I love my life, and I love my children. They need to have me in their lives for a long time. I want to see my daughter grow up to be healthy and strong, and a beautiful young woman, which she's becoming. And I want to see my son grow up to bring home girls that I think are generally unacceptable. I want to be here.*

I'd gone on the offensive. My doctor and I had talked about this surgery two years prior, when he'd first said it might be an option. We'd discussed it again. It had hardly been an overnight decision. I'd researched all the other options, nonsurgical and so on, and none of them had been right for me. So I'd made the decision to have the surgery, and I'd scheduled it for January 9, 2007.

I couldn't dwell on losing my job because I knew I needed to think about the surgery. I had to focus on staying healthy. I refused to be around sick people, and I didn't allow myself to get too stressed out.

In the meantime, I talked to Linda, my publicist, and Henry, my agent, and we decided I'd stay on the show until the end of the year. I promised the execs at CBS I would give them one hundred percent, and that's what I did. I never kept the fact that I had been fired a secret, because I hadn't done anything wrong. Nevertheless, we thought it best to say I was leaving to pursue other opportunities, which was true, as my book was being published.

My last day on the show was December 22, and I had my mastectomy two weeks later.

After my last day at CBS, I took my kids and husband on vacation to our home in South Carolina. I slept a lot, which I'm sure was the manifestation of some form of depression. I was dealing with three of the biggest life-stressors at once (we were also in the middle of renovating our house). I don't know how I pushed through it, except by taking things one step at a time. It was all I could do.

I had the initial five-hour surgery on January 9, 2007. I left the hospital on January 11. I went back to the hospital and then had a week off. The next Tuesday, I was back in the hospital. I had a couple of weeks off, and then, in the month of February, they put in temporary tissue (called expanders) beneath the chest wall. Every couple of weeks I'd go into the hospital, and they'd put a needle into my breast and blow the breast up like a tire to fill it with saline until it got to the size I wanted it to be. It was EXCRUCIATING!! Then they filled me one more time to overexpand my breast, and thirty days later I could have the exchange surgery, where they exchange the temporary breasts with the permanents. I had the exchange surgery done on March 8. As I regained my strength, I slowly began to comprehend everything that had happened to me over the past few months. It was a tough time, but I never cried. I focused on adjusting to my new reality.

I feel fantastic now. I have always been an athlete, and I am now physically stronger than I have been in many years. And I am relieved, knowing that I won't be on the table again this year. I still see my doctor a couple times a year, because though the cancer risk is greatly decreased, there is still a chance I could develop the disease. But no more mammograms, biopsies, or fear. And my doctor thanked me very recently. A young woman who had seen me on *Oprah* talking about my surgery had elected to do the same thing. Her mother had died of breast cancer when she was five years old. The woman was being closely monitored but had opted for the PBM. And when they'd taken the tissue out, they'd found cancer, which had been unseen on any of the other tests. My doctor sent me a note detailing this, and when I read it, I finally cried. I want to make a difference. I guess I have.

I've always thought of myself as a strong person, but I had no idea what I was capable of enduring. I feel like I can do anything now. When you've had the crap kicked out of you professionally, gone through a major surgery, and had the symbol of your femininity removed, there's not a whole lot else that can be taken away from you. I feel like there's no stopping me now. This experience was a huge wake-up call for me. Up until the time I went through all of this, things had come to me kind of easily. I've definitely learned that life isn't easy. But whatever comes my way, I feel like now I'm equipped to deal with it.

I know that there's going to be a tomorrow. And in many respects, tomorrow will be better than yesterday. This is going to sound crazy, but I feel great, perhaps because a change needed to happen in my life and I was too afraid to make that change myself; when it was made for me, I was liberated. But along with liberation comes fear. You get set free and you think, *Now what?*

I really feel that all of this happened to me so that I could feel lighter and truer to myself, even when faced with harrowing uncertainties. I don't know where I'm bound to end up in the future, but I look forward to figuring it out.

Note to Self

Hang tight. It's going to be an
exhilarating, terrifying, wonderfully
exciting—not to mention bumpy—ride.

A Testament to Change

MAILE M. ZAMBUTO

Maile Zambuto is the executive director of the Joyful Heart Foundation, a nonprofit organization that works to heal, educate, and empower survivors of sexual assault, domestic violence, and child abuse, and to shed light into the darkness that surrounds these issues. Born and raised in Honolulu, Hawaii, Maile now lives with her husband and two children in New York. The credo "Be the change you wish to see in the world" is posted on her desk, her dresser, even on her coffee cup— and it clearly drives everything she does. Like many of the women whose lives she has impacted, Maile is a true survivor.

When I was eight years old, I testified before a grand jury about the sexual abuse I'd suffered during kindergarten, second, and third grade at the hands of Mr. Bizzell, one of my teachers. He created a ritual in the classroom during which he would call female students up to his desk and ask us to sit on his lap while he checked our homework. Sometimes he would make us stand in line at the side of his desk, and other times he would call us up one by one. I was always a good student, and, like most little girls, I loved attention. Mr. Bizzell was very attentive. He told me I was smart, pretty, and creative. He also told me I was his favorite. He knew just what to say and how to make me feel like the most special girl in the world.

On some days, schoolwork was all that took place. On most days, however, he molested me on his lap, in front of the class. I was five years old when the abuse began. I did not know it was wrong for him to touch my breasts or my vagina, nor did I know it was abnormal for me to touch his chest or his penis. I thought this was the way everyone got their homework checked.

More than anything, I trusted him. The trust I felt was similar to the trust children feel for a parent. To complicate matters, the private school, where I attended classes, operated like a small community—some might even say a family. Mr. Bizzell was well liked and respected in our community. He played the role of a charismatic teacher and trusted friend to faculty and parents. He was well dressed, kept his hair neat, and wore professorial glasses.

By the time I got to second grade, I knew our ritual felt wrong, and I started to feel ashamed. I didn't know why, but I felt embarrassed and confused. About this time, Mr. Bizzell started telling me that we shared a special secret that no one could know. He told me that people wouldn't understand, and that if they knew about what we were doing, I would have to leave school and all my friends. He told me that without our secret, I wouldn't be special anymore. He also told me that my parents would be very angry with me and that I would get into a lot of trouble. I started to feel sad most of the time, and I lived in fear that our secret would get out.

It was hard to hide the way I was feeling inside. I remember standing in line at the side of his desk with tears running down my face. As Mr. Bizzell placed me on his lap, he offered me a handkerchief to wipe my tears with one hand, while with the other hand he fondled my vagina. Oftentimes afterward, I would ask to use the little girl's room. I would lock myself in a stall, hold my knees to my chest, and pray for a big storm or tidal wave to hit our school so that I wouldn't have to go back to my classroom.

When I was in the third grade, my mother started reading to me from the book *Where Did I Come From?* It answered a lot of questions kids start to have about their bodies. I knew deep down that what Mr. Bizzell had been doing to me for years didn't feel good, but it was during the conversations with my mom that I started to realize that what he was doing was actually wrong.

I also thought that what I was doing was wrong. By the time I recognized what was happening, I believed that it was also my fault, and I felt ashamed that I had allowed it to go on for so long. I wanted to tell my mom, but I was too afraid and too confused by what the consequences might be. My parents had gotten divorced, and I could feel that the adults around me were unhappy. I felt that their unhappiness, too, must be all my fault. I felt that if my mother knew the truth, it would make her sad or angry, and I just wanted to make everyone happy. I also felt that my parents wouldn't love me as much and that I wouldn't be special or smart or pretty anymore.

As I got older, the abuse escalated. It became more frequent, and Mr. Bizzell grew more aggressive. I started wearing shorts under my dresses and eventually began wearing pants, so that it was harder for him to get to me. I also started to feign being sick, and I would put the thermometer under the faucet or next to the lamp to convince my mom that I had a fever.

One day after school during a car-pool ride, one of the class moms overheard her daughter whispering to a friend in the backseat of her car about being molested by Mr. Bizzell. Later that night, the phone rang. I was in my room, and my mom was doing the dishes. Two mothers called to tell my mom about what they had learned. They told her that their daughters had said that it was also happening to me. They told her I was his favorite.

My mom came into my room and asked me if what they were saying was true. I told her that it was, and she started to cry. Then she called my dad, and we immediately drove to the home of one of the other mothers. Together, the parents called the school principal around midnight. After he denied the accusations and insisted we were telling stories and making it all up, the parents called the police. I remember that all the adults around me began to fight and cry. Everyone was so angry, and I really didn't understand what was happening. For years, Mr. Bizzell had told me, "If you tell anyone about this, everyone is going to be angry with you. You are going to have to leave school." His words, and my worst fears, were coming true.

After word spread about Mr. Bizzell, there were teachers, administrators, and even parents who insisted that we were making up stories and that the allegations against Mr. Bizzell were untrue. It was hard for them to accept that a grown man—their friend and colleague—could be responsible for such atrocities.

The story was covered on the morning and evening news, and in the local papers. The scandal seemed to divide the school in half. Those who had accused Mr. Bizzell were shunned. The three other girls who testified left the private school altogether, but I would not leave. I was stubborn even then. The boys in school teased me for years afterward, but somehow I was able to handle it. I grew stronger. There was such shame around what had happened that I think everyone just wanted it to go away.

My parents were certainly not equipped to deal with the situation. No parent is. It's painful and paralyzing to confront the reality that your little girl has suffered abuse by someone you trusted and that you could not protect her. They were filled with shame, regret, and blame. And there was rage. I remember a fight that occurred when my grandfather wanted to buy a gun to hunt Mr. Bizzell down and my dad had to stop him.

For my dad, the next best thing to killing Bizzell was to sue the school. This was a critically important step he took for my future. The school settled, and a trust was established in my name to pay for my therapy until I was an adult, and my private education through college. My mom took on the role of healer. She would talk to me openly about what had happened, asked me how I was feeling all the time, and insisted that I attend my therapy sessions. More than anything, she reminded me on a daily basis how special, smart, and pretty I was and how much she loved me.

In April of 1981, when I was nine years old, Paul Bizzell was indicted on four separate counts by a grand jury for the offense of sexual abuse in the first degree. Each count involved a different female student. In January of 1982 he pleaded no contest, and in March he was sentenced to prison for five years. He was also ordered to pay restitution to his victims. He never did.

Mr. Bizzell also never served the full term of his sentence. He was in jail for eleven days before he was attacked and beaten. He went into a coma for weeks and nearly died. His swollen, bloodied face was all over the news, which is how I learned about what happened to him. I felt sad for him and confused by my feelings. I believed that I was responsible for his coma and that his near death was all my fault. It is beyond the emotional and mental capacity of a third-grader to make sense of things like this, and even now, as an adult, it's hard for me to admit that I was sorry he was suffering.

Upon Mr. Bizell's recovery he filed for a motion for reconsideration of sentencing, and it was granted by the judge. He was released and sentenced to five years' probation. Mr. Bizzell made a statement to the court: "It is difficult to express in words the magnitude of sadness that I have for the poor parents of the girls and the girls themselves." He went on to say, "I knew my crime was deplorable and made many efforts at self-correction before it came to light. After incarceration, I will never forget why I was suffering in prison."

The abuse I suffered at the hands of Mr. Bizzell would not be the last time I was violated as a young girl. Although I grew up to be outgoing, popular, and overachieving at everything I did, most of the time I felt alone and insignificant.

During the years that Mr. Bizzell was abusing me, he was married to another teacher at the school. She was a quiet and sweet woman. Their marriage ended and when he was released from prison, he made his way to the West Coast. I tried to forget all about him and I tried to move on.

I attended college at a private Jesuit school in Los Angeles. When I was a sophomore, I went out for a night on the town with my girlfriends, and we ended up at a bar on the Sunset Strip that was the hottest spot in Hollywood. A group of guys offered to buy us drinks and chatted with us for a while. We were having a good time and my friends wanted the party to continue, but I was tired and wanted to go home. I said my good-byes and made my way to the parking garage alone. I noticed one of the guys hanging out near his car. He approached me. At first, I didn't think anything of it because he had been so friendly in the club. We talked for a minute, and then he leaned in to kiss me. I hesitated. I told him that he was cute and nice, but I had a serious boyfriend and needed to go home. He grabbed my hair and pressed me into the front seat of the car.

He raped me. I didn't scream and I didn't fight back. I just completely shut down. I remember lying on the front seat of the car as his hand struck my face and thinking, *I'm exactly in the place I'm meant to be.*

That night in the car, the rape was the physical confirmation of what I'd always felt and feared so deeply inside—that I was an empty vessel to be used and my purpose in this life was to please others.

When it was over, I went back to the bar and told the bartender what had happened. He didn't call the police, and I was too despondent to insist that he did. A hostess took me into the bathroom to clean me up, and a friend picked me up and took me to the hospital. I was poked and prodded for most of the night, but I felt nothing. The next day, the police came to my apartment to question me. They asked me what I had been wearing. Had I been drunk? Would the bartender confirm that I hadn't been? Then they asked me if anything like this had ever happened to me before. I lied and said no. I told the police that I wouldn't press charges, and asked them to leave me alone. I remember sitting in my living room and feeling like someone had turned out the lights inside.

The next year would be messy. I wasn't in therapy at the time, and since I was attending a Jesuit college, I turned to my faith. I made an appointment to see a counselor at school, and she suggested that I go to confession. I dropped out of school, and my relationships began to fall apart. I was reckless and disrespectful to others and myself. It was a very dark time for me.

In April of that year, the Rodney King riots devastated downtown L.A. Final exams were cancelled, so most of my friends spent the week glued to the television or going to parties on campus. I signed up to help repair some of the damage caused by the riots. The next day, I drove to South Central and spent the day cleaning up the streets. For a month, I helped those who had lost homes and businesses get back on their feet. I found myself under heaps of destruction, surrounded by people who felt buried and helpless. Eventually, I started volunteering in a clinic to care for babies born to abusive or drug-addicted mothers. I started to feel needed, and I drew great strength from the people I helped. I began to heal.

I went back to school and started to work on making healthier choices and respecting myself. When I was twenty-three, I moved home to Hawaii to be close to family and friends. I joined the Junior League of Honolulu and started raising money to respond to the needs of women and children. It was through this work that I was educated about the epidemic of violence and abuse in this country. What I discovered was staggering. I learned that as many as one in four girls and one in six boys will be sexually abused by the age of eighteen. That 95 percent of child-abuse victims know their abuser. And studies have found that abused children are more likely to experience such problems as teen pregnancy, delinquency, drug use, low academic achievement, and mental-health issues.

I was introduced to the Children's Justice Center, an innovative program for abused children and their families. Through my work with the league and the center, we created a self-esteem program in partnership with the Children's Alliance of Hawaii for teen girls who had been severely sexually abused and were living in foster care. It was through my work with these brave young girls that I realized this was the place I was *truly* meant to be, doing the work I was meant to do. I worked with countless girls who looked at me and thought I had a blessed life. They wished they could be more like me. It was the first time I shared my story.

During this time, I met a wonderful man named Jason, who would become my husband. One afternoon, we were driving to the beach and my cell phone rang. In that moment, my worst fears were realized as a kind voice at the other end of the line began to speak. He asked me if I knew a Paul Bizzell. I said I did.

The man explained that after Paul Bizzell left Hawaii, he remarried, this time to a woman with a young daughter. He started molesting his stepdaughter when she was seven years old and didn't stop until his wife walked in on them in the kitchen several years later.

The district attorney explained to me that the court initially intended to accept a plea bargain from Mr. Bizzell that included a stay at a treatment facility. Then they learned that he had a history of abusing girls, and, through his probation officer in Hawaii, they found my original testimony.

That same year, on the plane ride to testify in Mr. Bizzell's sentencing hearing, I wrote a letter to the court. With pen in hand, I opened my leather journal, and the words flowed onto the paper from someplace deep inside. What resulted was a twenty-page letter, most of which I read to the court:

> *Your Honor, this man has a serious and uncontrollable problem. He was given a second chance to rebuild his life, and here we are. I am certain that Mr. Bizzell has no concept of what my life or the lives of my classmates have been like since we were abused, and I'm convinced that he never will. The effects of the abuse and the breach of trust are devastating. I can assure you that they don't last for any term of sentencing, but forever. Here I am, twenty-seven years old, and I have to relive the abuse all over again.*
>
> *I remember learning as a child that this man was being released from prison after serving a fraction of his sentence. I had always been taught the difference between right and wrong, and that if you do something wrong, you must face the consequences of your actions. What Mr. Bizzell had done to me was the worst kind of wrong*

imaginable, and yet I was suffering the consequences. I felt the courage I showed to tell the truth meant nothing. I felt unsafe, powerless, meaningless, and completely insignificant.

Mr. Bizzell, you violated every faith and trust we gave to you. You took from me my innocence, my purity, most of my youth, and a piece of my spirit. Why was this not enough?

Apparently, facing the possibility of years in prison and being beaten nearly to death is not enough to stop you. The magnitude of sadness you claim you felt for my family and me was not enough for you to keep your hands off another little girl.

Your Honor, yesterday I met the girl who the court papers refer to as "the victim." She is an innocent, bright, and beautiful child, and I can only imagine that there have been others along the way. Please spare her from the torture of not knowing what justice is.

I stopped short as I neared the end of my letter. I faced my former teacher and abuser, looked him in the eye, and saw a pathetic, weak, sick, and powerless man looking back. I said, "I forgive you. I do not wish you harm. However, you have shown us that not even a second chance is enough for you."

I closed my tome, intending never to reopen it again. I wanted to preserve the power that lay in its pages. It had taken me almost twenty years, but I looked at him and thought, *I was wounded but I'm not broken. You didn't ruin me.*

Tragically, none of my former classmates came forward to testify. It was very important to me that Mr. Bizzell's most recent victim meet me and know that it was possible for her to feel safe, strong, and powerful again. I hoped she would see me and think, *If this happened to her, and she's okay, I will be, too.* To this day, I pray that I affected her spirit.

Shortly after the sentencing, I moved to New York City with my husband. Within a week, I was volunteering in the playroom of Safe Horizon's Jane Barker Brooklyn Child Advocacy Center, a program much like the one I worked with in Honolulu. Later that year, I accepted a position with the organization to raise awareness and critically needed funds. I worked my way up to become the chief development and marketing officer of Safe Horizon, and in the summer of 2008 I celebrated my ninth anniversary of service.

Today, I am the executive director of the Joyful Heart Foundation, the only organization in the country that provides groundbreaking retreat programs for survivors, to help them heal mind, body, and spirit.

My work adds value and meaning to my life on the deepest level. I believe that I could not do what I do with as much commitment and passion if I had not lived through these experiences. For that I am grateful. My work gives meaning to the senseless things that happened to me. It gives me purpose.

I heal every day in small and grand ways. It is a lifelong journey for me. Believing in the notion of trust is one of the most difficult concepts for me, and I work on that every day. I find that I like to control everything. I work at a pace and with a determination that sometimes scares me. I make certain that people know when I'm in a room—it's my way of never being mistaken for insignificant. My husband and children, my family, friends, and colleagues help to shine light in the darkest corners of my soul.

"Be the change you wish to see in the world." By telling my story, I hope to be the change I see. What I see is a community that is empowered with knowledge, compassion, and courage to support survivors and help them heal. I see a community that is dedicated to protecting its children so they can reach their full potential. I see a community that values and dedicates resources to individuals and families that have been impacted by violence and abuse. I see a community that seeks to ignite and foster an open dialogue about how to collaboratively end the cycle of abuse.

In 1999, upon hearing Maile's testimony, Judge Plotz sentenced Paul Bizzell to eight years in the Department of Corrections facility. Bizzell was released from prison in 2007, and in December of that same year he was arrested for drug possession and assault. In May of 2008, he pleaded guilty to the possession of narcotics and was charged with a felony. He was sentenced to three years in prison.

Note to Self

By helping to heal others,
you can heal yourself.

You are not alone. If you or someone you know needs help, call the National Domestic Violence Hotline at 1-800-799-SAFE or the National Sexual Assault Hotline at 1-800-656-HOPE. To learn about the signs of child abuse and how to report it, go to www.hopeshining.org. If you suspect a child is in immediate danger, please call 911.

Medicine Doctor

MAISIE McINERNEY

Maisie McInerney is the thirteen-year-old daughter of writer Jay McInerney, author of ten novels, including *Bright Lights, Big City, The Last of the Savages, Brightness Falls, Model Behavior,* and *The Good Life,* and Helen Bransford, artist and writer. She attends Ross School, she loves to sing, and her cat, Tillie, is among her best friends.

Fifth grade began as a really good year for me. In the beginning of the year I sprained my wrist playing volleyball. In fourth grade I'd hurt my Achilles tendon playing basketball, but as far as I could tell, I was going to coast through my last year of elementary school without injury. I was just a healthy, normal girl.

Then one day in the middle of fifth grade I came home from school and told Mom that my left knee and both ankles hurt. "My knees have been bothering me all day," I said. She asked if

I'd done anything in gym class to hurt them. I told her I didn't think so. "We'll see how it goes," she said.

That happened on a Friday, and we didn't think much more of it, but on Monday, when I was setting the dinner table, I told her, "Mom, I really don't feel good. I think I'm getting sick." I went to bed at eight o'clock that night, hoping to sleep it off, but by the next morning, I felt worse and had a fever. Mom said I could stay home from school until we figured out what was going on. We thought I would be back in a couple days, tops. But as the days went by, my joints became more inflamed, and a weird rash that had plagued me the previous year returned. Things didn't look promising.

We thought the rash, which was on my legs and stomach, was eczema, so I went to a dermatologist for a skin biopsy. The test came back negative, and the doctor couldn't figure out what was causing it. I got three more opinions, but the doctors all said I had "a mysterious rash." It remained a mystery to every doctor I saw.

With my swollen joints and recurring rash, I saw my pediatrician, who said, "You're a mystery!" She also noticed I'd lost a few pounds. I wasn't really eating, and I felt weak. She drew some blood and tested me for Lyme disease, mono, and who knows what else. As they took six vials of blood, I thought, *Oh, my God! That's so much blood!* Little did I know that there was *much more* blood yet to come.

The day after my visit to the pediatrician was the debut of my school play. We were performing *Theseus and the Minotaur*, and I had a pretty big role as a narrator. I'd worked very hard to memorize the lines, so I convinced Mom to let me perform. I still had a fever of one hundred degrees and I'd just gotten blood drawn, so I really wasn't my best, but I made it through the play. Afterward, I felt awful, and the next day my fever jumped to one hundred and two.

As the week went on, I just kept getting worse and the symptoms kept growing. First the rash would spread, another joint would hurt, then the fever would spike higher. By Sunday, my parents were very worried. We ended up at the South Hampton emergency walk-in clinic, and the doctor I saw thought I might have juvenile rheumatoid arthritis (JRA). At the time I didn't even know kids could suffer from arthritis. I thought it was a problem that grandmothers and great-aunts had.

Um, I'm pretty sure I don't have that, I thought.

The ER doctors repeated the mono and Lyme disease tests, but they also ran a Sed Rate blood test to detect the level of inflammation in my body. The normal level is about eight. Mine was ninety-seven.

At that point, they knew something had to be really wrong. My doctor set up an appointment with a rheumatologist in Commack, New York, which was two hours away. On the way, I sat in the backseat of the car thinking, *What could possibly help this?* I doubted anything could work. When we arrived, the rheumatologist said I had typical JRA symptoms—joint pain and a rash—and that I also had a soft lull in my heart. She did an EKG, and it was abnormal. She also said I'd have to wait six weeks to confirm, for sure, whether or not I had juvenile rheumatoid arthritis. She said that if the symptoms had lasted this long, it would confirm I had JRA. We didn't want to wait six weeks. I was really sick and felt weak, tired, and in pain.

Throughout this process, my mom was so amazing and supportive. Whatever I needed, no matter how far we had to drive, or how many doctors we had to see, she did everything in her power to help me. She went to great lengths to make me better. Mom heard about a top rheumatologist, one of the best in his field, named Dr. Thomas Lehman in New York City. We made an appointment. When I saw him, he took an X-ray of my hand and said, "You know, you probably have JRA, but as a doctor, I'm going to keep my mouth shut. We need to rule out anything else." So I had more blood drawn, and after two weeks it became apparent that I definitely had JRA.

There are three types of juvenile rheumatoid arthritis. The first is systemic, which is what I have. The second is polyarticular, and the third is pauciarticular. Systemic JRA is the most rare and most serious because it can affect major organs like the heart and kidneys. My whole family was really scared. Dr. Lehman put me on prednisone, which is a steroid. I thought at the time that it was a miracle drug, because it got rid of my rash right away. At eleven, I didn't really care about anything except the way I looked. (Actually, I am still that way.) But the rash was a huge bummer for me because it covered my entire body and I couldn't escape it. When it spread to my face, I was just really, really embarrassed and stressed out. So once the rash disappeared, I thought, *Wow! Prednisone is really going to cure me.* The thing was, I still couldn't get out of bed. I could barely sit up anymore because my joints felt creaky and painful, and my fingers swelled to the point where they were unrecognizable. They looked like balloons, and my feet were too sore to walk on. My knees were twice their normal size. It was impossible to function. I couldn't even open a bottle of water. I felt really helpless.

The isolation factor was also pretty awful. I missed my friends a lot. My cat, Tillie, was the only thing I could stand while I was sick. She was the only one I could be around when I didn't want to be around anyone. Tillie slept with me, watched movies with me, and curled up with me in bed—and I believe she played an important role in healing me. She helped me feel less alone.

After two weeks on prednisone, Dr. Lehman put me on something called Humira. I was very afraid of this, because I hated shots and had to be injected once a week. Normally, it's given to adults with moderate to severe arthritis. It had never been tested on kids, so we were scared to try it, but we had to do something. Unfortunately, it didn't really work, so we tried thalidomide. That was *really* scary. You know the whole thalidomide story, right? Mothers used to take it for morning sickness, and their babies were born with horrible birth defects. Now it's used to treat HIV, AIDS, throat cancer, and rheumatoid arthritis. You have to sign all these forms when you take it. I had to sign forms saying that I wouldn't have sex. It was ridiculous. Hello, I was eleven.

When the thalidomide didn't work, I was given a shot of anakinra, every day, which also hadn't been tested on kids. When my mother gave me the injection, it was a hundred times more painful than Humira. It was this chemically strong shot that we kept in the fridge. We had to use a very big needle. It was also really cold going in, which didn't help matters. I had bruises on my back, hips, and legs from always trying to find a new fleshy area where the needle could poke me.

Unfortunately anakinra didn't work either, and we had to switch to methotrexate, a pill, which was what really killed me. At that point I just stopped talking, because I didn't have any energy left. Methotrexate took out the little energy that I had left, and I felt helpless and began to give up hope. For seven months I'd had the same fevers, rashes (they'd only temporarily gone away with the prednisone), joint pain—and way too much medicine. I remember telling my godmother that I was losing faith. I wasn't feeling any better, and I was drowning in chemicals. I began to wonder if the medicine could have caused the symptoms in the first place (or at least continued them). There was no way to really know.

I also was really frustrated because this whole thing had come out of the blue. I'd been healthy my whole life. Then I found out that my father's first cousin, my second cousin, had systemic JRA and that I had gotten it through my genes. She was diagnosed at a slightly older age when she had measles, which triggered the JRA for her. In my case, the doctors thought puberty might have triggered it. Some people who are born with JRA never even show symptoms. At this point I wasn't talking a lot—I was just kind of there—and I was really pissed off. *Why did this happen to me?* I didn't even know who to be mad at.

Finally I came to the conclusion that everyone goes through something, and I had to get better. That was my motto for a long time. When things were hard, I kept telling myself, *Everyone goes through something difficult. . . . Everyone goes through something difficult. . . .* And then I'd get mad again when I'd remember that most people didn't go through something so difficult this early in life.

After five months, my mom and I were completely fed up with the doctors, the meds, the pain—and all the ways it affected our lives. Mom finally said, "There has to be a better way to do this."

So we went to two homeopathic doctors, but they didn't help either. Suggesting flower herbs to help my swollen and tender joints didn't cut it. We tried everything, though. During one trip to the health food store to buy emu oil, which is made from the fat of an Australian bird, we had to ask the owner to help us find it.

"Why are you here for emu oil?" he asked.

"I have arthritis," I told him.

"I do, too," he said.

My mom started talking to him, and he suggested that I see a physician named Dr. Sidney Baker, who was a doctor with an MD from Yale but who had decided over the years to take a more holistic approach to healing. He lived in Sag Harbor, New York. It was impossible to book an appointment with him, and it cost three thousand dollars just to walk though the door, but we managed to get me in. Dr. Baker examined me and had me fill out loads of paperwork. I told him my entire medical history.

He read about all of my horrible symptoms, extreme medications, and questionable diagnoses—and yet the first thing he said was, "You had acid reflux?"

"Yeah," I told him.

"Anyone with stomach problems has huge problems," he said. "Stop eating yeast. No bread, no vinegar, no wine. Let's see if that helps."

Dr. Baker told me to take *Saccharomyces boulardii*, which is a fungus in the form of a pill intended to treat and prevent gastrointestinal disorders—which, in my case, were the root of my disease. He also put me on arginine, which is a natural amino acid. (Arginine plays an important role in immune function.) Dr. Baker was trying to get me off the harmful drugs that my previous doctors had put me on, but at the same time he was replacing them with more helpful supplements that were better for my body. And he put me on a vegan diet because a vegan diet helps with ALL inflammatory diseases, including breast cancer, heart disease, stroke, and especially arthritis.

Four days after following Dr. Baker's regime, I was back to my normal self. Completely. It was almost like I had never been sick. He was a miracle doctor. Things had gotten so bad that I hadn't even been able to talk, and within a week I was running around at school with my friends. I almost completely forgot about the trauma I'd been through, because I felt so good.

Dr. Baker transitioned me off all my drugs over the course of three months. At the time, I was on methotrexate, anakinra, thalidomide, and prednisone. He wanted me off the methotrexate first because it can cause cancer. My hair was falling out in brushes and in the shower due to the drugs I was still on, so he put me on Armour Thyroid, and it stopped. It was like he knew all these hidden secrets that no other doctor could even think of. He gave me B-12 shots for strength, which I give myself, and they make me feel amazing. Dr. Baker is a miracle worker, and his office was only five minutes away.

It turns out that I'm really allergic to yeast. If I eat it, my fingers swell up and the arthritis returns, but it only lasts about a day. So now I'm a vegan. I don't eat yeast, bread, vinegar, dairy, eggs, or meat. I eat spelt bread, veggie burgers, and salads. I make cookies without milk and eggs. I love this diet. I feel a lot better and lighter.

Dr. Baker diagnosed me with systemic juvenile rheumatoid arthritis with a sensitivity to yeast. In the beginning of his treatment I was taking *S. boulardii*, arginine, B-12 shots, anti-inflammatory shakes, and fish oil. I no longer take any pills, but I do give myself the B-12 shot once a week. I wish I could tell you some amazing trick to make the pain go away, but the truth is I don't have any pain. In fact, half the time I forget I even have JRA. I have a healthy great life now, and I am fortunate enough to be able to move on from that time in my life. Because one thing I've learned is, a disease doesn't define you. I don't think people think of me as "that girl with JRA." I think YOU define yourself, and nobody else.

When I went back to school eleven months after being sick, everybody was really happy to see me. My friends had stayed the same, but I had become more mature. I have three friends I absolutely adore, who are really supportive and helpful, but five of my friends, who I'd thought were true friends, didn't really support me after I came back to school. It was really surprising and sort of hurtful. And after spending so much time leaning on people who cared about me while I was sick, I came to realize how important this quality is in true friends.

I asked Mom what I would have been like if I hadn't gone through my ordeal. She said, "It made you a much deeper person." Personally, I think I would have been fine without that. I wouldn't have cared whether or not I was a deeper person. But I guess that being more insightful has helped me see who my real friends are, which is important. I think it's better to know that sooner versus later.

Being sick has also made me a stronger person. I think I can really understand and support others who are going through a hard time. I think I was mature before I went through this, but I didn't have as much knowledge and respect and understanding.

I want to be a doctor someday, because of what I know about medicine. I believe that when you're sick, everything in your body is affected, physically and emotionally. I may become a psychiatrist, but I definitely don't want to be the kind of doctor that just needs a prescription pad and a pen to diagnose a patient. Those are the kinds of doctors I went to for a long time, and while I think that drugs can be good sometimes, I think it's wrong to just treat symptoms. I think you should really find out what causes them, which is what Dr. Baker did for me.

I have no pain now, and Dr. Baker says that JRA is something you live with. It never goes away. I'm always going to have to be aware of how I feel, but I don't have any symptoms that I know of anymore. I'm extremely active. I play volleyball, soccer, and I swim. I'm just a normal kid again.

Note to Self

**Tenacity is the root
of all wellness.**

Fear, Not

RHONDA BRITTEN

Rhonda Britten, founder of the Fearless Living Institute, an organization dedicated to giving anyone the tools they need to master their emotional fears, is the author of four national bestsellers, *Fearless Living, Fearless Loving, Change Your Life in 30 Days,* and *Do I Look Fat in This?* During her three seasons on the Emmy Award–winning daytime reality drama *Starting Over,* Britten was named "America's Favorite Life Coach" and was dubbed *Starting Over*'s "Most Valuable Player" by the *New York Times.* She is a globally recognized expert on the subject of fear and fearlessness.

A steady downpour pummeled the windowpanes of my childhood bedroom in northern Michigan on a chilly June morning. I snuggled deeper under the warmth and comfort of my blankets, wishing I didn't have to face what lay ahead. The year was 1975, and I was fourteen. It was Father's Day, and back then in my little hometown that meant families trooping to have brunch at local restaurants where buffets were considered the height of elegance. Part of me was looking forward to the salad bar and the slices of roast beef, but I dreaded the get-together. My parents had been separated for almost a year. This obligatory reunion with my father was sure to be strained.

I wondered whether my two sisters—and, for that matter, my mother—felt as uneasy as I did. Still, I told myself, nothing really upsetting was going to happen. We'd be in public, after all. Everyone would be on their best behavior. In spite of all that had gone on between my parents behind closed doors, they had always been very good at putting up a front. They cared too much about what the neighbors might think.

Reassured, I threw the covers off, got up, and picked out the white cotton dress my mother had finished making for me only days before. An accomplished seamstress, she took pride in outfitting her girls. I treasured everything she created, but this dress was one of my favorites. She had sewn me a long white scarf with black polka dots, an accessory that made me feel very sophisticated. I wrapped it around my neck as a kind of testimony of her love. In return, I loved her so much that it almost hurt. I have a photograph of just the two of us taken before my younger sister, Linda, was born. My mother was holding me on her hip. My little head was leaning on her shoulder. On the back she had written, "When you were the baby of the house, Rhonda." The image and the message gave me strength and a sense of being very special. I looked at the picture and read her words whenever the trials of teenage life started to get to me.

On that Sunday morning, I got dressed, and while my sisters

were still fighting over the bathroom, I walked by my mother's room. She spotted me through the open door.

"Oh, you look so pretty!" she said with a lilt in her voice. "Come in. I want to show you something."

My heart skipped a beat. As the middle child, I cherished every moment when I was alone with my mother. She put down her omnipresent coffee mug after taking one more sip and did the rest of her makeup. I perched on the bed, careful not to rumple the spread, and watched her smooth the rouge onto her cheeks after gliding the blue shadow over her lids. Even without the help of cosmetics, she was a true beauty. I wanted to grow up to be exactly like her.

"How's the new boyfriend?" she asked after she had put on her lipstick and spritzed herself with perfume.

Girl talk. I was thrilled by this private, intimate moment. "Okay," I giggled. "So far, anyway. How's Bill?"

Her eyes lit up. Bill was my mother's first attempt at finding love again, and my sisters and I approved. He was a big man with a heart to match. Since meeting him, my mother smiled a whole lot more.

"That's what I wanted to show you," she said, dusting off her hands and reaching for something in the basket beside her. She held up a blue and red striped polo shirt.

"I made it for Bill's birthday," she said. "Do you think he'll like it?"

I felt like my mother's friend and daughter all at the same time. I was safe and well loved and lucky to be alive. "Oh, yes! It's perfect!" I said.

That's when the doorbell rang, shattering the coveted one-on-one connection with my mother. "Your father is here," she said, quickly folding the polo shirt and hiding it under the bed. Neither of us wanted any evidence of Bill in the room. My father, unable to let my mother go, was wildly jealous of her relationship with Bill.

"Go let your father in. I'll be right there," she continued. Her expression said the rest: Be nice, put on a smile, give your father a hug, and keep our little secret.

I stood up. After a reluctant pause, I began moving toward the front door as my mother had asked. My father had called me a week before Father's Day, even though I hadn't spoken with him in months, asking me to come and live with him. I had begged off. Why me? He loved Linda, my little sister, the best. Once, when I had somehow irritated him, he had chased me and pinned me down, putting his hands around my throat. My screams had brought Linda to the scene. Because of her, he had released me. Yet now he wanted me, not Linda. He said I would thank him someday. For the suffering? Did he think that would make me a better person?

I opened the front door. The rain had slowed to a drizzle. My father stood on the stoop, a little damp but looking absolutely wonderful and normal—exactly the way I remembered him from when I was a little girl. There was no sign of the angry, troubled man I had come to expect. Pleased and relieved, I felt compelled to hug him after I ushered him inside.

As he entered, my mother came toward us, shrugging into her raincoat and saying something about wanting to warm up her car. The yellow 1972 Buick Apollo was a gleaming symbol of my mother's newfound freedom. Leaving my father after almost two decades of verbal abuse had proven to be an incredibly liberating experience for her. Mom was a farm girl who had never learned to drive anything other than a tractor. Getting her driver's license and buying that Apollo had been a key step toward her independence. I watched, smiling, as she dashed through the raindrops with her car keys in hand.

Then I glanced at my father. His eyes were following my mother, who was dodging puddles on the way to her car. Abruptly he said, "I'll be right back. I need to get my coat from my trunk."

He loped across the lawn to his car, which was parked inches away from my mother's. I opened my mouth to call to my sisters that we were just about ready to leave. Before I could utter a syllable, I saw my father pull not a coat but a rifle from the trunk of his car.

Every second that passed as I made my way from the doorframe onto the edge of the porch is burned into my mind forever. My breath stopped. My heart stopped. Time seemed to stop. My father was yelling at my mother, "You made me do this." His hand was wrapped around the rifle stock, the barrel aimed straight at her.

"Daddy, don't!" I screamed. "Dad, I'll live with you . . . Dad, I'll take care of you!" Oh, my God, I had to stop him. Maybe the rain was drowning out my words. Maybe he couldn't hear me. Maybe he didn't care.

My desperate cries did nothing to dissuade him. His hand tightened around the trigger as he trapped my mother between the two cars. Still, I kept pleading, hoping to stop him. But my voice was powerless. Why didn't he hear me? Why didn't Linda hear me? He would listen to her. Where was she? And where was my older sister, Cindy?

My mother said hoarsely, "Ron, don't you do this. Don't you do this."

"You made me do this," he countered. "It's all your fault. You gave me no choice. If I can't have you, no one can. No one will."

While he raged, she looked him squarely in the eye, showing her courage in the face of the man who had controlled her for so long. Instinctively, she wrapped her arms around her body in the vain hope of deflecting what was to come. As I watched, I kept running scenario after scenario through my mind. I had to save her. I could jump between her and the gun. I could do something to distract him, maybe throw a chair or bang on the metal garbage pail, and she could run. But my body was frozen. Much later I would learn that Shakespeare had put my paralysis into words: "Extreme fear can neither fight nor fly."

Crack! The sound of the rifle firing tore a hole in my life. Everything moved so slowly that I felt as though I could reach out and stop the bullet in flight. The way my mother looked right before and after the bullet entered her abdomen is my most vivid memory. She was so beautiful and scared and alone. When the bullet penetrated, she fell forward ever so slightly, her body wrenched in pain. She grabbed her stomach the way you would if you were going to throw up. I remember her face, twisted in agony, still eye to eye with her killer. She was silently begging him to stop. I think for one part of one second my father didn't believe what he had done. I know I must have been screaming, but all I remember is the surreal silence. I felt as though I'd been in a movie. This couldn't have been happening.

The click of the gun re-cocking broke the stillness. My father's gaze and the barrel of the gun turned my way. I was sure it was my time to die. But the gun swung back and found my mother again. As the second bullet hit, she fell through the open door of her prized car. The bullet went straight through her and lodged in the steering wheel. The nonstop blaring ripped into the quiet of a small-town Sunday morning. To this day, the sound of a car horn has the power to unnerve me unless I call forth all the inner resources I have stockpiled to free me from fear.

The horn was still keening its eerie death knell as my father ran toward me. Rain-soaked, he fell to his knees at my feet, the gun upright at his side. He rested his right temple directly against the end of the barrel and pulled the trigger. His every motion was seamless, as if he had planned and rehearsed diligently for this final act. The sound of the gunshot at close range was deafening. My father's blood splattered on the white dress that was my mother's last gift to me. His body collapsed beside me.

The only sound was my own harsh breathing, waking me up to the realization that what had happened was not a dream. It was real. I began to shudder. In that moment, I was gripped by a potent fear that I didn't deserve to be alive. Why was I still standing? After all, my father had proved that I wasn't worth living for. In fact, I wasn't even worth killing. And I—the only person on the scene—had failed as my mother's savior. What earthly use was I, anyway?

I turned and retreated into the house, heading for the sanctuary of my mother's bedroom, where just a few minutes earlier I had felt safe and singled out for her confidences. I got down on my knees and folded my hands against the bedspread. The scent of her perfume was still in the air. I prayed with all the faith I had ever had. "Please, God," I begged, "don't let her be dead." Yet I knew even then that she was already gone.

The news traveled fast through our little town. Arrangements were made, and within hours we were at my aunt's house. I am told that I was hysterical, then silent. I suppose I changed out of the bloodstained dress. I remember very little from the time I knelt to pray until hours later. I vaguely recall phoning my boyfriend and blurting out what had happened, but after that everything is just blank. My aunt had convinced Cindy to put me on medication. I took the pill, more for their sake than for mine. But I refused to eat. These people, my relatives, were convinced that if I would just eat, things would be better.

They had no idea. I had failed to save my mother. I didn't deserve sustenance. Each mental replay admonished me more. In a haze of medication and self-loathing, I kept thinking I could have done something to stop my father from killing my mother. I could have stepped in front of the gun. I could have figured out something better to say. At the very least, I could have run over to the car where she lay slumped against the steering wheel. Maybe she had been waiting for me to come to her. If I had gotten to her, maybe she would have pulled through. But I had left her there. Looking back, I know that part of the fear that was etching itself into the very essence of my being was the idea that everyone else blamed me as well. Perhaps they were even pointing the finger at me for what my father had done. After all, he had once told me that it was all my fault that my mother had left him. I had no idea what he meant, but that didn't stop me from being afraid that he was right.

And yet that evening, as I did every Sunday, I went to the local indoor ice rink. Continuing with the routine I had always known seemed like the only thing to do. I didn't get much skating in, though. Once I got to the rink, I had to take care of my friends. They had shown up not knowing what to do or say. At first, they shifted from one foot to the other and avoided my eyes. This was a pattern with which I would become all too familiar in the months and years ahead. In a world where almost nothing was unmentionable any longer, a murder-suicide—especially one involving your parents and certainly if you were the only witness—turned out to be the last taboo.

Finally my friend Julie let herself react. She hugged me, sobbing into my shoulder. I was glad she was crying. My fear was already hard at work, keeping me from sharing my real feelings. I held her, letting her vent her grief and fury, all the while keeping mine in. I was afraid that if I let them loose, the world would not be able to withstand my heartache. I was afraid of myself. Afraid to be human. The consequences were too terrible to imagine.

Nothing after that moment was perfect for many years to come. At the cemetery for my mother's burial, the emotional dam that had been holding back my tears finally broke. The brilliant sunlight and the fresh breeze off Lake Superior seemed to mock the unbearable ache in my heart. I threw myself on my mother's coffin, crying, "Don't leave me! Please don't leave me!" My grandmother, a formidable woman with a no-nonsense philosophy of life, wrenched me off the casket and said, "That will be enough of that. It's over." As she led me away, her hand in a viselike grip on my wrist, the fear that it was not right to be me took a firm hold over my life.

The more that people tried to shield me from my pain, the more frightened I became of my own feelings and the harder I worked at keeping them in check. Many relatives became remote. Friends disappeared. I felt totally left out. People hushed when I entered a room. I remember overhearing adults prep visitors. "Be careful not to bring up the subject of parents," they would say. I developed a sense of shame about sharing my story with anyone. I was terrified that I would be accused of not stopping my parents' deaths. I was afraid of who I was.

Much later, while attending college on scholarship, I was seen as normal, a high achiever with much to be proud of. No one would have guessed the fears that were running my life. I kept others at arm's length to avoid the fear of being discovered and to dodge the inevitable questions. Fear was my constant companion, giving me permission to lie. "How are your parents?" someone would ask. "Just fine," I'd respond. For a long time, my parents were "just fine." Eventually, in the briefest of terms, I began telling people what had happened, followed by ". . . but I'm over that now. I've handled it. I'm fine."

At the time, I had talked myself into believing that I was fine. But I wasn't. Fear was taking its toll. I was worried that I would never have enough money. I doubted my ability to succeed. I dreaded the responsibility of growing up. I was uncomfortable being alone. Yet I was anxious about falling in love because I was sure any man would discover what my father must have already known: I was unlovable. My expectations regarding friendships could never be fulfilled. Intimacy and trust were elusive. Love was never part of the picture. I was easily angered and, at times, suicidal. Although my intellect and body had survived, my heart and soul were deeply wounded. Happiness was beyond my reach.

Nothing I tried—not the therapy, not the books I read, not the courses I took, not the grief groups I joined—gave me the peace I yearned for. More than that, I noticed that people from all walks of life had the same challenges I had. I began to wonder if maybe this was all there was, so I took to rationalizing my fear away. *This must be the way life is,* I thought. *Everyone else complains, whines, and moans. We each have our lot in life, this must be mine.* I figured the best I could hope for was camaraderie through my pain. Maybe you've felt this same way. Maybe you have come to the conclusion that the best you can do is learn to deal with it and try to control it the best you can. Well, maybe there is another way.

I decided this couldn't possibly be all there was. If no one could help me, I became determined to help myself. I wanted more than understanding. I wanted actual things to do that would help me get through my doubts, worries, paralysis, defensiveness, and so on. I wanted to know that my fear hadn't eclipsed any good left within me. It was only after my third suicide attempt ten years after my parents died that I started to take action. It all started with a calendar and some gold stars. Each day I would write down exactly what I did that was kind and loving to others as well as myself. I was vigilant. At that point, it was all I had. At the end of the month my calendar was covered in gold stars. I knew I had a fighting chance. From the seeds of that first exercise, I have come to realize there is another way to get beyond the fear. I have figured out the pathway to fearless living. It is my purpose and my passage back to myself.

Note to Self

You are not your fears.

Of Stunts and Men

STACY COURTNEY

Stacy Courtney has worked in Hollywood as a stuntwoman for over a decade, starring in such films as *A Life Less Ordinary*, *Hidden Assassin*, *2 Fast 2 Furious*, and *Confessions of a Shopaholic*. She has jumped from an eight-story building, been set on fire, and reenacted a scene in which a helicopter crashes into the Harlem River—all in the name of a hard day's work.

I was twenty-five years old when I worked as a second camera assistant in Los Angeles. I liked learning new things and I was interested in the film business, but it was a physically demanding job, peopled mostly by men, whose end goal was to be a DP (director of photography). After two years, I realized I was climbing a ladder to a career that I didn't really desire, so I decided to try something new—you know, start fresh. I admittedly felt a little lost about my next steps, so my dear friend Kate, who lived in Santa Fe at the time, suggested I join her in the desert. At that point, I could still pack everything I owned into my car. When I put L.A. in my rearview mirror, it felt great!

At first, to make money, I waited tables. I'd done it in the past, and I was good at it. I also worked part-time in a gallery, where the owner introduced me to an actor/silversmith. He taught me how to make jewelry and sell it to the retail stores in the plaza. Odd jobs helped me get by, but moving to Santa Fe had cost me a big pay cut. So when a DP I knew asked me to meet him in Texas to work on a pilot, I couldn't resist. The show turned out to be *Walker, Texas Ranger.*

On set, I met Allan, the show's stunt coordinator and second unit director. Since I worked the camera on the second unit, where all the stunts were filmed, I worked with him. As I observed the filming of the stunts, I began to think that I would like to give them a try—especially since I saw stuntpeople flying in from L.A., being put up in hotels, and getting per diem, while I was packing heavy camera equipment and working as a local for a lot less money.

It turned out that the show's leading actress was exactly my size—little, and blond. In one episode, they asked her to do a stunt in a more dramatic fashion than she was willing to do. Usually in this situation, there would already be a stunt double on set, but since this was unexpected, they couldn't find someone on such short notice. At that point Allan pulled me aside and asked if I'd be willing to step in.

I thought, *Here's my chance,* so I agreed to run through the woods in heels and get tackled by this hulk of an actor. I was a tomboy as a kid, who grew up in a rural area and was used to playing rough-and-tumble games. I was the "Hell, yes!" girl—I would try anything, go anywhere. The stunt went well, so Allan said he would feel good about giving me a few more jobs to test my mettle and help me get some skills.

When I exited *Walker, Texas Ranger*, I didn't know if Allan would really call me to work again. *Out of sight, out of mind*, I thought. But when he came through Santa Fe a month later, he had a job for me. "I'm working on a show in El Paso," he said. "We're re-creating a chase scene; you'll be driving."

I was excited and nervous, as I hadn't done any driving stunts yet, but I wanted my shot at a new career. I asked one of the guys for a quick lesson in sliding a car with an e-brake. The chase looked great; I skidded the car to a mark at the Stop sign, Allan and the director were happy, and that is how my career in stunts began. After that, Allan called whenever he needed a double in L.A. I learned how to crash cars, take a punch, and use air rams and ratchets to fly through the air. I also rolled a car using a pipe ramp, which was a pretty big deal. The ramp is positioned at the end of the run-up to get just the right angle for the camera. Then you agree on a speed at which you will hit the ramp to achieve the desired effect. The faster the speed, the higher you go, and a metal "kicker" on the end of the ramp helps the car begin the flip. The control is in hitting your mark on the ramp at the correct speed; after that, you just go for the ride. It was exhilarating, and walking away from it built my confidence.

My next few years were spent mostly on location. I went to Prague for a movie called *The Shooter*, starring Dolph Lundgren. I doubled for a French actress Dolph chased throughout the movie. I was pushed out of a moving car, ran on the top of a

moving train, and jumped off the Charles Bridge into the Vlat-
ava River. It was October, and the water was freezing. I also did
a Hilary Swank movie before she was Hilary Swank, The Oscar-
Winning Actress. I doubled for a sorority girl whose sisters
make her lean over the ledge of a tall building and hang a banner before she plunges to her death. Here, I had to fall onto an
air bag the size of a postage stamp. We shot at the courthouse in
Salt Lake City, where the ledge was about seventy-five feet off
the ground. That was scary, because when I jumped, the banner
got twisted around me on the way down and screwed up my trajectory. I was heading for the side of the bag, when the stunt
safety on the ground yelled to move the bag enough so that I
landed on the corner. My elbow and head still hit the ground,
but an MRI showed that I only had a slight concussion. I began
to realize that injuries were part of the job description. That
same month on a Holly Hunter movie, I tore some leg muscles
doing an air ram over the cab of a truck. Working with Holly was
a high point, because she was so inclusive in her working process. I felt like I was working with her to help tell the story. But
on a bigger scale, I was really proud of how far I'd come, and
how hard I'd pushed myself in this field.

I had relocated back to California with more direction in my
life and more stuff in my car. I was working with Allan a lot, and
as a result we began dating. We had been together three years
when he planned a trip to Hawaii over New Year's Eve. We'd
worked very hard over the past few months, and we needed a
vacation. When we arrived, however, it rained for seven days
straight, and during this time I realized our relationship wasn't
working. We were arguing more often, and I was finally seeing

that we didn't really want the same things. I had left behind a part of myself that didn't fit into Allan's life, and I was missing that part of me.

During the months before Christmas we had bought a house in Park City, Utah, and moved in together with the intention of getting married. Allan had asked for my father's blessing, but months had gone by without an engagement. He was taking frequent trips, and he avoided spending that Christmas with my family and me. Our closest connection was our stunt work, and that wasn't enough to build our relationship on. On the seventh night in Maui, it stopped raining. We were sitting outside, staring up at the stars. "This isn't working, is it?" I asked him. "I'm not happy, and I don't think you are either." Allan agreed with me, and we decided to end the relationship. It was very matter-of-fact. Neither of us spoke about our intended engagement; we just went to bed. Of course, the sun came out the next morning. We'd resolved the night before to just pack up our stuff and go home, but with the sun blazing in the sky, Allan said, "Let's rent a Harley and go for a ride." We had fun and didn't talk about the fact that we were splitting up. At the end of the day, he said, "Look, we came here to go diving. Let's just go tomorrow." I didn't see the harm in it, and we both loved a good adventure, so I agreed. In retrospect, I wonder if it's any coincidence that as a stunt person I learned how to endure relationship bumps and bruises when I met Allan.

When we got to the water the next day, the ocean was murky and the currents were really strong because of the storm. I had indigestion that morning, which I never get, and I didn't feel so hot. I enjoyed the dive, but because of the water and my stomach issues, I would have happily gone back to the dock after that first experience, calling it a day. But Allan wanted to dive some more, so the captain took us to our second location. Despite how crappy I felt and how bad the visibility was, the "Hell, yes!" girl in me didn't want to bail. So when Allan egged me on to do the second dive, I agreed.

Swimming around, we saw an eel, when Allan gave me the signal that he was short on air and needed to head back. The dive master was in front, Allan was next in line, and I was behind Allan. As we were swimming back, I'm not sure if I heard a noise or if I felt the shadow of the boat come over me, but I remember being hit by something hard and then catapulted through the water. My first thought was that a shark had bitten me.

Turns out it was a huge catamaran with about thirty tourists aboard, having a good time. Earlier in the dive, I had seen them snorkeling from underneath, but they had been in a different area. When they'd been ready to head back to shore, the first mate had begun pulling the anchor, but a strong current had caused the boat to drift. In the time it had taken to pull the anchor, the boat had silently moved over me in the water. When the captain had started the engine on his boat, I'd gotten sucked up into the propeller. Later, he admitted to hearing a thump but he'd thought he'd just hit a coconut. So he'd kept on course.

Meanwhile, I was coming out of the spin cycle, choking and sucking down water because I'd lost my regulator when the propeller had tossed me. Allan swam to me and pulled me to the surface. I struggled to breathe and felt disoriented; the water was thick with blood. I saw my left foot come out of the water in a contorted way that didn't look physically possible. The seriousness of what had just happened was sinking in. Allan screamed to our boat captain that I'd been hit by the catamaran. The dive master stopped the boat from moving any further by yelling and waving his hands. Someone on the catamaran handed down a surfboard so that I could be lifted from the water. That's when I saw my twisted, raw, and exposed leg for the first time. I told myself that if I wanted to survive this, I couldn't look again. I had to stay calm. Panic was not an option, because help was far away and I was bobbing in the open sea.

The boat was total mayhem. There was a lot of screaming, and nobody knew how to tell the Coast Guard where we were because there was no GPS to give a position. The word was that the helicopter didn't have a swimmer's basket and wanted to go back for one. I heard someone yell that there was no time for that. Someone wrapped a belt around my leg to stanch the bleeding. I remember three or four women surrounding me, creating shade for my face by forming a little ring around my head. One of the women said, "I'm a nurse, we've got help on the way," while the others rubbed my head and held my hand, trying to calm me down. I could feel death hovering.

I remember thinking about my family as I lay there: my sister, mom, dad, and brother. I couldn't leave them, I wasn't ready to go. The last thing I wanted was for them to receive The Phone Call. So I sent a message out to my guardian angels, asking them to join the women there and surround me; as I was talking to them, I began to breathe very slowly and conserve my energy. I focused on my life here, and how badly I wanted to preserve it.

I heard the Coast Guard's Sikorsky helicopter coming from a distance. They dropped a basket into the ocean and Allan scooped me up and put me in it. The ride to the door of the helicopter was the most excruciating pain I've ever experienced. The blades created intense wind that would hit my exposed nerves, and my screams were swallowed up by the chopper noise. I prayed to pass out, but that relief never came.

It had taken over an hour for the chopper to meet the catamaran, and once I was on the helicopter, I thought, *Okay, I've made it this far.* The Coast Guard officer kept insisting I focus on his eyes: "Look at me. Look at me!" he repeated. If I lost consciousness and stopped fighting, I might die. There wasn't room for me to lie flat in the helicopter, so I had to hold my head up. But it was getting as heavy as a bowling ball, and I just couldn't keep it up. I remember thinking, *Holy shit, this is it, I don't have anything left.*

I resigned myself to the fact that I'd done the best I could and couldn't fight anymore. I felt surrounded by angels, and an incredible sense of peace came over me. I thought, *I'm done, and it's Okay.* At that moment the Coast Guard officer snapped me out of it. "Stay with me!" he said. "You need to keep looking at me," he repeated. He kept me awake and alert.

We landed in a parking lot, and I was transferred to an ambulance that took me to the hospital—yet another twenty minutes away. As the ER doctors cut away my wet suit, the EMTs pronounced my condition grave. I heard them mention that the suit's compression had probably helped slow the bleeding. Just before they put me under for surgery, I heard someone say, "Let's try to save the leg," which I immediately translated as,

I'm going to wake up without a leg. I was devastated. I later learned that the propeller had initially caught my heel, then moved up my leg, through my calf and thigh, and stopped just under my bottom. My femur was broken in two places, very close to the top of the bone and very close to the knee joint. The bone in my ankle was sliced almost clean through. My ankle was basically hanging on to the rest of my leg by a piece of skin and one bone.

After my surgery in Maui, I was MEDIVACed to Honolulu, where I was met by my parents and a reputable orthopedic trauma surgeon. Although he was pessimistic about my recovery, warning that he did not think I would ever walk without braces, he assured me he would do his very best work. He was young and full of himself, though I haven't met an orthopedic surgeon who isn't, but his confidence was reassuring. In fact, he seemed pleased to have such a complicated surgery on his hands, and he took care to research and plan for it. In the meantime there were several debridement surgeries and procedures to cleanse and cut away dead tissue. The hospital even sent lab workers to the accident site to collect water samples; they wanted to treat the specific bacteria that I had been exposed to before they started operating.

During surgery, the doctors filleted my knee to insert a rod through the center of my femur and grafted bone using scrapings they had removed from my hip. When I woke up from the surgery I was relieved to see my leg intact. Allan was crying at my bedside, asking for a second chance and for me to marry him. Barely coherent, with my pupils the size of saucers from my morphine drip, I said, "Yes."

An evaluation from the hospital psychiatrist showed I was suffering from severe post-traumatic stress disorder. I was terrified to sleep because I had nightmares about the accident and feared reliving the experience. Mom learned something called Healing Touch, which was offered at the hospital. It helped ease the pain, and it soothed my nerves. She was there night and day monitoring my care and being a healing presence. I recovered for two weeks in the hospital before I was MEDIVACed to L.A., to be near the doctor who was going to do my follow-up surgeries. By that point I'd beaten the odds and was determined to push the limits. "I still have my leg," I said. "I'm going to walk and I'm going back to work."

Our home in Park City, which had two flights of stairs, was covered in snow. This was problematic, because I was going to be in and out of a wheelchair for a while. So my friend Ashley turned her apartment into a recovery unit, complete with hospital bed, so I could begin my rehabilitation. In the meantime, Allan said he would look for an apartment for us. I was still in a state of stress. What's more, the nightmares continued, so sleep was a struggle. Mom had traveled by train to San Diego to take advanced classes in Healing Touch and Reiki and was using the techniques to help me with sleep and healing. Even worse, I couldn't eat. Ashley, Mom, and my brother took care of me—and noticed the extent to which Allan had dropped out. He always had excuses for why he wasn't around, and he dumped me with others while he took jobs out of town or flew down to the islands. While they were questioning his actions, I spent my energy just getting through each day.

I couldn't stay with Ashley forever, and Allan had done nothing to find us a new home, so Ashley and another friend searched until they found us a place. Every day I had a doctor's appointment or physical therapy, and I needed a car that was easy to drive so that my mom could taxi me around the city. At this point I owned a '73 Bronco with loose steering, manual brakes, and no air-conditioning—not exactly luxurious or easy to handle. Allan's truck was off limits because he used it for work. So my parents loaned me the money to buy a more practical car, and Allan took it upon himself to use his car dealer connection and buy us a Mustang convertible. It was a car he had always wanted, and he bought it with no regard for my current needs for practicality. I was incredibly disappointed by his actions, until one day he went on a drive in my new car and came home in a Porsche—his ultimate dream car. His selfishness was in full gear, and I was left behind in the rearview mirror, hazy from all the drugs I was using to manage my pain.

I sought help for weaning myself off my pain meds, and I began seeing a holistic nutritionist to help me regain my appetite and a therapist to help with the post-traumatic stress and depression. Allan went with me for some of the sessions because I was starting to feel suspicious about his actions. She explained that there was a part of me that thought that if Allan wasn't there I would die. In a breakdown session of his own, he admitted lying to the therapist and told me he'd been cheating on me—throughout our entire relationship! We took a break, and I went to Chicago with Ashley. The doctors told me not to do it, but I insisted. "I need a life," I said. "I need to do something that doesn't make me feel broken." Allan followed me out there, confessed his undying love, then announced that one of the last girls he'd been with was pregnant. He hid his money and planned to deny paternity. But the baby was his, and I once again felt deceived and confused. Though my body was physically healing, my mind still clung irrationally to a future with Allan. I was stronger in many ways, but I was always an emotionally weakened version of myself with him.

It wasn't until I was in New York several months later, visiting my brother, that the pieces fell into place. While I was there, Allan had his lawyer inform me that he was going to sue me for $50,000 for his pain and suffering during my accident. I'd already given him $100,000 from the settlement money I'd received after the accident. Also, by keeping track of all our expenses while we'd been together, I knew I'd paid him back for half of everything—rent, groceries, utilities, etc. This was my final breaking point. Until that moment, I had let him get out of jail free. But when I opened the attorney's letter, it was like an emotional cord linking me to Allan was severed, and in a crystal-clear moment I said, "I'm finally done!" And I meant it this time. I called a friend's husband, who is a lawyer, and he wrote Allan a scathing letter to shake him off.

I didn't speak to Allan for years after, but I am actually thankful that he sued me. It hadn't been enough for us to be incompatible or for me to have felt deserted after the accident. I'd had to see, on paper, that he was nothing but a taker—a sociopath, according to the therapist—who would continue to lie and manipulate. I didn't need him for my survival. Even though he'd come to my rescue in the water, ultimately I'd saved myself. I was back.

When I think about the accident now, I think of everyone

who has struggled and survived something traumatic. I remember watching documentaries about people who survived terrible scenarios; I'd insist, "I could never survive something like that, I'm just not that strong!" But now I just smile. *I'm one of you*, I think instead. The accident, the Allan ordeal—it's all made me realize that nobody's hardship is worth more or less than another's. And for those who don't hold on, it doesn't make them weak or less capable. We are all on our own unique journey, and sometimes part of that journey is letting go.

In an effort to leave all ties to Allan behind, I left for New York and another fresh start. It was there that I went back to doing stunts. In fact, my first job was during an episode of *Third Watch*, in which I played a helicopter traffic reporter. The chopper went down in the river, but both the reporter and the pilot made it out. She went back to reporting, but the second time it happened, she didn't make it. All things considered, I couldn't believe that this was *my first job back*! The coordinator who hired me was the same friend who'd been instrumental in moving the air bag. "I don't know if you want to do this stunt," he warned me. "And if not, I'll understand and call you for other jobs. But for this one, the helicopter will be submerged into the Harlem River, there will be a pony bottle of air in case we can't get to you in time, but there will be boats all around."

I immediately thought that I couldn't do it, but I trusted him like a brother and I told him I'd think about it. *I am being offered the chance to get back on the fucking horse in the biggest way possible. I'm going to be in the water, around boats, doing an insane stunt. What better way to make a comeback?*

So I did the job, it went great, and I was so in the zone while

I was working that I didn't have a minute to be anxious. Instead, I had this huge sense that I could do anything after that. I'd survived the real thing *and* the reenactment! It had been four long years since the accident, and I was back. I walked with a limp and had limitations, but I was back! Accepting the job helped me realize that I didn't want to go back to physical therapy every day, that I was done feeling injured. I just wanted to work and feel normal again. I'd endured eleven surgeries in three years, and so many alternative means of healing. For so long I felt like Frankenstein, with staples and scars up and down my leg. I worked really hard to heal, and I felt incredibly proud of how far I'd come. It was time for me to get on with my life.

Until the accident, my life was golden. I came into the world with good parents and lots of love. I was given a healthy and tough little body. I'm smart, capable, affable, and I did well at almost everything I tried. But then I got smacked down. I felt weak and disfigured, like damaged goods. Emotionally I still struggle to know that I was so wounded that I would let Allan take advantage of me, time and again. I thought I knew myself better, then. What I know now is that making Allan comfortable was more important to me than my own well-being. Had I been listening to my own voice the day he'd asked me to go diving, and had I paid attention to the signs—my suspicions about his integrity, his lack of emotion around breaking it off, feeling sick after the first dive—none of this would've happened.

I've since promised myself that I will never disconnect like that again. I know my worth now. I am not damaged goods; I'm a survivor. I believe we participate in designing our life plan based on what our soul needs to learn in a lifetime. And there are exits placed along the way should we stray too far from our plan and need to come home. It was my will to stay, my deep connection to the people I love, that gave me the strength to hold on. The accident was a gift because it taught me to listen to and trust my inner voice. I'll never drown it out again.

> *Note to Self*
>
> Trust your inner voice.
> It just might save your life.

Unexpected Guests

SUE SANDFORD

Sue Sandford lives in Dallas with her four kids, two dogs, three cats, and a hamster. She made headlines most notably in the *Dallas Morning News* when she adopted the McCray family as her own after they were displaced from their home by Hurricane Katrina. Sue is a proud full-time mom to her four amazing kids.

once read a beautiful prayer that said, "Bring a stranger into your house for three days and at the end of those three days, you'll know their true colors. Either ask them to leave, or you'll be friends for life." I had run across the passage quite randomly while reading one night before bed, and I thought it was an interesting theory. I certainly never expected it to foreshadow one of the most moving experiences of my family's life.

I had always hoped for a fairy-tale marriage, but my reality was far from it. I was engaged at nineteen and wed two years later to a good man who was responsible, funny, and kind. We had kids two years apart, which began when I was twenty-five—then at ages twenty-seven, twenty-nine, and thirty-one. I figured that if being a mom was bound to tire me out, I might as well stay tired until I'd completed my family and stayed in the rhythm of childbearing.

I entered into adulthood with steadfast convictions that I would not end up like my parents: divorced and angry. I was determined to have the fairy tale, and everyone believed I had it. People put our family on a pedestal, and who was I to let people down? My days were spent smiling and laughing and putting up a good front, while my nights were full of loneliness and desperation. The real story was that my husband's issues were tearing him and us apart, and they transformed him from the man I fell in love with to another person altogether. He had become a tormented stranger full of lies and deception. He stole not just my trust but also pieces of my dignity, my self-respect, my hope, and my dreams. Nonetheless, I believed that if I worked hard enough, loved big enough, and hoped strongly enough, I could drag the marriage to the finish line on my own.

Then, one day, I got tired of trying to cover up the lies and deceptions. There would be no finish line for me, and I figured it would be less exhausting and painful to allow myself to fall off the pedestal. I have always been told that when you take a big fall, you grow wings on the way down. I believed this to be true, but I never expected to have to fall so far before sprouting my wings.

Part of this might have had to do with all the weight dragging me down—literally. I'd put on forty pounds of depression weight in one year. Right before we got divorced, I confronted my husband. "Look at me," I said. "You see a heavy, dour woman. Doesn't it strike you that something is wrong?" Marriage had squeezed myself out of me, which, I think, is a common (and very sad) female predicament. We throw ourselves into our kids and our husbands and forget that it takes a lot of energy just to walk around and be alive and be ourselves.

Our divorce took only four months. He signed the papers without an attorney and accepted my terms as they were—fair and equitable. He didn't fight at all, which made me feel like I was not worth fighting for.

After my divorce, I had to rebuild myself, my life, and my ability to trust others. There are twenty-three cousins in my family, and we are very close. I am the only one who is divorced. It's a dubious distinction, and one of which I'm not especially proud. I often felt like an outsider when it came to my own family, but my outsider status was further highlighted by my Pleasantville-esque neighborhood. I live in University Park, which is in the heart of Dallas, Texas. It's like Wisteria Lane from *Desperate Housewives*, with a Southern twang. The neighborhood is a slice of Americana, complete with apple pie and Fourth of July parades. The streets are lined with trees, happy children, and neighbors who wave to you from the porch when you drive by. Everyone knows each other, and most people who grow up there never leave.

As one might imagine, University Park is a nuclear-family kind of place, and my divorcée status makes me stand out in the crowd. It's also 98.5 percent white, a product of economic segregation, very Christian, and extremely wealthy. Living in my neighborhood is like living in a bubble that doesn't naturally belong in real life. In 2003, when the first African-American family bought a house in University Park, it made the front page of the local paper. For me, moving here meant exceptional schools for my kids, but it also meant financial hardship.

In August 2005, I had eleven dollars in my bank account, thanks to a hospital bill for my daughter that I hadn't budgeted for. I was broke, but my brothers supported us financially so the kids could live in a nice neighborhood and I could stay home with them (my brothers have taught me a lot about kindness). I wasn't the only one who received a crash course on being broke and relying on the kindness of others: 2005 was the year Katrina struck, and I wanted desperately to pay forward my brother's kindness but had no idea what I could do with eleven dollars and a credit card.

When I saw footage of the hurricane on TV, I knew I needed to do something to help. I couldn't have written a check even if I'd wanted to, but I wanted to take action; I had to do something hands-on. When the levees broke on Tuesday, the local news station announced that Reunion Arena in Dallas, the defunct sports megaplex seven miles from my home, would act as a makeshift shelter. My kids and I had a powwow to talk about taking in a family, and we decided that we could handle it. My kids were ten, nine, seven, and five at the time, and our plan was to have them sleep in my room on two inflatable mattresses. We figured we could put a family in each of the remaining four bedrooms and one in our living room. We had no furniture, so we imagined that we could fit twenty people in the house, total. I called the Red Cross the next day and became certified to work with the refugees at the shelter that very weekend, which happened to be Labor Day. I went to Big Lots, maxed out my credit card, and bought hundreds of mini toothpastes, toothbrushes, and deodorant for the evacuees.

That weekend, my kids went off to their dad's house and I headed down to training at Reunion Arena. Hundreds of people had approached the Red Cross about taking in Katrina victims, but there was no way to connect the evacuees with these people. I recognized the problem on Thursday night, and with the help of a complete stranger I met on the sidewalk, I began a foundation called Lending Hand. We launched a website in twenty-four hours that allowed evacuees to get out of the overcrowded shelter and into a home. I had never done anything like this in my life, and yet it seemed so effortless. I was high on adrenaline from springing into action; my brain was engaged and thinking about positive outcomes instead of the negative ones I had experienced through my divorce.

I met the McCrays through Lending Hand. Chris Minks, the wonderful stranger who'd set up the website, his wife, and I were handing out paper flyers to anyone we could. One of those flyers made it into the hands of a McCray family member, and they explained their situation. That when fate stepped in. Chris walked over to me and explained that he had met a great family, who had just arrived that day. The McCrays were a large family, and they refused to separate. When I asked him how many there were, he shook his head and replied, "Twenty." They wanted to stay together as a unit, and this was making it very difficult to find them a place to go. The McCrays had safely escaped New Orleans—all eleven of them, crammed into a five-seat sedan—and had met up with the rest of their family, who had evacuated earlier, in Jennings, Louisiana. The family had then decided to head to Dallas to find help and shelter. I asked if I could meet the McCrays, and from that moment, I knew they were meant to be with me.

James and Linda McCray, the couple who headed up the family, were a formidable pair. Linda proudly told me later that James hadn't let her open a door for herself in thirty-six years, and that James hadn't made a meal in that long either. The two took care of each other, and by listening to their stories and watching them interact, a new standard would be set for me about what a marriage and family should be.

With James and Linda were four grown children and their husbands, fiancées, boyfriends, and ten beautiful grandchildren. The littlest McCray was just three weeks old, and the family had no luggage, no spare clothes, and no hope. Having lost every material possession they'd had, they refused to lose each other and were determined to stay together in whatever shelter they could find. What I saw the first evening I met the McCrays was a family that knew the only thing worth rescuing in New Orleans had been saved, and that everything else could be replaced.

As we stood in the middle of the chaotic, makeshift shelter in Dallas, we were brand-new friends but indeed total strangers. I took Mr. McCray aside and gave him the lowdown on where his family would be living for the next few weeks—maybe months. I felt it only fair to be open and honest with the McCray family before they made their decision to come and stay with me. I explained that I lived in an all-white neighborhood. I told them that they'd be fine, but that they needed to know this before we arrived, because people would likely stop them on the street and ask them who they were. It wasn't so much prejudice, it was protection. My neighbors knew I was single and they would want to know who was in my house. This was on a Friday night, and I had committed to volunteering at the shelter until Sunday. The McCrays would have the run of the place for two days. I didn't have time to tell my neighbors that a family of twenty African-Americans were moving in. I would learn later that the McCrays didn't even know my last name.

When I arrived home on Sunday, I found that the McCrays had spent their own money to stock my pantry with food. Linda had prepared a buffet fit for a queen, with slow-cooked baby back ribs, potato salad, and BBQ chicken. She taught my oldest daughter how to make homemade peach cobbler and spectacular bread pudding. The neighbors started dropping by with gift cards and diapers, anything they could do to help. My girls quickly adopted the tiny newborn McCray grandchild as their own, and my son became fast friends with their grandson, Shaun. The McCrays even threw my daughter an eleventh birthday party while they stayed with us. To this day, it astonishes me that a family who had everything taken from them gave so much.

I watched Linda McCray navigate the tragedy of losing everything with love, commitment, trust, wit, and respect. She told me that Katrina hadn't taken anything that was of value to her, that the things in her life that mattered most were gathered around her in my home. Even in the aftermath of such a catastrophic event, she instilled in her family a sense of normalcy. She encouraged everyone to do their hair, play games, and maintain a sense of optimism. I never saw her frown, and I never heard her complain. Linda's entire family sought refuge in her love, and I sat in awe of her strength. Linda taught me by example that the only pedestal worth being on is one built by faith in God and a love for each other.

Even though we were together only ten days, the McCrays and my family became one extended family. We weren't the nuclear kind, but one that is chosen out of love, trust, and faith. We became the kind of family that has one common interest, which is to care for one another and hold each other up when you're down. It was the family I had always dreamed of having, and I was finally home.

After the McCrays left, a few neighbors said things to me like, "You're lucky you weren't robbed, attacked, shot, or raped." I knew that no such thing would have happened in my house. I tell my kids that if you took all the bad people in the world and wiped them off the face of the earth, the majority of the population would be left standing. I would hope that if I was forced out of my home, with nothing but the clothes on my back and my four children, that someone would help me, too. I have been asked countless times how a single white mother of four could take in an African-American family of twenty strangers. That question never occurred to me at the shelter. Instead, I asked myself, How, as a woman who had ventured out on her own and was helped by so many, could I turn my back on a family in need? When I decided to take the McCrays into my home, I saw no differences in skin color, economics, or faith. It was the right thing to do.

As crazy as it sounds, I really think that it took Katrina to heal my heart and my family. Linda calls me her angel, but what she doesn't realize is how great an impact she and her amazing family had on me, my children, my extended family, and my town. She has no idea the grace she bestowed on my weary soul, and the gratitude I will forever have for her unexpected love.

In February of 2006, despite my begging and pleading for them to stay, the McCrays moved back to the Ninth Ward. Before leaving, James and Linda wrote each one of my nineteen neighbors a thank-you note. They were the only people starting to rebuild on their street, but James knew that if he went back he could help watch his neighbors' houses and, hopefully, bring them back as well. Their house was rebuilt, board by board, by James and his family. Patience was their constant companion as they waited eighteen months for electricity and two and a half years for federal funds. I can hardly put into words the rage that rose in me as I watched them fight for every small step. I remember so clearly James's frustration at not being able to provide a place for his family. One of his daughters had thirteen addresses in one year. Meanwhile, Bourbon Street had an instant makeover after the storm.

My kids and I visit the McCrays about twice a year and have the great joy of sleeping on inflatable mattresses on their floor! They come up for the anniversary of Katrina, and we always go down for Mardi Gras. We have helped them celebrate two weddings—with my littlest as a flower girl—and sadly watched them bury James's mother a week before her house was completed. They send me a card every birthday, Mother's Day, Valentine's Day, and sometimes just because. I do not know what I have done in my life to deserve them, but I will never let them go.

We should all be lucky enough to have people like the Mc-Crays in our lives, friends who teach and remind us what's most important in life, and how to face uncertainties with grace and dignity.

> *Note to Self*
>
> Never turn your back on someone in need. You may find that you need them as much as they do you.

A Moment of Truth, a Matter of Choice

MARIANNE WILLIAMSON

Marianne Williamson is a spiritual activist, author, lecturer, and founder of The Peace Alliance, a grassroots campaign supporting legislation to establish a United States Department of Peace. She is also the founder of Project Angel Food, a meals-on-wheels program that serves homebound people with AIDS in the Los Angeles area. She has published nine books, including four *New York Times* number one bestsellers. She has a weekly radio show on Oprah and Friends, which airs on XM radio.

I think I remember the moment when I decided to survive. Which is the same thing as saying I remember the moment when I decided to not be pathetic.

I had gone through a very down time. It was something the world might define as a nervous breakdown, but I see that merely as a label. The point is that I was deeply depressed. The drama I was playing out was very "Anna Karenina"; the drama,

of course, was centered around a man, my drug of choice at the
time.

So I remember a moment when I considered suicide. And
my pathetic thought was, *And then he'll be sorry.* But then right
after that what flashed into my mind was, *No, he won't. He might
be sorry for about five minutes and then after that he'll think, "It's
too bad about her," and that will be the final say: that "It really is
too bad about her."* And it won't be people looking back like I was
a romantic tragedy so much as people looking back and thinking I was weak somehow. In that moment I thought about my
father and all he had been through in his life and the strength
he had summoned from somewhere. And I thought about my
mother and the love that she had given me. And it wasn't so
much, *Marianne, you can't kill yourself because it will break their
hearts,* though of course that was there. But in that moment it
was more, *You can't kill yourself because that's not who you were
born to be.* And it wasn't like I knew what to say yes to in that moment. It simply meant that in that moment I knew what to say
no to. No, I will not be weak. That doesn't mean I knew how to
be strong, but it meant I made a decision not to be weak. It
wasn't that I knew how to not be pathetic but in that moment I
said no to being pathetic. And coming to that point in my life,
where I could summon up whatever that moment of strength
was in which I could say no to being who I didn't want to be,
opened a space in my mind where I could finally be seriously
available to finding out what I did want to be and who I could
become.

The world knocks us down sometimes, but God is always
there to lift us up. It's simply the nature of Reality, like a code

imprinted onto the universe. Just knowing that has made all the difference for me at times when I thought that some pain or another was too hard to bear. I've lived through a lot of dark nights, but for every dark night there was ultimately a dawn. And that has given me tremendous faith.

Note to Self

God creates only greatness,
and God created you.

My Lush Life

CANDY FINNIGAN

Candy Finnigan, CADC, is an interventionist on A&E's top-rated reality program, *Intervention.* In its sixth season, the show chronicles the "rock bottom" for addicts of all kinds. Finnigan and her fellow professionals organize interventions for the families of the addicts featured. Finnigan is also the author of *When Enough Is Enough,* published in 2008 by Penguin/Avery. She lives in Los Angeles with her husband of forty years, acclaimed musician Mike Finnigan.

I didn't really start drinking until I was in my thirties, and I didn't think much about alcohol before then. But I went down the path of addiction quickly, and it took me less than five years to fully develop my disease into a debilitating disaster. Before that, my association with booze was more about the pretty dress and matching purse and heels one might wear while sipping a martini, rather than the martini itself. I have my mother to thank for that—she was a refined lady living the life of a fine glass of champagne.

My mom died in 2005 on Mother's Day. ("Just so you won't forget me," she said, and meant it.) Her personality was larger than the house she raised me in: 5,000 square feet, complete with an elevator and two rooms dedicated solely to gift-wrapping. She was the epitome of Kansas high society, which meant she sent out five hundred Christmas cards every year, as well as two hundred birthday presents to all the other rich folks in the area. The façade that everything was divine was driven home by the classy cocktail in her hand. So when I told her I was an alcoholic, her façade remained firmly intact though it went against all her plans. She even confused Alcoholics Anonymous (AA) with Triple-A car insurance (AAA) on a regular basis. She claimed to have never known an alcoholic, even though her brother had died of the disease. And even when I went to rehab with a grocery bag full of clothes, a half-empty vodka bottle, and a concussion, she remained deep in denial, saying I simply needed a vacation.

I grew up in a very privileged family in Kansas that was fueled by oil money; which is to say, I didn't want for anything. As a child, I had many personalities, and I owned enough clothes to costume them all. I was a Junior Leaguer, and my family was well known in *Who's Who in Society*, the tome for the elite. I was a Waldorf debutante. Where I'm from, the more clubs you belong to, the better your circle, but I hated groups of any kind. Maybe that's because my parents adopted me after they lost their biological daughter to polio and I never truly felt as if I belonged to any group. The death of their biological child broke my mother in half, and I don't think she ever recovered. In an effort to save my sister's life, my parents flew in Sister Kenny from Philadelphia, and she brought with her an iron lung. They donated a great deal of money to the hospital that tried to save her life; there's now a playground and children's playroom named after her—the Sharon Derby playroom.

When my parents found out they couldn't have more biological children, they adopted my brother and me. I was told I was picked, like a tomato, from a handful of redheaded, freckle-faced girls from a high-end adoption facility called the Golden Cradle; I was also told my biological mother had died. I didn't find out that this was untrue until my biological mother died at ninety-four in 2004; I think my parents knew that if they'd told me my real mom was still alive, I might have run away to find her when the social pressures of high society became too much.

My mother wanted me to be the daughter she'd lost, but I couldn't have been more different. It was clear from day one that I didn't fit into her Daughters of the American Revolution lifestyle. If she was Neiman's, I was Target. Don't get me wrong, I love having money, and I had it to burn growing up. But I felt that the pomp and circumstance that came with it—referring to friends by their last names, bragging about one's summer house—wasn't a very sincere way to live. I never felt comfortable with it.

My dad was a great man who was the exact opposite of my mother. He made his money in dry goods and as an oil investor. He spent as much time on the golf course (he was on the executive committee of the USGA) as he did anywhere else, and he put many of his caddies' kids through college. At his funeral, there were seven black men sitting at the back of the church—an odd sight at a rich white man's service in Kansas circa 1994. When I thanked them for coming, they said, "We just want you to know that your father put a roof on every single one of our churches." My dad was understated, tasteful, and couldn't have cared less about acquiring material things. Upon a first meeting, you would never have known he was loaded. My mother, on the other hand, was like Elizabeth Taylor—all hair, furs, and diamonds. They were a curious pair, who loved each other through fifty-six years of marriage. They had a good marriage that made me want to settle down and start a family of my own.

When I was eighteen, I met my future husband, Mike, at a fraternity party and thought to myself, *I'll take him.* He was a Big Man on Campus, with a full basketball scholarship at Kansas State University, and he was from a very different world than mine. His family lived in Ohio, and they were a good, blue-collar, hardworking Irish Catholic family. Really wonderful people. At some point, Mike got put on the bench because he developed mononucleosis, so he started playing music at fraternity parties to supplement his scholarship. Eventually, the coach gave him a choice: play music or basketball. Mike picked music, and he never looked back. I thought he would eventually outgrow living the life of a musician, but the next thing I knew he was making an album in New York and recording *Electric Ladyland* with Jimi Hendrix. I still lived in Wichita, attending dental hygienist school, when he played on that album.

Mike and I had a society wedding in 1969 that appeared in

Town & Country. We promptly moved from Wichita to San Francisco. Our first apartment had a couch, a Murphy bed, and an aluminum kitchen table.

Even though Mike was on the road a lot touring, when we were together we stayed at home and drank like we were at a bar. We enjoyed our fair share of all-nighters doing drugs in the homes of random rock stars and with random strangers, but drugs never really appealed to me. I preferred to drink.

We moved from San Francisco to Los Angeles in 1975 in our orange Karmann Ghia with two screaming cats in the back. I thought we would buy a house in the suburbs, I would get pregnant, and we would make our life work. Instead, we moved into a huge mansion. I had my daughter Bridget after we had been married for eight years. I thought it would make me feel better and more normal to have a child, which was what I wanted more than anything.

After my first child was born, I remember the feeling of really needing a drink, because I wanted to celebrate. But I also needed some relief from not knowing what to do one more time. I was never really sure how solid I would be as a mother, because I had not experienced a maternal upbringing and Mike was on the road a great deal. So I set out to create my own stable world. I saw how everyone else was doing it and followed suit. I moved into the San Fernando valley and bought a Volvo station wagon and set out to create this perfect family. I became a stay-at-home mom, and my kids went to private schools, where I was vice president of the PTA. When the other school moms heard my husband was a rock musician, they were shocked. Everyone thought he was an attorney, and that pleased me. There was a big part of me left over from Kansas who just wanted to fit in so that I would be safe.

After my daughter was born, I started drinking in earnest. I drank every day, and alcohol dominated my life. I scheduled my days around it. There were times I considered skipping a movie because it might be too long to wait for a drink. I very rarely drank during the day, but when five o'clock came, I was so horribly lonely that I turned to wine as my companion. I could stay up until two o'clock in the morning just talking on the phone, smoking cigarettes, and playing solitaire. I would drink four bottles of wine a night, and after about the second one, I would go into what I call "a brownout." The next day, I'd find a glass in the kitchen, in the bathroom, behind the bed, but I would never remember putting them there. I'd toss the evidence and promise I'd never drink again, and then I'd start all over again at five o'clock that same afternoon.

Drinking was always my little secret, and I don't think my husband had any idea how much I drank, because he was never there. I went to bed drunk at 2:00 a.m. and woke at 6:00 a.m. to take my kids to school, so I was still tipsy behind the wheel. Meanwhile, my husband was touring every summer with Crosby, Stills and Nash. He would leave in May and come home in October. The rest of the year, he was busy climbing the music industry ladder, and we partied together. I always felt like music was his mistress, but I was determined to make things work.

When my husband would arrive home after months on the road, exhausted, he didn't want to hear about parent/teacher conferences, baseball games, or my endless meetings with therapists to help with our daughter's congenital speech impediment. Though he loved our children, he only wanted to hear about the glorious things they had done and not about the day-to-day minutiae involved with raising them. He was tired, and he wanted home cooking and his clothes washed. He needed to be king of the castle. None of it came easily to me, though. I was hardly domestic when we married; I had to call his grandmother to learn how to boil water.

I hit rock bottom as a mother and wife when I began asking myself, *Is this all there is?* I know a lot of mothers who think that raising their kids and taking them to baseball, ballet, and church is enough to feel fulfilled. It wasn't enough for me, and I worried a lot about what I was going to do when my kids left home. That was the question that would lead me to open that fifth bottle of wine.

At the height of my alcoholism, now with a four-year-old son and a daughter who was eight, my marriage became very volatile. My husband and I were two Irish drunks. We broke a lot of dishes during this time. My pain and discomfort grew from a longing to be needed. I drank because I was crying out for purpose and relief from loneliness. But I didn't voice this properly, so I'd reach a certain point where any attention was better than no attention. I would push Mike to the point that he'd lose it verbally and emotionally—which wasn't the desired result, but at least it was a side of him that nobody else ever had. I brought that anger out in him. I created it. I invented it, and I'd push his buttons just to prove I had some kind of power over him, *over something*, because my life was otherwise out of control.

After one particularly bad fight with Mike, I decided to leave him. I called my mother, who loved coming to my rescue at times like these. She came riding in on her white horse and whisked me away to the La Jolla yacht and tennis club for five days. I sat in the bar and drank. My mom was the best at enabling my addiction, and I was grateful for her denial. She hired a nanny and a driver to take the kids to Sea World and anywhere else they'd want to go, and I'd power through Jose Cuervo at the bar.

The kids were freaking out, and I realized I needed to get my act together. When I went home after seven days, I decided to stop drinking—and this time, I meant it. I went four days without a drink, which in my mind meant I didn't have a problem. I decided that I would make *Mike* the problem, and that I couldn't live such a lonely, empty life anymore. I was going to get a divorce, go home to Kansas, and be treated in the manner to which I was once accustomed. I had no idea that drinking was the root of all my problems. I thought it was living in Los Angeles and being a mom, and not living up to what everyone else thought a rock 'n' roll wife should be. I was convinced that *everything* was someone else's fault.

My mom called a big-shot divorce attorney. When we went for a meeting, he asked, "Who's been drinking?"

My mom said, "Not I."

I said, "I haven't had a drink today. Yet." The attorney said, "If you want to get through this like a lady, I suggest you stop drinking."

I told him that I didn't drink that much, and that I only drank wine, but he didn't care. He was the first person ever to say anything to me about drinking. He said he'd do everything he could to help me out, but I had to get it together. It was a harsh reality check, but what he said was true, and I began to seek help. My husband had no idea I had visited an attorney and was contemplating a divorce.

All of this happened in the mid-1980s. Alcoholism as a disease wasn't talked about as openly as it is today. I reached out to the "Local 47," the musician's union in Los Angeles where Mike belonged, and they informed me that there was nothing they could do to help me. They told me to call my doctor. That gave me permission to drink for another six months, because there was no help. I was hopeless. My mother-in-law had become a member of Al-Anon (the twelve-step program for the families of alcoholics and addicts), and she was determined to keep her grandchildren safe. She gave me three months to get it together to get help to stop drinking, or she would take action to take my kids from me. One night, Mike came home from a session and I had drunk all the liquor in the house, including the cooking sherry. I proceeded to run to the park and hide, because I knew he would be angry that I'd left nothing for him. I promised God that if Mike didn't find me, I wouldn't take a drink again. I walked down to the house of a woman I knew and knocked on the door. We had a couple of drinks, which I told myself were going to be the last drinks I ever had.

When the sun started coming up I called the Betty Ford Clinic. The woman I spoke with said I needed to stop drinking first, and then I could show up with eight thousand dollars and be admitted. This seemed a little odd, since I clearly was going to need help in order to stop.

"I need to be admitted this very second," I said.

She said, "It doesn't work that way. You need to show your commitment first."

In May of 1986, I was desperate for a solution. I called a number I'd seen on television offering an aversion program, which meant there was spiritual guidance and they didn't use a twelve-step program to help people get sober. It was radical treatment. Attendants gave me injections until I projectile-vomited for hours, and then they told me that I would never drink again. They also gave me a cocktail every day made of fifty-eight ounces of alcohol mixed with lukewarm salt water. Along with that, they gave you fake cocaine, which was really baby laxative and gave you explosive bowels. At one point, the nurse made me sit in a small room for several hours with 267 open bottles of alcohol while I vomited and had diarrhea into a large tin bowl.

During the final three days of the ten-day program, I was given "truth serum" (sodium pentothal) to help me spill my deepest, darkest secrets. They wrote everything down and then shared it with me when I came to. Apparently, I'd told an elaborate story about how I'd robbed a grocery store while my kids had waited in the car, which I've never done in my life. Maybe I told that story so that I would seem bad enough for them to help me—I don't know. Looking back, I think I would have done anything to have someone pay attention to me, including lying under truth serum.

When I was released from that hellhole, I immediately began attending twelve-step meetings every day in Los Angeles. After thirteen weeks of my sobriety, my husband got sober, too. And being the overachiever that Mike is, he also lost sixty pounds and went to two meetings a day. I was still just finding my sea legs, but I realized that no matter what he did, it didn't mean I was less sober. With the kids still at home, I started hosting twelve-step meetings for recovering female alcoholics. We provided childcare, and at the end of the meeting we always had the kids join in the Serenity Prayer. It was an amazing group of women, and from those meetings came other opportunities to help people find sobriety. Before long I realized that I wasn't only good at helping others but I also loved it. I now understood the saying "I had to give back so freely, what had been given to me."

In 1990, my husband and I, along with David Crosby and Buddy Arnold and a few other musicians, began a support group called The Musicians Assistance Program (MAP). We wanted to help musicians get sober. Buddy would tell me about someone who needed help, and then I'd knock on each one's door and introduce myself. "Hi, I'm Candy," I'd say. "My husband's a musician, and I'm sober, and I'm here to help you." Of course I got elected to the job because the guys were out on the road. That's all it would take for the person who answered the door to burst into tears; nine times out of ten, they would confess how badly their life was falling apart. We'd wait until the musician came home, and then MAP would usher him/her into treatment. That's the simple version of how I started doing interventions.

I received formal training at UCLA, and by the mid-1990s, I was performing about fifty interventions a year. I was an aftercare provider for Betty Ford for ten years and trained at The Meadows Institute in Wickenberg, Arizona, to learn how to help people. I now have a vast amount of knowledge that I really honor. For instance, 85 percent of what makes an intervention successful is the surprise; you don't invite somebody to his or her own hanging and ask her to bring the rope. If an addict thought you were about to do an intervention, he might get higher than ever and die. The psychology behind the process is amazing.

One in twenty-five thousand people in the United States seek help for addicted love ones on a yearly basis. Most people don't have resources, money, or knowledge about what to do or how to do it effectively. My biggest challenge is to encourage both the loved ones and then the addict to really trust me. Addicts are so raw that they can identify authenticity right away. I've seen it happen over and over again. The hopeless alcoholics and addicts I work with don't care where I come from. They have no idea that I grew up rich in Kansas, or that I'm married to a musician and sent my kids to private school. I simply show up, walk into their homes, and say, "The only thing I am here to do is help. None of you have to live like this anymore. I represent hope."

I have learned how to be true to myself by being an interventionist, and I know that if I walk through a stranger's door, no matter what I am not going to fail. After an intervention is complete, everything has changed—there are no more secrets, no more whispers. Though I know my mom did her best, I am not the enabler she was. In fact, I'm entirely the opposite. I no longer crave the attention from others that I once did, because my husband and I are now a very active team that works hard every day toward a mutual goal. Sobriety. The best part is that while reaching the goal improves our relationship with each other and our children, it brings other couples and families together, too—and that much closer to healing open wounds. It's a perfect circle, and one I would have never drawn had I stayed in Kansas, sipping martinis in a pretty dress. And for that I am eternally grateful.

Note to Self

Vulnerability is a sign of strength,
not weakness. Help others,
help yourself.

LIFE'S CONSTANT COMPLEXITIES

Achieving Harmony

SHERYL CROW

Sheryl Crow is a nine-time Grammy Award–winning artist, an advocate for breast cancer research and environmental issues, and a loving mother to her son, Wyatt. She is also one hell of a horsewoman who enjoys a cold beer after a long ride. Her huge heart and limitless compassion cannot be underestimated.

Although the first album I recorded never saw the light of day, my first album to hit music stores knocked the wind out of my sails. I don't think I was prepared for what I was about to learn about human nature, the music business, and ultimately about myself. It's pretty amazing how a high point in your career can clash with a low point in your life. But maybe that's how we gain perspective.

I was brought up with the core belief that if you do the right thing and are a nice person, others will treat you the same. That said, being nice always came easily to me—almost to a fault. And throughout my life, I've always taken care of others' needs before my own. I think being the middle kid in a family of four helped define that part of my personality. My first album, and my relationship to the guys who worked on it with me, underscored this truism in a big way.

While my life hasn't been without challenges, breast cancer being the biggest, I've been very blessed. When I left my job as a schoolteacher in Missouri to move to L.A. to pursue music, I was as naïve as a person could be. However, I think it worked to my advantage—especially since the alternative was facing the truth about how hard it is to make it in the music business.

After years of singing backup, I was introduced to Bill Bottrell through a very dear musician friend. (Bill's a maverick music producer, who's worked with Madonna and Michael Jackson, who, coincidentally, was my first big gig as a backup singer.) At the time, he was looking to get back to his roots and produce music in a noncommercial way.

Bill was hanging out with a group of incredibly talented Los Angeles musicians who were very counterculture at the time, and really up on what was happening politically. The lot of them liked to hang out at Bill's studio in Pasadena. I was invited to come out and jam with them one Tuesday night. Because the first session was so fun and, actually, pretty fruitful, we decided to make a weekly happening out of it—thus the name Tuesday Night Music Club was born.

These sessions were extraordinary for me in that I suddenly found myself embraced by what felt like a community of real artists at a time when my career seemed to have been in the dumps following the shelving of my first record. All the guys had some success under their belts—and I, the new kid on the block and the only woman—was less naïve than before, but still very green.

The whole lot of us liked to hang out in local bars until the wee hours of the morning and conspiracy theorize about all sorts of things. This was 1993. Reaganomics, the JFK and MLK assassinations, and whether the government was covering up alien invasions in Roswell were all topics of lively and heated discussion. We shared the same admiration for our favorite writers, Jon Fante and Charles Bukowski, and we did our best to uncover the underbelly of L.A. they so beautifully depicted.

The group of guys and I shared a lot of similarities, but deep down we were vastly different. They were truly against the grain, wildly talented, somewhat bitter artists. I was just beginning my career and trying to make an album. They made it look "cool" to suffer for your art, and they had an "us against them" mentality. They acted as if the music industry, which had ironically made them successful, was the enemy and any commercial success equated with selling out. I found myself joining in. They'd had enough success to feel like they were being overlooked and misunderstood when things weren't going well.

The very first time I jammed with the TMC, we collaborated and wrote "Leaving Las Vegas." One of the guys, David Baerwald, pulled the title off the bookshelf at the back of the studio. The experience was lightning in a bottle, with a few tequilas being the chaser. We had maybe two or three more successful Tuesday nights together, but when Bill and I decided to continue on during the days making my solo record, the guys became very competitive.

Although the Tuesday night jam sessions came to an end, Bill and I continued to work in the studio on the album that would ultimately be called *Tuesday Night Music Club.* During the day, the guys would stop by to see if we needed a bass player or a guitar player. I was so intent on making everyone happy because they were my friends that I'd give away equal writer's credit to the guy playing the bass line or the drums. I've learned a lot about cowriting since then: there is a formula to writing that keeps everyone honest. At the time, however, my friendships were what I cared about.

Bill and I finished the record, and I put together a band I could afford. We hit the road. We drove a van that pulled a U-Haul full of equipment, we stayed in cheap motels, and we played really small gigs in bars and dives across the country. Slowly, by word of mouth, our audiences began to grow. The day we graduated from a U-Haul to a bus was cause for a huge celebration.

When "All I Wanna Do" became a single, the record became a hit. What seemed like overnight success to so many people felt like a lifetime of touring to me. We'd been sweating, humping equipment, and playing everywhere for at least a year before we picked up speed and finally had a fan base to back up our credibility when the album took off.

Once the song took off and we were enjoying some success, the guys who were with the Tuesday Night Music Club wanted in the band, but I felt a deep loyalty to the young guys who'd stuck it out with me. We weren't the best band, but once again my loyalty and caretaker instincts said not to hire the guys who didn't want to be in it from the start.

In my first interview with *Rolling Stone,* they published very little about all the writers from the TMC days. I went in-depth as to who they were to better explain the album's title and what amazing careers they'd had, but nobody wanted to hear about them because nobody knew who they were. Readers wanted to hear about the name on the record—mine—so I found myself between a rock and a hard place.

Suddenly, rumors flew that I was somehow taking everybody's music and becoming famous with it, when my first album was always supposed to have been my solo record. And the TMC guys started becoming mouthy to the press about me, which, I later learned, is how the negativity started.

I started to read everything that was written about me, which was a mistake. I was deeply hurt. I'd hear or read things like, "Hey, did she really write the record?" "A bunch of guys wrote and she took the credit." "Sheryl wasn't even there when they made it." All of this was incredibly hard to endure, because anyone who knows my work ethic is aware that I arrive early and pick up the coffee cups at the end of the night.

At this point, I felt I'd done everything right and yet had ended up on the bottom of the pile. I lost faith in those around me, but mostly I lost faith in myself. I started to believe to some degree that maybe the naysayers were right. What if I didn't have talent, and I couldn't do it on my own? In many ways, my first great success was the end of my innocence.

The experience really set me up to make my second album in the right spirit. When I went into the studio to record, I felt like nobody believed in me, so I had nothing to lose. I figured I'd make the record I wanted to make. I couldn't wait to get in, close the door, and purge myself.

Twenty-four hours after I shut the studio door, my producer

left. I called my manager. "I'm screwed," I told him. "What should I do?" "Do it yourself," he said. "You know what you're doing. You've always demoed your music well enough that it sounds like records." We hadn't okayed this change with the label, because we'd thought they would never let me, a woman, produce on my own. So feeling like I really had nothing else to lose, I just did it. My second album created a big opportunity for me and—I'd like to think—for other women to produce their music. When one door closed, another opened. Literally.

When I listen to the album today, I hear the scrappy, frustrated voice of a woman who thought her career was over and then proved that she was just beginning. It was a nice opportunity to turn a horribly negative experience into a positive, self-affirming one and learn to believe in myself again. The process toughened my skin, and it made me much more protective of my own talent. I'm no longer afraid to own it. I called that album *Sheryl Crow* for all the obvious reasons—it was my statement, for better or for worse. Happily, it was received for the better.

I always said that if my first record had sold ten thousand copies, I would have still been in good graces with those misunderstood artists. Instead, I became the "them" in the "us against them." It didn't feel great at the time, but in hindsight, I realize how much it prepared me for the future. The lessons that come with breaking free, in many ways, carry over in all areas of one's life. I'm not nearly as gullible, and I have a lot more savvy when it comes to running my business like a business. Ultimately, I can't make everybody happy.

The amazing and beautiful thing about life is that there will always be a time and a place to heal old wounds and practice forgiveness and compassion. I hold no grudges against anybody for anything, and my days are better lived that way. This reality was never more clear than when I had the amazing opportunity to reunite with my producer, Bill, fifteen years later on the album *Detours*. The title says it all. We laughed, we cried, we got to work, and we made some really inspired, kick-ass music.

Note to Self

When you try to please everyone,
you risk losing yourself
along the way.

Jerry Versus Carrie:
A Story About Something

JENNY BICKS

Jenny is a screenwriter and television producer. She's written
for several television series, most notably the four-time Emmy
Award–winning *Sex and the City*. Jenny also created and
executive-produced the ABC series *Men in Trees*. Her short
film, *Gnome,* which she also wrote and directed, appeared at
the Berlin Film Festival, Aspen Comedy Festival, and L.A. Film
Festival, among others.

In 1997 there was probably no job more sought after if you
were a sitcom writer than a job on *Seinfeld*. It was the pinnacle.
The golden ticket. Like getting to design Porsches after you
spent years toiling away in a matchbox factory. It was the last
season. The last chance to work on a piece of history! And I got
the job. Me. But like any good story, this one has a whole bunch
of twists and turns before you get to the end.

Let's back up.

When I was in second grade and my teacher asked, "What do you want to do when you grow up?" I told her, "I want to write"—and meant it. But more than *wanting* to be a writer, I *had* to be a writer. It was the thing that kept me sane. And I sucked at math.

I grew up in Manhattan, in a comfortable world of private schools and nuclear families (this was the early '70s—before people realized that divorce wasn't a dirty word). My parents—still together—raised four kids in a nice Upper East Side home. Opportunity was plentiful. But emotional openness was not. I was a very emotional kid. This led to a lot of overwrought poetry for a fourth-grader. I had a very rich, elaborate fantasy life. I created characters, worlds, and entire scenes that played out on the page. Most of all, I liked to make people laugh. Luckily, I went to an all-girls school, where no one told me women couldn't be funny. We all got to play boys in our stage shows. I got to play the grave digger in *Hamlet.* I used a great cockney accent (well, *I* thought it was great) and a limp. I bet Shakespeare was turning over in his own grave.

After graduating from Williams, a small liberal arts college, with an English lit degree, I came back to New York and worked in advertising for five years. I was an account executive, which is as far away from being a writer as one can be. It took me a long time to understand that I could actually make a living by writing. I thought when you grew up you had to carry a briefcase, like Darrin on *Bewitched.* It took me half a decade to realize I should at least be writing ads, rather than selling them. When that happened, I quit. I moved to Italy for a few months, ate a lot of pasta, flirted with Italians, and came back to New York without a job. It was freeing and scary. A friend of mine spotted an ad in the back of a trade magazine looking for writers of radio comedy. I had never done such a thing, but I did have an odd knack for writing song parodies, so I sent one in. I got the job. And thus began a year and a half of commuting to Bridgeport, Connecticut, to work with a bunch of DJs writing jokes. I loved it. Not the commuting part. But the getting-paid-to-write-comedy part.

I knew, though, that TV was where I wanted to be. I wanted to see my characters talk instead of just hear them on morning drive radio. But I knew no one in Hollywood. Well, except some guy who was a friend of my ex-boyfriend's. And I had never even met him. But I contacted him, sent him my *Seinfeld* spec (see! Even back in '92 I knew I wanted to write that show!), and somehow the fates were kind. He got me signed with his agent.

By 1993 I was working on my first sitcom in L.A. It starred Faye Dunaway and Robert Urich. You can guess how that went. But it got me to L.A., got me my first credit, and got me some really great stories I still tell at cocktail parties. Every year I worked on a pretty bad new sitcom that would invariably end after a season. Slowly, though, I moved up the food chain to better sitcoms that only lasted a season. Then I got on one that lasted three. I started to get a little more confident. Maybe I was good at this job. I worked in rooms full of men, usually as the only woman. At first they wouldn't know what to make of me (women aren't supposed to be funny in the real world, fyi), but after I got a few good jokes into the script they would accept me. I had a great time.

And I guess my work was paying off. While I was working on *The Naked Truth* with Téa Leoni (the three-season show), I got a call from my agent. A spec Larry Sanders script I had written had gotten the attention of someone at *Seinfeld.* They wanted to meet me. My head exploded. *Me?? The hottest show on TV wanted to meet me?? Do they know I worked on all those bad sitcoms??* So, back to the designing Porsches part of the story. This was 1997. *Seinfeld* didn't reflect the zeitgeist; it defined it. So if a writer, namely me, could get a credit like this, it would be more than a calling card. It would prove that I'd officially arrived. I could say the name of my show at parties and people would not just recognize it—they might perhaps even fawn a little. Old boyfriends would rue the day they broke up with me. My streets would be paved with gold. So I waited for the meeting. That never happened. Because Jerry was off on vacation in Europe. I had a phone call, but not with him—with some executives. Maybe I should have taken this as a bad sign. I didn't. I got the job. I was thrilled. I remember thinking, *Thank God, I've made it.*

I, like everyone else in America, loved *Seinfeld.* I thought it was the most brilliant twenty-seven minutes on TV. The show "about nothing" struck a chord with a pre-9/11 country in a thriving economy. There was no war to fight, no half-cocked president to figure out. Things were fairly carefree. That's one of the reasons I love television so much. It's truly a time capsule for the country, a microcosm of a bigger picture.

The word around town was that *Seinfeld* was a Harvard "boys club," stocked every year with guys fresh from Cambridge. I didn't care. I was used to the boy domination of comedy rooms at that point. Plus my dad had gone to Harvard, so that had to count for something. But right away, this job felt different. It was myself, one other woman, and these boys. Most had worked on the show for years. And there was no writer's room, that great bastion of comedy shows. There were just individual offices and a blank chalkboard staring at you every morning. It was intimidating, but I was too excited to care. I had a reputation for getting along with everybody, and I liked a challenge. Bring on the chalkboard and the boys. We would be in preproduction for the first two months I was there; this meant I didn't have to write a word—nobody did—for sixty days. There was no basis for criticism yet. We were gearing up for the season. It would be a dream come true.

Yeah. Here's where the story takes that dark turn.

So I start to hear the whispers: "Jerry had to hire a girl." Apparently the studio had told him he had to hire a female. I was a token. A token he hadn't even met before hiring. He'd liked my script, I guess. But maybe they had put a Harvard boy's name on it for it to go down easier.

And then I finally met Jerry in the cereal room. (Seriously, a room stocked with twenty brands of cereal. You were expected to eat it—mixed in various combinations—every morning. Forget the writing, the cereal room was its own form of intimidation.) I remember kind of leaving my body when I met him. *This is friggin Jerry Seinfeld standing in front of me! JERRY SEINFELD!!* He seemed nice and smart. And then he told me a story about how he had gone out the night before for dinner with a friend, who had gotten up to use the bathroom. A girl he didn't know had slipped into his friend's chair at the table just to sit with

Jerry. I thought that was creepy and, frankly, pretty ballsy of the girl. I asked him if he had told her to get lost. He looked at me and said, "You can't do that! Women are *craazzzyy*." Hmm. I laughed. "Well, not *all* women are crazy. . . ." And he just stared at me. I guess you aren't supposed to question Jerry about his POV on women. I guess I should have just shut up and agreed with him. Yes, all women *are* nut jobs. But I didn't. And that was pretty much the beginning of the end.

A few weeks later, Jerry called me into the conference room. I thought he might compliment me on my chalkboard, which was filling up with some fun ideas. Instead, he fired me. But it felt more like a breakup. "It's not working out between us," he told me. "You'll be financially taken care of"—as if he wanted a divorce and had his attorney on line one. I was confused. I told him he hadn't even read one word of my writing yet. The writing he had hired me for. But it didn't matter. It was over between me and Jerry before it had even begun.

I'd been blindsided. I was humiliated. I thought, *If Jerry Seinfeld fires me, my career is over—and then what will I do?*

I refused to cry in front of him. That was important to me, because I didn't want to give him the power of having made me cry. It helped that I was in shock. *Jerry Seinfeld just fired me? Where are the show runners? The show runners are the ones who do the firing . . . did my agent know about this?* (This is one nice thing about paying people to handle your career—usually they are the ones who hear about you getting fired long before you do. So at least you end up hearing the news from someone whose job it is to make you feel better.) When I told my agent how everything went down, she said, "What? What are you talking about?" I remember thinking I was going to throw up into the trash can in my quiet little office with my chalkboard. I didn't. I hadn't thrown up since tenth grade. Jerry Seinfeld might have cost me my job, but he wasn't going to make me lose my cookies. All I kept thinking was, *Oh, my God. I am going to have to call everyone I know and tell them I was just fired from the most popular show on television. My career is over.*

I went home and cried. And might have gotten drunk. And called some friends who said the appropriately unprintable things about Jerry. I love my friends.

Two weeks later, I received a call from Michael Patrick King, a writer I had worked with on a CBS sitcom in 1995 called *The Five Mrs. Buchanans* (one of those one-season wonders). I loved Michael. He was funny and smart and laughed at Hollywood. "Darren Star [of *Melrose Place*] and I are working on this new show for HBO, but it's not on the air yet," he explained. "I want you to write a script for it." He was talking about *Sex and the City*. It was dirty and funny and real and about single women like me in their thirties. Did I want to write a script for it? Hell, I wanted to roll myself up in it and live there forever. It gave me the perfect opportunity to showcase who I was as a person and the kind of material I wrote best. Of course you see the irony here—had I stayed with *Seinfeld*, I would never have been able to take advantage of Michael's offer.

HBO shoots its episodes so far in advance of airing that I wrote episode eight of the first season, and it didn't even air until after we were long finished writing the first twelve. So even as the debut season aired, we had no idea if it would last eight episodes. Looking back, it wouldn't have mattered to me

if nobody had watched and it hadn't become such a great success. The writers who worked on the show were this wonderful
lot of wounded individuals, all having faced and triumphed over
rejection; this made us able to write so openly, which is why the
show resonated, I think, with so many people. We also loved
what we were writing, and we loved working together—and I
think all of that came through. It's what made it possible to have
an impact on so many viewers, and it certainly had an impact on
me. I was able to return to the reason I wanted to write in the
first place.

The key to a great work environment, especially as a writer,
is collaborating with people who understand you, who get you,
and thus get your writing. That's what I'd been looking for since
I'd penned those maudlin poems in fourth grade—and I found
it twenty-something years later. I was finally writing with my
own voice and not for somebody else's. The funny thing is that
Sex and the City turned out to be the *Seinfeld* of its time. The difference is that I ran to *Seinfeld* because it was so prestigious; I
was drawn to *Sex and the City*, however, because it was so me. I
would never have appreciated one experience so much without
the other.

So apparently that saying about a window opening when a
door shuts may actually be true. Who knew? Maybe Jerry did,
though I doubt it. He seemed pretty pessimistic to me. But in
the end, I guess I have to thank him. I found the best work of my
career, the best friends of my career, and the couple Golden
Globes and Emmys don't hurt either—all because Jerry Seinfeld
fired me.

Thanks, Jerry.

Note to Self

Be true to your voice,
and always demand to be heard.

The Day I Stopped Being Professional

ANDREA SEIGEL

Andrea Seigel is the author of the novels *Like the Red Panda* and *To Feel Stuff*. She lives in the servants' quarters of a famous dead author's mansion in Altadena, California.

As I was about to graduate from college, I began to get emotional phone calls from my mom, all focused on a consistent theme. "You don't have a suit!" she'd cry in the tone of voice someone might use if the ozone layer had disappeared completely and her child was about to step outside without protective gear. "You need a suit!"

I couldn't imagine myself in one. The closest I'd come to slacks was a pair of tailored vinyl pants, which had finally split that recent winter when freezing air had shocked them as I'd left a heated building. They'd responded like glass, cracking straight down the ass.

Upon my return to Southern California, my mom practically

took me straight to the mall from the plane. "They're having a sale, and there will be suits!" she exclaimed, her delivery alarmingly evangelical for a Jew.

"I bet I could get away with a top and pants if the top's really nice," I mulled. "And the shoes have closed toes."

"Andrea," she said as if I had not just come out of an Ivy League school with a near-perfect GPA but was instead the just-discovered little sister of Jodie Foster's forest-dwelling character in *Nell.* "You need to look professional."

I don't bring up the Ivy League and the near-perfect GPA to sing my own body electric. They were both logical extensions of a religion I'd followed since even before I understood the concept of God, that religion being the game you played to succeed in life. While still in school, doctrines of that game had included: exceptional—not good—grades, essays written with great care at least three days before they were due, and some low-grade professor-asshole kissing.

This ass kissing was never performed outright. Instead I paid close attention to how each of my instructors believed the world should run. I became particularly attuned to individual font preferences. The first day of class I'd examine handouts and syllabi, noting whether the professor leaned toward Courier, Helvetica, Arial, etc. Then I'd execute all my papers using the favored typeface, which reflected the subconscious impression of authority back at authority. This was the academic version of what psychologists refer to as mirroring.

When I came home from Macy's with an interview suit that day, my mom was certainly happy, but she wasn't responsible.

The suit was only a finishing touch. I'd had a professional life since kindergarten, which is where my memory of the game begins.

I wore the suit. I got my first real job. If you're curious what the suit looked like, while in it I felt convinced no guy would ever want to sleep with me again. And that's all you need to know.

Two years later I became a professional writer. One of the first items of business upon selling my first novel was donating the suit to Goodwill. Working from either my bed or an armchair, I adopted a uniform of booty shorts and halter tops knotted under my boobs.

Still, I was inescapably bound to an updated set of my doctrines. I turned in projects at least two weeks before their due dates, this being less a result of inspiration than discipline. If a contact asked me to call her at four o'clock in the office, I dialed at 3:59 and fifty seconds. I never lost patience with artistic compromises. I never threw the kinds of tantrums creative people are supposedly entitled to. I never stopped thinking of it all as a game that I had a mortal obligation to play well. Far beyond courtesy or OCD, these were calculated decisions, intended to keep myself gliding up and up and up toward heaven on earth, which looked a lot like a Ralph Lauren interior when I bothered to picture it.

I giddily told my best friend Geoff, "I'm a machine!"

A production company hired me to adapt my first novel for film. The original was the piece of writing that had brought me the closest I'd ever come to explaining myself. In the book, the protagonist becomes so immune to the charms of

the game that she sees no other option than planning her
suicide.

What followed the signing of the deal was a year of development hell, which I described in my first attempt at writing this
essay. In addition to laying out precisely, detail by detail, all the
hurdles the production company set up for me, and the professionalism with which I either straddled or jumped them, the
essay also included a description of the suit my mom bought
me. The earlier version was driven by that old impulse to cover
my ass, so I had to go back and delete three pages.

In the version that now stands, I decided just to skip to the
outcome, which will maybe seem unwarranted without that
rigor. But whether I've properly grounded my actions has become, since last December, irrelevant to what I did.

Last December, the situation with the production company
got so dispiriting that I walked away from the final payment on
the contract. The parting was handled very professionally, with
my agent communicating my regret from the distance of New
York. The production executives went silent after I gave up the
money. It was all very civil.

Soon after, a small but thick envelope arrived in my mailbox. Opening it on the walk back to the door, I found a note
written on brown card stock. The production company's name
was stamped in red capital letters across the top; over the name,
a splashy "2007" was printed in purple glitter.

Handwritten, the note read:

> *Dear Andrea,*
> > *happy holidays.*
> > *thanks for all your hard work.*

All the best,
Bob + Joe.

What made the envelope so thick? A square white box hold-ing the bullshit kind of chocolate bar you find only in Whole Foods. The brand was called Vere. A chocolate-colored circle on the front of the box boasted, "chocolate with benefits. 75% CACAO. Low Sugar · Gluten Free · Rainforest Chocolate Single Origin." In perhaps the classiest touch, a graphic spatter of liq-uid chocolate swung across the white background, making like a Marimekko print.

I walked upstairs and unearthed a Ralph's paper bag in the gap behind my fridge, comparing its shade of brown to the card stock. They were a close match. I traced the size of the produc-tion company's note onto the underside of the bag, then cut it out.

From my craft cabinet I pulled out my box of Prisma Pencils, locating a red that matched the red of the production company's name. I wrote "ANDREA" in a nearly identical font across the top of my paper. Happily, I already had a purple glitter glue pen in my possession, so I squirted a jaunty "2007" across my N, D, and R.

Tracking down a Rollerball in my junk drawer with the same line thickness as the one on the model, I wrote, doing my best to match penmanship:

> *Dear Bob + Joe,*
>   *fuck you*
>   *All the best,*
>   *Andrea*

Then I blew on the paper for a few minutes to speed the drying of the glitter glue.

I got in my car and drove over to my nearest Ralph's (I'm a loyal customer), where I bought an original Hershey's bar, 100% no-bullshit chocolate. When I returned to the car, the glitter glue was sufficiently hard, so I drove to the post office to weigh the contents of my envelope.

After affixing the appropriate postage to the envelope, I dropped it in the nearest mailbox without a second thought. There were no belated qualms, no twinges of self-doubt. The only feeling I had on the drive home was that of a job well done.

That night, while running through my day during a phone call with my mom, I told her, "I made some pancakes for breakfast, and I finally got the blueberry-to-batter ratio right. Went running at the gym. Lots of email. Huge nap. And I sent a candy bar and a card that said 'fuck you' to the people who optioned my book and ran the project into the ground. All around, I feel like I was fantastically productive."

"Andrea," she said in the same way she'd probably say my name had I just copped to arson. "What are you doing burning bridges?!? That's so unprofessional!"

But she was wrong. I'd done an incredibly professional job on the card's lettering, using a ruler to keep the letters straight. A painstaking job on the red shading. I'd applied the glitter glue with the lightest, most deft touch. The Hershey bar had been a thoughtful reference to the Vere box, the colors on its wrapper a near perfect inversion. The end product had been a skilled piece of work, created with the same meticulousness I applied to everything else that bore my name. I was proud of it.

If civilization is pretty much the construct that keeps us animals from flinging feces at one another—and it needs to be, because we can't walk around with feces in our hair (or rather, we can't *all* the time)—then professionalism was the veneer that had kept me from flinging shit in the face of school, employment, and a checking account: all the bastions that combine to form the temple of "making a living."

It took sending that card to realize that by eschewing professionalism I could only hurt myself, and when I balanced that damage against that which had been done to my "hard work," so casually mentioned in the company's note, I came out even. Starting from zero was someplace I probably hadn't professionally been since preschool, and if my shit got flung back at me, that really wouldn't be so bad, because, hey, at least it was mine.

And it wasn't that sending the card launched me into an attitude of total abandon, a Matthew McConaugheyish existence where shirtlessness *is* a suit. I still believed and believe that that game has a certain romance to it. I still beat deadlines, and I still carry out even the littlest task with the utmost care. The difference is that now I'm fully aware that there are some bridges that connect me to places I don't even want to go.

So what was the fallout of the envelope? There was none. The production company executives never said a word about the card to me, my agent, or anyone else, as far as I know—meaning that even in the very end, they remained consummate professionals. And also, gigantic pussies.

Note to Self

Along with the suit,
sometimes the gloves
have to come off, too.

Life of Pie

KATHY NAJIMY

Kathy Najimy (*Ms.* magazine Woman of the Year) is a writer, director, and actress who has been published in several books and has starred in more than twenty films, in two long-running TV shows, and on Broadway. She is most known for her original feminist comedy *The Kathy and Mo Show* as well as *Sister Act, King of the Hill, Veronica's Closet, Numb3rs, Hocus Pocus, Ratrace,* and, on Broadway, *Dirty Blonde.* She has won more than $300,000 on game shows for her favorite charities. She lives in L.A. with her husband of thirteen years and their glorious daughter.

As a lower-middle-class, not thin, frizzy-haired Lebanese girl, I stood out among a sea of bronze-bodied, beach-volleyball-playing blondes in my hometown of San Diego when I was growing up. I don't mean that in an *Afterschool Special,* syrupy sad kind of way. I had lots of friends and lots of fun, but I wasn't like the other girls. I never wore the coolest clothes, and I was clueless when it came to boys. I was always thought of as "fun cousin Kathy," who'd tag along to events for comic relief—or, in some cases, play babysitter to my wilder cousins. I was not the girl who would go to the beach in a bikini and get asked out by a boy. I was the girl who would go to the beach *with* you, in order for you to get permission to go to the beach with boys.

I had one particular cousin who literally couldn't go out of the house unless I was with her. She had a thing for boys who were older and of a different race—and color (she *loooved* black boys). Her mother didn't know about any of the specifics, but in order to get permission to leave the house she would drag me along, and I would sit in the car and wait until she was done fooling around with whomever she fancied at the time.

Because I wasn't a key player in the boy-girl game (I tried and failed miserably at it), I observed everything. I noticed how girls moved through the world. I watched them see themselves through the eyes of a cute boy, teacher, or media images and sensed the changes they made in themselves. I was fascinated by the adjustments they made to fit in. I noticed how girls were treated, how they acted, and what they thought of themselves.

At a young age, while I didn't have the faintest idea of how to get a boyfriend or wear a thong bikini, I did have a keen sense of what didn't seem fair, what felt right and wrong. I watched my mom—who spoke five languages and had graduated early from college—swallow her voice to marry young and have four kids. (It was her only option, really. The Lebanese culture is beauti-ful, rich, and loving, but it can also be very sexist by tradition.) I saw her stay in an unhappy marriage because she didn't have the resources and opportunities to earn her own living. I was not bothered by Mom's choice to be a stay-at-home mom but rather by her lack of choices in general. I watched the women in the family cook and clean while the men went out to smoke cigars. Outside of my home, I watched the difference in the ways boys at school were *encouraged* to be and girls were *allowed* to be. Roles were dictated to women, while allowances and opportunities were offered to men. Consequently, I developed a very low tolerance for injustice of any kind.

I always knew I was different, but nothing underscored this more than the day I went to the House of Pies with my cousins.

I was fourteen and in the prime of awkward adolescence. As I mentioned, I hung out a lot with my cousins; it was fun having me around, and I really loved being with them. We were a very tight group, but we looked and acted nothing alike. I was heavier than they were. I had the frizzy hair (they ironed theirs—no, literally . . . IRONED!), and I didn't have the right clothes. They shopped at the then hip Lerner's or Hartfield's. I shopped at what our budget would allow . . . Kmart. They all knew how to bleach and wax. I didn't know the first thing about hair removal.

One too sunny California day, we were sitting in the House of Pies, a chain restaurant akin to Denny's (but with a lot more meringue). Although I really dug my aunt (she was fun and spontaneous and taught us all how to belly dance), she was, well, VERY *into* her girls and quite competitive about their achievements. In my house, she was known as "Aunt Bragger." That day, my aunt decided to go around the table and ask each of us what we wanted to be when we grew up. Her youngest, who was twelve years old, said she wanted to be a cheerleader. Her middle daughter hoped to become a stewardess (it was the '70s, so "flight attendant" wasn't even a term yet), and the oldest wanted to be a model. And then my aunt finally turned to me and she said, "Kathy, what do you want to be when you grow up?" And I said, "I want to be an actress." There was a very long pause, then they all almost choked, did a double spit take, dropped the German chocolate pie out of their mouths, and rolled their eyes . . . suppressing laughter.

My aunt and her daughters didn't react this way to be mean. They loved me. Remember, I was the fun cousin, and their ticket to Boyfriend Land! In their world, there were just a couple of ways you *had* to be if you were going to be an actress, and it certainly wasn't a poor Lebanese fat girl with frizzy hair from San Diego with no training, no money, and no connections. I remember having this very internal dialogue with my very young fourteen-year-old self and then . . . I just smiled.

It was from that moment that I knew my destiny. I *had* to be an actress. To this day, I'm still not sure if it was because I had a burning, insatiable desire to create and act or to prove them wrong. Or to prove myself wrong or right. Or maybe it was an unconscious response to the world's expectations of us based on our bodies—on how we look. Maybe it was a combination of all of that . . . or maybe it was the sugar high I had from the banana cream. Who knows.

I knew from my experience as an astute outsider that it would be a tricky journey to the top. Wanting to be an actress and actually being an actress are two very different realities, but with some grueling hard work, a surprisingly unwarranted dollop of self-confidence, and a lot of denial about reality . . .

I became a working actress.

I am grateful to say that I've never taken a role described as "fat." I think of myself as having a different kind of beauty: the difference between key lime and coconut cream, maybe. In my career, I have never chosen to take the part of a pitiful fat girl, a part where a large-size person is downtrodden and a victim, or even more damaging, a part where the girl is dying to be skinny—and in the third act gets a makeover, loses weight, and is magically happy. It does not interest me. That's been done, and I wasn't put on the earth for that. I was put here to dance and have a fantastic husband, to wear tight, low-cut dresses on the cover of magazines, to work, write, perform, give speeches, and try to be a good mother.

Yes, I know that the worst thing you can be as a woman in our society is fat. I used to joke that there was a giant scale at the border of Los Angeles that women were required to get on before they entered the city. If you were ten pounds overweight, you got a citation. If you were fifteen pounds over—charged with a misdemeanor. Thirty pounds overweight—well, they would just shoot you.

So if I had a magic wand that would make me into a comfortable size 6? Shit yeah, I'd wave it. Without a doubt. But until that wand comes, I try to make what I am and what I have work.

I would have loved to have known earlier in my life that it's possible to achieve so much, despite such a limiting and yet far-reaching POV—especially in the TV and movie business. We say to girls, "The thinner you are, the more valid and valuable you are." Instead, we should be saying, "The happier and healthier you are, the more valuable you are, at the size you are."

Against all odds, here's what I've learned to be true:

1. Most of the women I know spend a good part of their thought processes and energy on how they look. That leaves little time to think about the world and how to change it. We spend so much time walking on broken glass, trying to figure out how we can be acceptable and DIFFERENT from who we are, that we risk letting our lives pass us by.

2. No matter what size we are, the media still insist we are not "right." On the same cover of *People* magazine, editors chided Mary Kate Olsen for being too skinny and Kirstie Alley for being too fat. No matter what we are—it's just not right. We are just never, ever how *they* think we are "supposed" to be. And we waste the real purpose of our lives trying.

So what do I do? I try to bypass the brainwashing by embracing the power of positive thinking, *MY* thoughts, and what *I* believe in *my*self. It's none of my business what others think of me. I'll never walk into a room wearing boxy, oversized clothes that scream "SHAME" or sit on the couch with a pillow over my stomach. Instead, I walk into a room with the knowledge that I deserve to be there—and I do. And others respond in kind. I've always tried to move through the world with a fair amount of confidence and grace. I'm not saying it's easy. I doubt myself—a lot. Many, many things have happened in this long quest to be what I was meant to be, and though I try not to dwell on definitive dates and times, I believe it started with my cousins at the House of Pies. On that day, I realized that in order for me to be successful at anything, who I *was* needed to surpass how I *looked*. And what became valuable to other people was no longer how I looked but who I was. Through my creative and political work and family, I've found a way to offer myself to others in a way that feels authentic.

Alas, I never did become a model, a cheerleader, or a stewardess. But I still love me some German chocolate cheesecake.

Note to Self

You can only command an audience when you know your self-worth.

In Treatment

KATHLEEN DENNEHY

Kathleen Dennehy is the author of *Adventures in Poverty.* She has published self-deprecating stories in *Fresh Yarn,* the online salon for personal essays, written *Princess Tale* cartoons for Disney, cowritten salacious specials on celebrity scandal for the E! Channel, and writes screenplays when no one is looking. Kathleen also runs Tuesdays @ 9 LA, a writers-in-process series, and is a proud mentor to teen playwright Anna Geare, who just won the Rubicon Festival Young Playwright award.

My therapist didn't go crazy overnight. I'd like to think it was a slow and steady process, a mental crumbling that occurred over seven years of weekly sessions. In my version of events, she lost her own personal movie plot incrementally, in almost imperceptible movements. Because if she was certifiable from the beginning, well, I don't really want to know what that says about me.

I am a distinct blend of Irish Catholic/German Jew, which

means my youth was spent volleying between shame and guilt. For twelve years, Catholic school nuns trained me to obey, fear, and spell. Yet trust and personal boundaries were life lessons neither the Josephite nuns nor my family managed to teach. (They managed to skip over balancing checkbooks, too.) This perfect storm of obedience, shame, guilt, and fear taught me to trust too easily, fully, and deeply—and to establish boundaries as easy to invade as the Falklands. I grew up unable to say no to telemarketers, Jehovah's Witnesses, or men who were wrong for me. Physically incapable of saying, "I don't see this relationship going anywhere," I would move in with the guy, knowing that sharing an East Village cold-water flat with a virtual stranger that I barely liked would quickly hasten the relationship's demise. I was so afraid of confrontation that I would lug a futon up four flights of stairs to cohabit with someone I just didn't have the guts not to date. Lest one think I am exaggerating for comic effect, I have lived with seven men. Seven.

By my late twenties, I professionally aspired to misery. I thought part of my job description, as a poor and frustrated artist, was to tend and nurture the neat rows of my flowering depression. I had never been in therapy but was heartily encouraged by teachers and friends to give it a try. I eventually stopped becoming insulted by this and assumed they saw something I didn't. A comparatively well-adjusted friend from the New York theater world urgently recommended I see her therapist, Paula Brown, MA, MFT, who specialized in "creative types." This isn't her real name, but it's real-name adjacent. After months of putting off my friend's pressure to the point where I almost decided it would be easier to date or move in with her, I caved and made my first appointment with the therapist.

I was nervous about our first session and had no idea what to wear. I was afraid that my new shrink would take one look at my outfit and declare me criminally insane. Finally, I settled on a look that said I was playfully neurotic and creative if a tad uncomfortable with my hips and thighs. I arrived late, which only made me more panicky, and her fancy office, in a tall tower overlooking Central Park, decorated with framed diplomas bearing various capital letters trailing her name, intimidated me into sullen silence. I refused the couch and sank into the chair opposite her instead. After a dull pause, I churlishly asked if I was supposed to just start talking. When she snapped back that she would talk, too, I instantly relaxed. Snottiness I could deal with. I'd imagined therapy would be like talking to my mother, except my therapist would kick me out after fifty minutes instead of begging me to move back home. I instantly loved my shiny new therapist because she was reasonably priced and let me smoke. I now realize that when a handy ashtray and twenty-five-dollar sessions are one's reasons for choosing a mental health practitioner, one's issues might be a bit deeper than initially expected.

Paula Brown, MA, MFT, was an aging Jewish hippie. Stacks of books filled her office, books that looked like she'd actually read them. Paula smoked expensive English cigarettes, which I interpreted as Continental and discerning. She was funny, quoted her obscure books, swore like a sailor, and spoke passionately until foamy moisture collected in the corners of her mouth—all of which I found deeply reassuring. She was like the older roommate you share a one-bedroom apartment with in the West Village who teaches you how to sound great in a drunken bar conversation. After my first session, where we laughed and smoked and I cried and learned that my childhood had been treacherous and Dickensian, I was hooked on therapy and rewarded with a regular time slot, which nothing—not even waitress shifts, real job interviews, or total poverty—could interfere with.

Thanks to Paula's unbridled attention, my trust issues pulsed like new muscles. I was like an addict, and blind faith was my drug of choice. I believe therapy is one of the best methods of seducing those of us who trust others too easily. Therapy, followed by cults, followed by multilevel marketing ploys, thrives in no small part due to over-trusters. And how can one not over-trust a woman with a master's degree and five beautifully fonted letters after her name?

Paula encouraged me to clean out the cobwebs of the rarely visited attic of my chaotic childhood. She defended me to myself in ways that I could never do on my own. Nobody had ever advocated me to myself, and I really needed to be convinced that the way my life was turning out wasn't even remotely my fault. It wasn't my fault I had no employable skills. It wasn't my fault I kept dating cruel, cold men who gave me presents that required a course of antibiotics to get rid of. It wasn't my fault I couldn't wake up in the morning or walk down the streets without sobbing. Paula took away all my self-blame and convinced me that my parents and conveniently deceased grandparents were the reason I had relationship and financial problems. I was only too happy to pay her to keep telling me this.

Since I can't keep anything to myself, soon all my poor artist friends were going to Paula, too. We all loved her cheap prices, funky clothes, and how her poodle snoozed in our laps as we performed our fifty-minute monologues about how unfair life was. Paula would laugh and clap, encouraging us to rag on our nemeses as expensive English smoke curled in her hair. Analysis? Self-examination? That was for crazy people. I didn't know that this wasn't actual therapy—mostly because I felt so good and cocky afterwards. I trusted her because she reflected back at me what nobody else was seeing. In front of Paula I was brave, I yelled back at the people who really had a thing or two coming, and I reveled in my pretty victim-hood tears. It was only many years later, when I had to undergo real therapy to recover from Paula's therapy, that I learned I had no idea how real therapy worked. Only then did I realize that Paula had had no vested interest in helping me better myself. Since I hadn't known any better myself, I'd settled for a very entertaining form of enabling.

One day I realized I was twenty-nine years old and single. Since puberty I'd been primped and pimped for matrimony by my resourceful mother; now I was convinced that if I didn't find a man, stat, I'd be a barren spinster forever. So I met the man who I decided would become my husband. My pliable intended had parental and financial baggage that matched mine, so we fell in love in a week and he moved in after a month. After four months, we were engaged, with a twenty-dollar fake pearl ring sealing the deal. When he popped the question on Valentine's Day in a crowded restaurant, I could feel my mother's sigh of relief from deep within my psyche.

About a month into our engagement, it became clear that my fiancé needed therapy, too. Not because of the insane velocity of our courtship—no, I never questioned *that*—but because of his sudden fits of rage, not to mention the occasional flying hairbrush, aimed toward me. He had never sought psychiatric help, so I dragged him kicking and screaming to Paula Brown, MA, MFT.

To her initial credit, Paula said she couldn't ethically council us as a couple and continue seeing me and/or him as a private therapist. It was a legal or ethical breach of something, but in my furtive, denial-laden mind, I wondered who else could help me, help him, and help us remain a couple. Friends who'd had more "conventional" therapy warned me about Paula's unorthodox treatment and procedures, but I couldn't be deterred in my quest for colossal unawareness. So Paula suggested what seemed like a healthy compromise: she'd see him until she determined the best therapist to whom she could refer him. It wasn't long before my fiancé also loved her poodle, pandering, and prices.

To someone like myself, who was ignorant of personal and professional boundaries, a therapist who gossiped about other patients—patients who were not only my friends but also friends I'd brought to her as clients—didn't seem at all unethical. In fact, it made me feel better about my own shortcomings to know that Mindy couldn't orgasm even through masturbation, that Rebecca was twenty-five thousand dollars in debt, and that Will slept on the couch because his wife couldn't stand the sound of him breathing while she was trying to sleep. In the meantime, Paula never found another suitable therapist for my husband,

and I couldn't find any reason to object to her seeing him. Plus, he'd already drunk the Paula Kool-Aid and was now a devotee of the highest order. Maybe she'd talk nicely about me to him, and actually get him to stop throwing things at me.

Saddled with a hasty marriage, a flailing career, and money woes, I failed to notice that Paula's stacks of books had grown to a precarious height; that her therapy poodle had grown matted fur and developed a horrible smell; and that the jackalope-size dust bunnies in the corner of her office were stuck to piles of dog poop. I ignored the troubling knot in my stomach as I dutifully made my way to her office every Thursday morning. Even when I learned from my husband during a fight that Paula was telling him deep secrets I'd confided in her about our troubled marriage, I kept seeing her. I'd placed too much trust in Paula to stop believing she could help me. I saw what I chose to see and was only troubled by what I chose to find troubling.

A year or so into my crumbling marriage and two years into my bizarre "analysis," I realized Paula was chain-smoking her Dunhills rather oddly; she had decided that the first five drags were the safest parts of the cigarette. So, after five puffs, she'd stab her cigarette out and light the next one. We'd developed a routine in which I'd buy her two packs so she wouldn't have to leave her office in the middle of a session, and she'd deduct the cigarette cost from my fee. Paula's office space had a small sitting area, a bathroom, her office, and another door in between; this last door always remained closed. One day I used her bathroom, and as I lowered my pants, I watched a plume of cigarette smoke trail upward, behind the shower curtain. I figured Paula had left a cigarette burning in the tub. Still seated, pants undone, I pulled the curtain back with the intention of putting out the cigarette. I found her husband standing behind the curtain smoking, amid a tub full of pots and pans. He calmly explained that it was too cold to smoke outside—as if he didn't have anyplace else to go, like a home. I nodded politely, and because I didn't want *him* to feel uncomfortable, I crossed my hands in my lap and pretended I hadn't been trying to urinate but had just been sitting there, as if we'd been awkward acquaintances at a cocktail party. Her husband finished his cigarette and left the room, and I tried to quiet the alarm bells in my mind and stop my hands from shaking.

After the bathroom incident, I began to allow myself to see Paula's psychiatric and environmental decay. I believe that there is often a pinnacle moment in a child's life when she realizes her parents might not have always had her best interest at heart. It could be the first time she sees a parent drunk, or having sex with or flirting with a neighbor; but every person experiences that first rift in which they realize that grown-ups don't always know what they're doing. I was a late bloomer, and this realization came at the hands of my therapist.

I became obsessed with the closed door in her office. During my sessions I'd smoke and blather on with Paula, all the while plotting how to find out what lurked behind it. As if she'd read my mind, one day I showed up for my appointment to find that a note had been taped to the door, ordering that it never be opened. That was it. The door officially became the lid to my Pandora's box. I knew nothing good would come of it, but I had to open it: I was convinced it would lead to the information I needed to make a decision about my life.

One day, as I tried not to listen to Paula cackle with another patient behind her cracked and peeling office door, I tiptoed over and opened the forbidden door. Inside was an active volcano, ten feet high and twenty feet wide, of shoes, books, clothes, pots, newspapers, sheets, lamps, files, and underwear. It touched the ceiling. The mound echoed the obsessive towers Richard Dreyfuss built in *Close Encounters of the Third Kind*— sure, his Devil's Tower replica was made of mashed potatoes and chicken wire, but he knew in his heart that "this means something." Similarly, I knew Paula's tower meant something too, as I was hit with the sickening realization that something was not right.

And yet I kept seeing Paula. Even given what I'd found, which I kept private from her, I still hadn't developed the ability to protect myself—even after most of her other patients had given up on her. Somehow, *their* "therapy" had worked, since these people had been able to walk away from her as soon as they'd become aware of her insanity. My husband and I remained strangely loyal to her and were even determined to help her, even if she was unable to help us. Though the discovery of Paula's volcano made me less convinced of her abilities, my husband was still a believer. This led to fights over my lack of faith in Paula, which were actually a nice change from our usual fights about money and our marriage.

Paula began calling us at home at all hours to see if we had any pain medication she could borrow or, when she was evicted, time to help her move out of her apartment—and then out of her office, when she was forced to leave there, too. We listened to her spittle-riddled tirades about her family, her landlords, and her narcoleptic husband. Suddenly, the patient became the therapist, and we were about as helpful to her as she'd been to us—which is to say, not at all.

Without a home or office, Paula now lived in a storage unit. She treated patients there, and they'd bring her groceries. Because I was still a firm believer in loyalty over pain and suffering, I refused to leave my marriage or my therapist—so they both left me. My marriage finally croaked when Paula told my husband, "If Kathleen was on a plane, and she knew it was going to crash, she'd still board the plane and not tell anyone." My husband believed her, and I did, too. She might have been deranged, but she was right, because she was the crashing plane, and I was still securely fastened into my seat. And when I heard that my husband met someone the day after he left me, and that Paula told my friends who were also her patients that I owed her thousands of dollars in back fees, my groundless magical faith in fancy cigarettes and capital letters trailing Paula's name finally evaporated.

I moved from New York to Los Angeles, where I avoided men and therapy like the plague of locusts I'd allowed them to become. My new life was mine to rebuild from the ground up. It was very crunchy and healing in Laurel Canyon, where I was surrounded by trees and dogs and other people's money—until the throes of grief over my divorce finally kicked in and overwhelmed me. I found a new therapist, a lovely Englishwoman whose office was clean, bright, and smoke free. There was no extra room full of secrets, no feces, no narcoleptic husband. Just Anne Klein separates, unscented candles, and Abyssinian cats chosen for their inability to shed.

By this point my biggest issue was that the young woman who'd trusted far too much was now the older woman who trusted no one, especially herself. It took me years to open up and divulge, and even longer to accept the role I'd played in a seven-year relationship with a bizarre therapist and dying marriage. But as I spoke, and the lovely Englishwoman listened in discreet horror, I discovered just how much magic I'd placed on five random letters after a charismatic woman's last name. I'd been raised to defer, to bestow trust and belief in my betters, but in my adult life I'd taken these lessons to self-abnegating heights. Through the grueling and painful work of real, honest therapy and bracing, unflattering self-knowledge, I grew up and found self-love and self-esteem. I became my own kind of better. I learned to trust others once I learned to trust myself.

To me, a good life is about determining the borders of yourself. It takes a long time to find out where those boundaries lie, and that these boundaries are mutable, not fixed lines like those in atlases or Thomas Guides. But once I determined where I ended and others began, and I really grew to respect that, I found myself on solid ground.

Note to Self

**Trust is not bought or borrowed
or imposed. It is earned.**

Beauty and the Inner Beast

GRETA GAINES

Greta Gaines is a southern rock musician who has made four albums. She is also a television host (she hosted *Free Ride with Greta Gaines* on Oxygen for three years and has been a correspondent on ESPN2) and internationally recognized pro-snowboarder and fly fisherman (Women's World Extreme Snowboard Champion '92). She lives in Nashville, Tennessee, with her husband, Michael, and two children, Cassidy, four, and Ryder, two.

My mother is both beautiful and brilliant, but she often told me that when she was growing up in the '40s and '50s in the Deep South, these two qualities could not comfortably live side by side within the same woman. You could be Flannery O'Connor or Miss Alabama (as she was in 1961). You couldn't be both. Since beauty fades, my mother instilled in me the notion that your actions and not your looks would get you noticed. I took this to heart, but secretly I always wanted to grow up to be beautiful like my mother, because to me she was Flannery O'Connor *and* Miss Alabama in the same woman.

I grew up in central New Hampshire, where being "hot" was second fiddle to being athletic—and, more specifically, a good skier. In fact, girls gained instant status as "hot chicks" if they were also great skiers. I excelled on the ski team and was considered to be pretty good looking as well, so I had a fairly easy time of it. At a time when most girls struggle to find their own identity, I was trying to run with the boys, trying to be noticed. Now, I have two brothers and an ultra-sportsman for a father, so I earned their respect on the slopes. Becoming a good skier was important for me, but even more so for my father. I skied hard and learned to do things that inwardly scared the shit out of me, but I never let it show.

While my father was pushing me athletically, my mother encouraged my artistic side. We didn't own a television until I was nine or ten, our entertainment was the great outdoors by day and the fireplace at night. We would sit around the fireplace and jam on the guitars, playing classic songs as well as original works by the Gaines clan. The winters were long and, I thought, a bit boring and depressing, but my father made a house rule that we had to fight boredom with our own brand of fun. One winter day, in 1982, my little brother ushered in what would become my best skill as an athlete when he brought home a couple of prototype Burton boards from Stratton Mountain after a ski race. We made jumps in the front yard and got pretty decent on these crude rides, years before snowboarding was allowed at most ski areas. By 1989 I had graduated from Georgetown and was ready to leave New Hampshire for bigger mountains and more snow; that's the year I moved to Jackson Hole, Wyoming, and got serious about riding big powder and steep terrain on my snowboard. I felt like I had really found my calling. In Jackson I hung out on the mountain with guys who were making all the right moves, and it motivated me to learn great technique quickly. I shared the mountain with some of the guys I had read about in *TransWorld* and other snowboarding magazines, people like John Griber and the late, legendary Craig Kelly. There were only a handful of women riding at Jackson Hole back then, like Julie Zell. Others, like Morgan Lafonte and Barrett Christy, would pass through town and visit. We were a little band of outsiders, boarding at the same level, and we went on to become internationally recognized pro-snowboarders. But we had no idea that we would shape one of the world's biggest new action sports.

The Tetons taught me to be an "extreme" snowboarder. I didn't realize it at the time, but I was shredding the steepest ski area in the lower forty-eight states. It was the Tetons that inspired me to start jumping off big cliffs, attempting first descents on untouched terrain. They also gave me the confidence to accompany nineteen men up to Alaska to compete in what would be the first world extreme snowboarding championships. Snowboarding rapidly exploded onto the mainstream sports stage in the early '90s, and many of us tried to make it a career. Prior to that we'd mostly been getting "paid" in swag: T-shirts, free gear, and stickers. I started to think about how to actually make a living as a pro. By going to Alaska championships as the only female, I pioneered a way for women to be visible in this sport at the very beginning. There was great tradition in women's skiing, but snowboarding was born from the male skateboarding/surfing cultures. Fitting in meant breaking down those barriers. I knew in my gut that I was only going to be a decent ski racer, but snowboarding had limitless potential for me. I was hooked. In a short three years, I was better on my snowboard than I was after twenty years of skiing; boarding fit me like a glove. It was like dancing on powder. It was all in the hips, and I had those. I'd followed my calling to the mountain, and it had the rising promise of a great career.

My passion wasn't exactly profitable at first. Snowboarding was still a new sport, and corporate sponsors didn't understand the business opportunities. However, I started the Wild Women's Snowboarding Camps in 1993 with my best friend, Mary Seibert Simmons. During the next ten years we taught hundreds of women how to ride. It was a great business, and I was part of the next generation of girls who could become action sports stars. It was uncharted territory, very different from my mother's generation.

This all changed when I got pregnant and gained fifty pounds. I had always been a woman on the move, and being pregnant was a state of suspension, a woman on hold. It gave me time to think about what I had and what I wanted back. And then I felt guilty because I was torn between wanting my body back the way it had been when I'd been a competitor and feeling incredibly blessed that I could carry a child. I was ashamed to admit this truth.

I'd become this cute, cuddly blob. I was just another pregnant lady for people to gush over. The world-class extreme athlete and hot blonde had left the building. I was bored and lonely during a lot of my pregnancy. I went from 135 to 190 pounds, and I went from sexy to matronly in only nine months. I began to fantasize about what life would be like after the baby arrived. I was determined to have kids, but I was also determined to re-boot, before my first child was born, the person I had been.

While pregnant, I continued to push my boundaries. It was my way of reclaiming power. I competed on the first Women's Bassmaster Fishing tour when I was in my seventh month, in one-hundred-degree heat. A lot of women found it inspiring, but I could only imagine what the guys were thinking: *Why are you out here fishing when you're this huge? You should be home with your feet up!* I was on a mission to shatter this image.

I snowboarded and skied when I was six months along. "I can't believe you're going to take that risk with your baby," the skeptics said. But I had an answer for everything.

With respect to my mother, I learned to live comfortably with all the sides of myself in the same body: snowboarder, musician, and mom. Since the births of my two sons, I'm a lot easier on my self-image nowadays. I love my womanly body. At forty-one years old I can still out-board and out-fly-fish most folks out there.

Being a mom has given me new and better priorities. Though it was difficult, pregnancy got me less obsessed with the physical and more interested in the spiritual. I believe that for the most part, soul-building comes when you have to go deep inside yourself and endure some silence. I always ran hard and fast and long and loud until I got pregnant. But thanks to the struggles of feeling uncomfortable in my own skin, I was given a second chance to grow into a new and improved version of myself, taking less for granted. I just try to do what I'm good at and enjoy what I have.

Note to Self

Treasure your virtues,
from the inside out.

Heart Opening

MARISKA HARGITAY

Actress Mariska Hargitay, a Golden Globe and Emmy Award winner, is best known for her role as Detective Olivia Benson on Law & Order: Special Victims Unit. She is the founder of the Joyful Heart Foundation, an organization committed to healing, educating, and empowering survivors of sexual assault, domestic violence, and child abuse and shedding light into the darkness that surrounds these issues. Her mission is unstoppable and her devotion to helping others an inspiration. She lives in New York with her husband and son.

I think I'm having a heart attack!" I gasped as I treaded water in the Pacific, a mile off the Hawaii coast. I was surrounded by a school of more than a dozen wild dolphins. "I'm seriously having a heart attack!"

My mind raced through the symptoms: chest pains, shortness of breath, dizziness, nausea. *This is it*, I thought.

Except that it wasn't. I was not, in fact, having a heart attack.

I was, as a dear friend who was in the water with me that day put it, having a "heart opening."

I hadn't known at the time that my heart needed opening. But that moment in the water still stands as one of the clearest and most profound of my life. In that instant I experienced possibility—not just an understanding that things were possible, but the essence of *possibility itself.* The armor of limitation lifted, and I knew beyond a doubt that anything I set my mind to, I could accomplish.

That moment informs my choices and actions every single day.

I hadn't always felt so empowered, so free. Yes, the months before my trip to Hawaii had been incredibly rewarding professionally: I had landed a kick-ass role on the latest installment of the wildly successful Law & Order franchise and moved to New York, my dream since I started acting. To the outside observer, my future couldn't have looked brighter.

But New York City overwhelmed me. Someone else might not have been as affected as I was, but I felt like I was drowning. I had left behind an extraordinary group of friends in LA, as well as my family, and I felt lost without my familiar network of support. All of that might have been okay if I could have gotten up every morning and gone to work on a sitcom, but the subject matter of this new show I was on—rape, incest, child abuse—was so disturbing and so foreign to me that its residual effects weighed on my psyche long after we'd wrapped for the day.

There I was, awash in a sea of noise: the noise of New York City, the noise of my show, the noise of my own emotions, the noise of fear and self-doubt. Luckily I had something to look forward to, to keep me going, the one quiet time I indulge in every year: my trip out west, *way* west, past Los Angeles, all the way to Hawaii with my friends. I was counting on the sun, the water, and that blissfully slow pace of life to turn down the volume and give my spirit a chance to take a nice, long, easy breath.

In Hawaii, at a friend's urging, I started going on group dolphin swims off the coast of Kona, one of the main cities on the Big Island. A wonderfully skilled and very knowledgeable captain would take a group of us out early in the morning and find a pod of wild dolphins. We'd scramble to get our snorkels and fins on, wait with bated breath for the captain's signal, and drop over the side of the boat into the water.

The moment I entered the water, the moment I crossed the threshold from the world above to the world below, the noise in my head quieted. Looking into the deep, contemplating what was beneath the surface, seeing these beautiful creatures that thrive in the world below, *and then entering their world with them* took my breath away every time. Without fail, the descent calmed and humbled me.

The dolphin swims were always fun and invigorating, and my fellow swimmers and I would compare notes when we got back on the boat, grinning from ear to ear.

And then one day, during a swim, something altogether different happened. I had slipped into the water near a pod of dolphins. I had seen their fins from the boat, but now that I was in the water, they were gone. The sun's rays pierced the surface of the water, sending long cables of light past me into the deep. I looked over my shoulder to see if the dolphins might be behind me. They weren't. But when I turned back, I found them. In fact, a whole group of them—a squadron, a little platoon, a posse, I don't know what to call it—was heading straight toward me. And fast. Just one of these creatures alone, fun-loving and benign as they are, can fill you with a kind nervous amazement when you encounter it in the depths of the ocean. Now I had a dozen of them, swimming right at me. I froze. Was I in their way? Did they not see me? Would they swim past me and disappear? No, their appointment was with me.

They surrounded me, swam around me in circles over and over, missing my nose by inches, as if they meant to keep me in place. Everywhere I turned, these animals were jumping up out of the ocean and then diving back in and darting past me. And this wasn't like some beautifully choreographed show at Seaworld. This was messy and spontaneous, raw and real. All I saw were bubbles and dolphins and the cables of light.

The entire encounter lasted only about fifteen seconds. And then, as quickly as they had come, they were gone. I finally came up for air.

"I think I'm having a heart attack!" I cried.

And then suddenly I just started talking, and I couldn't stop. "I'm going to start a foundation! I'm going to help people! I'm going to do all of it!" As I was speaking, I let go of fear, I let go of the limitations I'd placed on myself—and there were many—and I voiced what was in my heart. Actually, I *saw* with my heart—and for the first time, my heart was fearless. I also cried. A lot.

I got back in the boat, headed back to the mainland—and eventually, a few days later, back to New York. My first day of work, the alarm rang at 5:30 a.m. I remember looking at my tired face in the make-up trailer mirror as the hours on set dragged on. I was back in the noise and the grind, back in the deep. But this deep was different from the calming expanse of the ocean. No cables of light here. And no dolphins.

I started second-guessing myself. "What was I *thinking*? That a swim in the ocean with some dolphins was going to change my life? I don't know anything about starting a foundation! I'm an actress for crying out loud." Lines from the script I had been reading from all my life re-entered my dialogue with myself: "You're not good enough. You're not going to be the best at it, so why try? You're not smart enough." The limitations I put on myself were creeping back, and the clarity I had after those fifteen seconds in the water was fading.

I saw I had a choice: I could either go back to what I knew—fear and doubt and dissatisfaction with myself—and write off the experience in Hawaii as an interesting episode that I had over-invested with meaning. Or I could take the plunge, trust what my heart saw, and head toward the future I had glimpsed in that moment.

So I made my choice. I started pounding the pavement, trying to raise money for my "foundation." I say "foundation" in quotes, because in the beginning, there wasn't really any foundation to speak of. I had no background in nonprofits, and I'd never really encountered—nor thought much about, to be honest—the epidemic of sexual violence that exists in our culture. But in the first season I'd spent on my new show I had started getting fan mail that made the epidemic hard to ignore: "I am sixteen years old and I was raped last year and I'm really scared." "My mother's boyfriend is doing stuff to me that I don't like, and I wish Olivia Benson"—my character on the show—"would come and help me." "My sister told me our dad touched her between her legs and I don't know what to do." I was getting pain-filled, courageous disclosures of deep trauma and violation, confessions of heartbreaking scope and proportion. Here was the epidemic, arriving one letter at a time. I didn't seek out the cause, it found me.

At the time, my foundation consisted of just me, my friend Lisa Denning—a truly remarkable soul—who had been in the water with me that day, and a few other people who believed in what I had set out to do. As I made the rounds, trying to drum up interest and financing for my foundation, people gave me a lot of weird looks. ("You want to start a foundation that takes sexual assault survivors to swim with wild dolphins? We'll . . . um . . . that's great. We'll get back to you.") I realize now we were actually facing two obstacles in the early days of our foundation. First, our approach to healing survivors was clearly unorthodox, and people listening to our pitch couldn't wrap their heads around what we intended to do. Secondly, and perhaps even more problematically, *nobody wants to talk about, have any association with, or otherwise acknowledge the epidemic of sexual violence.* The topic makes people extremely uncomfortable. I was asking people to think outside the box about something they didn't want to think about in the first place.

But the obstacles only galvanized me more. I worked hard to gather all the knowledge I could. I surrounded myself with people who possessed the skills and information to get this foundation built—even if none of us knew for sure what it would look like when it was finished. However, the core of the foundation—the foundation's foundation—was always clear to me. What I read over and over again in all these letters, what I encountered again and again when people told me their stories in person, were broken hearts. Thousands and thousands of broken hearts. I knew my experience in the water had been a renewal, a baptism of a sort—a heart opening. And I know now what I allowed into my heart that day: the possibility of joy. That is the gift I wanted to share with survivors, and that experience gave me the name of my organization: the Joyful Heart Foundation. Before I even reached the mainland in Hawaii that day and got off the boat, I knew that's what it would be called. There was simply no other name for it.

Five years down the road, I find myself with an actual, operational foundation, staffed and supported by a group of visionaries working to heal survivors of sexual assault, domestic violence, and child abuse. Joyful Heart is more real, more vibrant than I ever dared imagine. Through the healing work of our retreat programs and other direct services we have helped more than *1,200 people* find the courage to heal and recover a sense of joy. We have heard survivors say, "You have helped me find peace." We have also heard them say, "You make me feel victorious." And one of our favorites: "You helped me learn how to dance again."

Thinking of the lives we have changed and the hearts we have helped heal humbles me the same way the expanse of the ocean humbles me. In both cases, I stand before something that is so much bigger than I am. What humbles me most, actually, is the courage of these survivors. Opening up to the possibility of joy again requires a well of strength, determination, and perseverance; I feel so honored to have encountered so many survivors who have all three in abundance.

I know I could have come home from that heart-opening experience and allowed the voices of self-limitation and self-doubt to take over again, allowed my eyes to be drawn away from the promise I saw in a moment of clarity. If I had listened to those voices, I would have decided I couldn't possibly succeed, so why even try. And Joyful Heart would never have been born.

That decision to forge ahead was crucial. But looking back, I also realize that facing the moment of decision—*Do I move ahead or do I turn back? Do I settle back into the fear I know, the fear I've been carrying all my life, or do I move forward into an invigorating life of not knowing what's next?*—is a daily occurrence, and it takes daily discipline to keep moving forward. There are so many opportunities to stop running during a race; and every step you take is a small, individual decision to keep on going. We definitely have a long way to go, but it's certainly nice to look back occasionally at the distance we've already traveled.

Note to Self

It is by living courageously—daily—
with a deep belief in our personal
vision that we achieve true success.

If you would like to learn more about the Joyful Heart Foundation, please visit www.joyfulheartfoundation.org.

ACKNOWLEDGMENTS

Our lives never go as planned. The proof of that statement lives on the pages with each story in this book. And mine has been no exception. During the course of editing and writing this book, I have experienced some of my most challenging moments, and I am deeply grateful to those who stuck by me and helped me both personally and professionally.

Thanks especially to my editor, Emily Westlake, whose even-keeled attitude and super-smart, highly organized, and creative brain was the perfect energy for this book at the perfect time. What a blessing. To the dynamic duo, Jen Bergstrom and Trish Boczkowski, who never stopped believing and put the professional behind the personal when I needed it most. A hearty thanks to the many talented folks at SSE: Cara Bedick, Kristin Dwyer, Michael Nagin, Linda Roberts, and Jennifer Robinson. To Kristina Grish, thank you for your care and your words. And to my fearless agent, Andy McNicol, thank you for your guidance.

To my parents, Buck and Sue, the best! Thank you for your love. I am grateful to be your daughter. And to my sisters, Cindy, Beth, and Allyson, thank you for your support and unconditional love. So much gratitude goes out to Beverly and Neal for helping to build and hold down the fort, and for your unwavering support.

For my dear friend, Meredith, who nudged—no, forced—me to write my story for Word-O-Rama, the seed that sprouted this book. My dear Leelee, who introduced me to the keeper of the book and whose creative genius has been invaluable. And for my dearest Kristin, the one who has gone before me, thank you for sharing your priceless wisdom . . . beginning, middle, and end.

And to my trusted tribe: Michele, Drea, Daryl, Thom, Tom, and Rich Shainee, who have given so much of their time, opinions, advice, and encouragement, and who helped me in more ways than I can count. . . . Thank you! And to Lizzie and the moxie gang, thank you.

This book would not be possible were it not for two people: My beautiful friend Lis Peery, who has been my right hand, my left-brain, and my trusted adviser every step of the way. And to my husband, Jason Berkin, whose calm guidance, eternal optimism, fierce loyalty, and deep intelligence carried me over the finish line and inspires me every day.

Finally and most important, I would like to thank the women who have told their stories in this book. You are such an inspiration to me, and by sharing your stories you have committed to inspiring others. I am honored to have your trust, grateful for your friendship, in awe of your bravery, and humbled by your wisdom.